2024 교원임용시험 전공영어 대비

Build Up New

박현수 영어교육론 Ⅲ 기출문제

박현수 편저

박문각 임용

동영상강의 www.pmg.co.kr

Guideline for Pre-service Teachers

2011~2023학년도 기출문항 분석

PMG 박문각

친애하는 예비 교사 여러분, 여러분을 열렬히 응원하는 박현수입니다.

Build-up Ⅲ의 시작에서 제가 삶에서 중요한 지표로 삼고 있는 글귀를 나누고자 합니다. 다음의 글귀는 제가 가고자 하는 길에서 저에게 무한한 용기와 인내를 갖게 해주는 마법의 한마디입니다. 그 마법이 여러분에게도, 여러분의 삶에도 녹아내리기 바랍니다.

좋은 마침이 있어야 새로운 시작이 있습니다.
There have to be good endings for there to be new beginnings.

늘 우리는 새로운 시작을 꿈꿉니다. 하지만 우리가 꿈꾸는 새로운 시작은 지금 여러분이 서 있는 그 자리에 좋은 마침이 있어야 가능합니다. 좋은 마침을 위해 여러분은 오늘도 당당하게 자신을 마주하며 또박또박 하루 속으로 걸어가시기 바랍니다. 좋은 하루의 마침은 또 다른 좋은 하루의 시작으로 이어져 여러분의 꿈으로 열릴 것입니다.

너무 힘들어 여기까지인가 그만 등 돌리고 싶을 때, 힘든 게 아니라 간절하지 않은 것입니다.
When I feel that's enough, it's not too hard, and want to turn back, it' not that it's hard, it's that I'm not in earnest.

끝날 것 같지 않은 임용을 준비하면서 이미 여러분 중 누군가는 겪었을 테고, 어느 누군가는 겪고 있을 테고, 다른 누군가는 겪을 슬럼프라는 늪에서 여러분이 가고자 하는 그 길에 대한 간절함을 생각해 보십시오.

그 간절함이 끝없어 보이는 그 슬럼프로부터 여러분을 구할 것입니다. 우리는 사실 삶의 최종 목적지에서 지금을 바라본다면 현재의 고통과 어려움은 신비한 계획 속의 어느 지점을 통과하고 있는 것인지 모릅니다. 또한, 여러분이 겪는 현재의 고통과 어려움은 여러분의 뿌리 속 자양분이 되어 훗날 제자들 앞에서 보다 당당한 모습의 여러분을 만들어 줄 것이며, 지혜가 가득한 성숙한 어른의 모습으로, 그들의 신뢰가 가득한 멘토로, 그 자체가 될 것이라 자신합니다.

여러분이 지금 지나는 이 길을 좀 더 당당하고 기쁘게 마주하실 수 있도록, 그리고 여러분의 간절함이 꿈을 실현시킬 수 있도록 New Build-up Ⅲ와 함께 박현수가 도와드리도록 하겠습니다.

임용 시기의 중간 점검에 해당하는 5~6월은 영어교육론의 기본적인 이해와 주요 교실지도에 대한 원리를 이해한 후, 실전 기출문제를 토대로 key concepts에 대한 재확인은 물론 data processing 및 direction analysis에 대한 훈련을 하여 정확한 답안쓰기에 주력을 해야 할 때입니다.

2023년 New Build-up Ⅲ는 Part Ⅰ과 Part Ⅱ로 이루어져 있으며, Part I은 2014~2023년에 이르는 서답형 기출문제를 통해 1~4월에 진행한 기본이론 및 실전 수업원리를 다시 한번 점검할 수 있도록 주제별 묶음으로 정리해 놓았습니다. 또한, Part Ⅱ는 논술형 문항 data를 수록해 실전 수업의 whole picture를 그려보고 영어 교수 및 학습상 발생할 수 있는 여러 가지 문제점과 issue에 대해 고찰할 수 있도록 하였습니다.

이번 2023년 New Build-up Ⅲ 개정에 애써주신 박옥진 선생님과 변영경 선생님, 함초롬, 유다현 선임 연구원과 유채원 연구원에게 감사를 전하며, 교정지 작업에 애써준 조교 명주, 정곤, 은정, 다은, 유진, 그리고 지우에게 고마움을 전합니다. 또한, 새로운 가정 속에서 한껏 에네지 넘치는 송은우 선생님, 더 강력하고 응집력 있는 팀을 만들어 주시는 유희태 선생님 그리고 앤드류 선생님과 한 팀으로 올 한 해도 힘차게 보낼 수 있음에 무한한 감사를 드립니다. 한 해 한 해 쌓아둔 서로 간의 신뢰와 배려로 2023년도 우리 제자들의 꿈을 가뿐히 이뤄 나갈 수 있길 기원해 봅니다. 아울러 꼼꼼한 편집으로 2023년 Build-up Ⅲ를 반짝반짝 다듬어 주신 변수경 편집위원에게도 마음 깊은 감사를 전합니다.

마지막으로 한결같은 사랑으로 늘 지지해주고 응원해주는 사랑하는 가족이 있기에 오늘 하루도 최선을 다할 수 있는 박현수가 될 수 있음에 진정 감사합니다.

여러분의 6월이 되길
박현수

2024학년도 대비 영어교육론 시험 전략

2023년 대비 중등 임용시험에서 영어교육론은 2022년 중등 임용시험보다 1문항이 더 출제되어 11문항(총 23문항 총 40점)으로, 역대 최대 출제 영역이 되었다. 이것은 중등 임용시험의 정체성에 따라 영어 교사의 필수 자질인 how to teach에 대한 자필평가의 중요성이 반영된 것으로 판단된다. 전체적인 출제 항목을 보면 2022년 개정 교육과정의 주요 개념들이 반영되어 보다 생동감 있고 학생 중심의 수업으로 진행하기 위한 교사의 역량 강화가 가장 큰 특징으로 분석된다. 따라서 각 출제 항목 안에서 교사의 역량에 따른 학생들의 자율성이 극대화되는 실제적인 교실 수업 data가 주를 이루고 있으며, 또한 디지털 리터러시 역량을 키우고자 하는 교실 수업 방향에 맞춰 교실 내 수업활동뿐 아니라 평가에 적용하는 사례로 computerized adaptive testing이 출제되었다.

A형과 B형의 문항 유형에서 살펴봤듯이, 2023년 기출은 현재 진행되는 교실 수업 방향을 가늠할 수 있는 주요 교육론 개념들을 실제 교실 지도와 연결하여 구체적이고 다각적인 임용 지원자들의 how to teach에 대한 역량을 간접적으로 측정하기 위한 의도가 명확히 보인다. 따라서, 2024년 중등 임용의 방향 역시 현재 진행되는 교실 지도 중심으로 national curriculum의 개정인 2022년 개정 교육과정의 주요 과제에 따른 교실 지도에 대한 whole picture를 그려보고 그 안에서의 주요 교육론 개념들에 대한 정리가 반드시 이루어져야 할 것이다.

─ A형 문항

A형 문항들의 출제 항목을 중심으로 살펴보자면, 기입형으로 언어 습득 과정(U-shaped learning) 중 교실 수업에서 흔히 보이는 과잉일반화 오류에 대한 현상으로 backsliding과 대규모의 교실 수업에서 학생 개개인에 맞춰 평가를 진행할 수 있는 computerized adaptive testing 등 2문항이 출제되었다. 서술형으로는 textbook adaptation의 사례와 group work에서 개인의 역할 및 reading comprehension을 보다 효과적으로 이해하는 도구인 graphic organizer에 대한 문항, 학생들의 언어 발달 상황에 따른 학습자 언어의 구체적 특징에 관한 문항, 그리고 문화 지도와 병행된 언어 지도에 대한 원리 및 분석 등 총 6문항이 출제되었다.

Read the conversation and follow the directions. [2 points]

(Ms. Kim, a new teacher, and Mr. Song, a head teacher, are discussing Ms. Kim's concerns about her student's writing performance.)

T1: Ms. Kim, did the process-oriented evaluation in your writing class go well this semester?

T2: I'm still making comments to students, but there is something I'm worried about.

T1: What is it?

T2: I'm afraid that one of my students is making more errors now than he was at the beginning of the semester.

T1: He got worse as the semester went on?

T2: Yes. He turned in the writing assignment. However, there were so many errors in his writing.

T1: What kinds of errors?

T2: Unlike the beginning of the semester, now he has problems with irregular verbs.

T1: Can you give me an example?

T2: When the semester began, he wrote words like "drank," "wore," and "heard" without errors. Now I am seeing errors like "drinked," "weared," and "heared." He is suddenly treating irregular verbs like regular verbs.

T1: Hmm. Now that I think about it, he is probably progressing!

T2: What are you talking about?

T1: Well, according to U-shaped course of development, he is starting to understand the rules of the past tense.

T2: Oh, I see.

Note: T1 = Mr. Song, T2 = Ms. Kim

Fill in the blank with the ONE most appropriate word.

In the above conversation, Ms. Kim's student seems to regress, making errors with irregular verbs that he used to use correctly, due to overgeneralization. This phenomenon is commonly called _____, in which the learner seems to have grasped a rule or principle but then moves from a correct form to an incorrect form.

모범답안 Backsliding

– B형 문항

B형의 문항들을 분석해보자면, 교실 지도에서 교사의 역량 강화 및 학습자 중심 수업과 관련된 내용이 문항의 공통적인 특징이며, 그 예로 기입형 1문항으로 action research, 서술형 문항으로 classroom observation(reflective teaching)와 사지선다형 문제 개발과 관련된 문항 등 2문항이 교사의 역량 강화를 위한 문항으로 출제되었으며, 학습 과정 및 평가에 관련된 서술형 문항들로는 writing 첨삭으로 content 와 organization에 대한 1문항, 어휘 지도에서 concordancer를 사용하여 진행되는 수업 과정 1문항이 출제되어 총 5문항이 출제되었다.

2023학년도 기출 | **전공B 서술형 ⑪**

Read the passages in <A> and <B>, and follow the directions. [4 points]

A

A high school English teacher, Mr. Choi, wanted to learn how to write selected-response items (e.g., multiple-choice items) more efficiently. He wrote several items before the workshop began, and found some of them were flawed according to the guidelines he learned during the workshop. The following are some of the guidelines along with examples of flawed items.

> **General Guidelines for Writing Selected-response Items**
> ① Make certain that there is only one, clearly correct answer.
> ② State both the stem and the options as simply and directly as possible.
> ③ Present a single clearly formulated problem to avoid mixed content.
> ④ Avoid negative wording whenever possible. If it is absolutely necessary to use a negative stem, highlight the negative word.

Item 1

My forehead itches every day during the summer. Using sunscreen hasn't helped much. I think I'd better go to the _____ to get my skin checked.

    a. dentist
    b. optometrist
    c. pediatrician
→ d. dermatologist

Item 2

Where did Henry go after the party last night?

    a. Yes, he did.
    b. Because he was tired.
→ c. To Kate's place for another party.
? d. He went home around eleven o'clock.

Item 3

I never knew where _____.

    a. had the boys gone
→ b. the boys had gone
    c. the boys have gone
    d. have the boys gone

Item 4

According to the passage, which of the following is not true?

  a. My sister likes outdoor sports.
  b. My brother is busy with his plans.
→ c. My sister and I often do everything together.
  d. My brother is more energetic and outgoing than I.

Note: '→' indicates the key; '?' indicates a possible answer.

B

    After the workshop, to improve the quality of the items, the teacher revised some items according to the guidelines. The following are the revised items.

Item 1

I think I'd better go to the _____ to get my skin checked.

  a. dentist
  b. optometrist
  c. pediatrician
→ d. dermatologist

Item 2

Where did Henry go after the party last night?

  a. Yes, he did.
  b. Because he was tired.
  c. It was about eleven o'clock.
→ d. To Kate's place for another party.

Item 3

I never knew _____.

  a. where had the boys gone
→ b. where the boys had gone
  c. the boys where had gone
  d. the boys had gone where

Item 4

According to the passage, which of the following is NOT true?

  a. My sister likes outdoor sports.
  b. My brother is busy with his plans.
→ c. My sister and I often do everything together.
  d. My brother is more energetic and outgoing than I.

Based on <A>, identify the ONE most appropriately revised item in <B> according to guideline ②, and the ONE most appropriately revised item according to guideline ③. Then, explain each of the items with evidence from <A> and <B>.

모범답안　Item 1 in <B> is appropriately revised based on guideline ② in that the original complicated stem is changed into a simple and direct one sentence. Also, following guideline ③, Item 3 in <B> presents a clear single problem about an 'indirect question' by changing tenses in the original options into the same past perfect 'had gone'.

Contents

차례

Part 01

Topic별 문항정리

박현수 영어교육론 (III)

기출지문 분석

Build Up New

박현수 영어교육론 Ⅲ

Part

01

Topic별 문항정리

Chapter

01 Second Language Acquisition – Theoretical Background

01 **Read the conversation and follow the directions.** [2 points] 2023 전공A 1번

> *(Ms. Kim, a new teacher, and Mr. Song, a head teacher, are discussing Ms. Kim's concerns about her student's writing performance.)*
>
> T1 : Ms. Kim, did the process-oriented evaluation in your writing class go well this semester?
> T2 : I'm still making comments to students, but there is something I'm worried about.
> T1 : What is it?
> T2 : I'm afraid that one of my students is making more errors now than he was at the beginning of the semester.
> T1 : He got worse as the semester went on?
> T2 : Yes. He turned in the writing assignment. However, there were so many errors in his writing.
> T1 : What kinds of errors?
> T2 : Unlike the beginning of the semester, now he has problems with irregular verbs.
> T1 : Can you give me an example?
> T2 : When the semester began, he wrote words like "drank," "wore," and "heard" without errors. Now I am seeing errors like "drinked," "weared," and "heared." He is suddenly treating irregular verbs like regular verbs.
> T1 : Hmm. Now that I think about it, he is probably progressing!
> T2 : What are you talking about?
> T1 : Well, according to U-shaped course of development, he is starting to understand the rules of the past tense.
> T2 : Oh, I see.
>
> T1=Mr. Song, T2=Ms. Kim

Fill in the blank with the ONE most appropriate word.

In the above conversation, Ms. Kim's student seems to regress, making errors with irregular verbs that he used to use correctly, due to overgeneralization. This phenomenon is commonly called _____, in which the learner seems to have grasped a rule or principle but then moves from a correct form to an incorrect form.

Your Answer _____

1. Topic : The learning phenomenon

2. Focus

성공적인 학습자들이 겪는 여러 가지 학습 현상 중에서 목표언어의 규칙을 습득해 나가는 과정을 흔히 U-shaped learning이라 일컫는다. 그 과정 안에서 보이는 overgeneralization의 예와 backsliding 현상에 대한 이해를 하고 있는가?

3. Three phases of U-shaped learning

Children overgeneralize in the early phases of acquisition, meaning that they **apply the regular rules of grammar to irregular nouns and verbs.** Overgeneralization leads to forms which we sometimes hear in the speech of young children such as *goed, eated, foots*, and *fishes*.

This process is often described as consisting of three phases:

Phase 1 : The child uses the correct past tense of go, for instance, but does not relate this past-tense *went* to present-tense *go*. Rather, *went* is treated as a separate lexical item.

Phase 2 : The child constructs a rule for forming the past tense and begins to overgeneralize this rule to irregular forms such as go (resulting in forms such as goed).

Phase 3 : The child learns that there are (many) exceptions to this rule and acquires the ability to apply this rule selectively.

Note that from the observer's or parents' perspectives, this development is 'U-shaped' that is, children can appear to be decreasing rather than increasing in their accuracy of past-tense use as they enter phase 2. However, this apparent '**backsliding**' is an important sign of linguistic development.

4. Keyword list

process-oriented evaluation, U-shaped course(learning, behavior), overgeneralization, backsliding

---

Answer   Backsliding

02 **Read the passage in <A> and the conversation in <B>, and follow the directions.** [4 points] 2023 전공A 10번

| **A** |

Second language learners pass through a predictable sequence of development. Since the early 1990's, some research has investigated the acquisition of pragmatic abilities in the L2. 'Requesting' is one of the pragmatic features that has received attention. In a review of studies on the acquisition of requests in English, six stages of development were suggested.

Stage	Characteristics	Example
1	Using body language or gestures	*Sir (pointing to the pencil).* *Teacher (holding the paper).*
2	Using verbless expressions	*A paper. / More time.*
3	Using imperative verbs	*Give me. / Give me a paper.*
4	Using 'Can I have _____?' as a formulaic expression	*Can I have some candy?*
5	Using 'can' with a range of verbs, not just with 'have'	*Can you pass me the book?*
6	Using indirect requests	*I want more cookies.*

| B |

(Students are doing a problem-solving task in groups. S1 plays the role of moderator in the activity.)

S1: We have to find some ways to make the environment more sustainable. Suhee, what's your opinion?

S2: I'm sorry, but nothing comes to mind now. I need more time to think.

S1: Okay. Tell us if you're ready. Minho, how about you? Can you share your ideas with us?

S3: We should use one-time products as less as possible.

S1: Hold on, Minho. What does 'one-time products' mean? Can I have some examples?

S3: Well, paper cups, plastic bags...

S2: Ah, I see. You mean 'disposable products', right?

S3: Yes.

S1: Minho, I like your idea.

S2: I'm ready. Driving electronic cars reduces air pollution.

S3: Sounds great.

S1: Now I think we have enough opinions for the presentation. Suhee, can you speak for us in the presentation session?

S2: I'm afraid not. Minho can do better than me.

S3: Umm. Okay. I'll take the speaker role. I'll do my best.

S2: Thanks, Minho. I'll write the presentation script for you.

S1: Wow, thank you.

S=student

Based on <A>, identify the developmental stages where S1 and S2 are, respectively. Then, explain your answers with evidence from <B>.

Your Answer

_____

_____

_____

_____

문항분석

1. Topic : Learner language (Interlanguage)

2. Focus

2언어 학습자들의 중간언어 발달 단계에 대한 이해를 점검하는 문항으로, 특히 'requesting'에 관한 화용론적인 능력에 대한 발달 단계를 토대로 담화 안에서 각 학생들의 중간언어 발달 단계에 대한 분석을 요구하고 있다.

3. Frequency of strategies used by students

- Direct imperative : *please*
- Performative : *I'm asking you to*
- Implicit performative : *I want to ask to*
- Obligation statement : *you should*
- Want statement : *I want you to*
- Indirect preparatory questions : *could you*
- Suggestions : *How abou*t
- Permissions : *May I*
- Mitigated preparatory : *I'm wondering if you could*
- Mitigated wants : *I'd appreciate it if you could*
- Non-conventional indirect strong hint : *my pen just quit. I need a pen.*
- Mild hint : *can you guess what I want?*

4. Keyword list

pragmatic ability, predictable sequence

모범답안

While S1 belongs to Stage 5, S2 is in Stage 6 as the developmental stage. S1 uses 'can' with various verbs such as 'share' or 'speak' for requests. On the other hand, S2 uses indirect requests like "I need more time to think". (or "Minho can do better than me.").

03 **Read the conversation and follow the directions.** [2 points] 2022 전공A 2번

> T1: Hello, Ms. Kim. You seem to be in deep thought. Anything bothering you?
>
> T2: Good morning, Mr. Lee. I'm thinking of how to make my English class more effective.
>
> T1: Yeah, I've been thinking about that, too.
>
> T2: You know, our textbook is organized by separate language skills. But the four skills are rarely separable from each other, I think.
>
> T1: True. Speaking almost always implies a listener, and writing and reading share obvious links.
>
> T2: That's exactly what I mean.
>
> T1: Actually, I've been adapting the textbook since last semester so that my students can be exposed to the language they will encounter in the real world.
>
> T2: Sounds great. How have you been doing it?
>
> T1: For example, I usually have pre-reading discussion time to activate schemata. It helps to make links between speaking, listening, and reading. My students actively engage in those kinds of tasks.
>
> T2: That can be a good way. Or I could create a listening task accompanied by note-taking or followed by a group discussion.
>
> T1: Great idea. I think just a slight change can make a big difference.
>
> T2: Right. I'll try to make some changes and let you know how it goes. Thanks for sharing your experience!
>
> T=teacher

Fill in the blank with the ONE most appropriate word.

In the above conversation, the two teachers are talking about the _____ approach, which is now typical within a communicative, interactive framework. The approach can give students greater motivation and make them engage more actively, which can convert to better learning outcomes.

Your Answer _____

1. Topic : Communicative and interactive framework

2. Focus

구성주의는 총체적인 언어 접근(whole language approach)을 취하고 있으므로, 언어는 분리할 수 없는 한 덩어리로 인식하여 실제 교실 지도 안에서 언어의 기능, 듣기, 말하기, 읽기, 쓰기 등이 통합되어 지도된다.

3. Why is it useful to integrate skills?

통합 수업으로 진행되는 언어 학습은 학생들에게 실제와 근접한 언어 사용의 기회를 제공해 줄 수 있으며, 하나의 주제를 토대로 여러 언어 기능을 사용하게 해줌으로써 다양한 언어 활동을 할 수 있게 해준다. 또한, 주제에 대한 충분한 탐구와 해당 주제와 관련한 어휘가 반복적으로 사용되어 연습이 이루어진다.

- An integrated skills lesson allows for the practice of language in a way which is closer to 'real world' and assists in the development of a full language user.
- A lesson which integrated a number of skills has more variety.
- It gives an opportunity for a topic to be fully explored and for vocabulary connected to the topic to be practised and recycled.

| Classroom Examples |

(1) **Intermediate level** : A lesson for intermediate level students based around a newspaper article might the following stages: speaking → reading → writing

① **Step 1** : The teacher introduces the topic (perhaps by showing pictures) and elicits what the students know and/or think about the subject.

② **Step 2** : The students could discuss what they would expect to find in an article on the topic in question.

③ **Step 3** : The students read the newspaper article. Tasks could focus on assisting comprehension and perhaps a more detailed study of some of the vocabulary, or on the style of the article.

④ **Step 4** : The students could write a letter to the editor in response to the article, or write an article on the same subject from a different perspective, or in a different style.

(2) **Lower level**: A lesson for <u>lower level</u> students about finding accommodation.

① **Step 1**: Start with the reading of a newspaper advertisement (with a focus on some of the special vocabulary).

② **Step 2**: Go on to a roleplay/information gap activity in which the prospective tenant telephones the landload/lady to ask questions and to make an appointment to see the flat.

③ **Step 3**: Listen to a text of someone being shown round the flat.

④ **Step 4**: Write a letter to a friend describing their new flat.

Such a lesson would have the following stages: reading → speaking → listening → writing

4. Keyword list

integrated, four skills, integrated skills lesson

Answer integrated

04 **Read the passage in <A> and the conversation in <B>, and follow the directions.** [4 points] 2022 전공B 6번

| A |

Conversation is co-constructed by two or more people, unfolding dynamically in real time. For conversational discourse to be successful, the participants have to know how to organize the events in it; that is, they need to achieve cohesion. A cohesive relation is one in which the interpretation of one element in the discourse presupposes, and is dependent upon, another. In English, along with the grammatical cohesive devices such as reference, substitution, ellipsis, and conjunction, cohesion in conversation can also be achieved using lexical cohesive devices.

Lexical cohesive devices by which links are made across a conversation include the use of synonyms, antonyms, repetition of the same content words, words exhibiting general-specific relations, and words displaying part-whole relations. The use of lexical cohesion is an indicator of topic consistency, and hence contributes significantly to the sense that speakers are talking to topic, and the talk, therefore, becomes more coherent.

B

(Two friends are having a conversation in the wallpaper aisle at a hardware store.)

S1 : Isn't it funny that wallpaper is in fashion again?

S2 : Yeah, I thought it was gone forever.

S1 : Me, too. So, you are redoing your kitchen?

S2 : Yup. And I want to use one of these.

S1 : Good idea. *(pointing to a roll of wallpaper)* How about that?

S2 : You mean the one on the top shelf?

S1 : Yeah, do you like it?

S2 : Uh-huh. It will go with my dining table.

S1 : Have you been to Lesley's new office?

S2 : I have, actually. It was huge and everything was so well organized.

S1 : Yeah. And she had the same wallpaper.

S2 : Oh, that's right. I remember that.

S=speaker

Based on <A>, identify TWO lexical cohesive devices used in the conversation in <B>. Then, provide evidence from <B> for each identified lexical cohesive device.

Your Answer
_____

_____

_____

_____

_____

_____

1. Topic : Discourse analysis

2. Focus

학생들이 성공적인 의사소통 능력을 갖도록 하기 위해 교사들은 담화적 능력(discourse competence)을 기를 수 있는 기회를 교실에서 제공해야 한다. 즉, 목표언어 사용을 극대화 할 수 있도록 다양한 pair work이나 group work를 토대로 spoken discourse와 written discourse의 특성과 유형들을 익히도록 해야 할 것이다. 특히, 담화상의 주요한 2가지 요소인 문장 간의 관계나 토픽의 일관성에 관한 cohesion과 coherence에 대한 파악이 무엇보다 중요하다.

3. How to construct the cohesive and coherent discourse

Cohesion, as one of the most important components of a text, contributes a lot to the coherence of a text. Cohesive relations include grammatical and lexical cohesion. Lexical cohesion is considered the most important one in various means.

Halliday and Hasan(1976) classify lexical cohesion into two main groups‐reiteration and collocation. Reiteration is a form of lexical cohesion which involves the repetition of lexical items, at one end of the scale; the use of a general word to refer back to a lexical and of a item, at the other end of the scale; and a number of things in between‐ the use of a synonym, near‐synonyms, or superordinate. They use this table to explain them more clearly. As far as collocation is concerned, it doesn't simply mean the lexical cohesion between pairs of words but over a succession of a number of nearby related words spanning a topical unit of the text, and these sequences of related words are called lexical chains. There is a distance relation between each word in the chain and the words co‐occur within a given span. Lexical chains do not stop at sentence boundaries; they can connect the adjacent words or even the entire text. In 1984, Halliday revised his classification of lexical cohesion. There are altogether four types: repetition, synonymy/ antonymy, hyponymy/meronymy and collocation.

4. Keyword list

discourse competence, spoken discourse, written discourse, cohesion, grammatical cohesion, lexical cohesion, reiteration, collocation

---

모범답안

The conversation in <B> uses two lexical cohesive devices: repetition of the same content words, "wallpaper" and words displaying part-whole relations such as 'kitchen' and 'dining table'.

05 Read the passage in <A> and the scenarios in <B>, and follow the directions. [4 points] 2022 전공A 10번

| A |

In most intercultural conflict situations, interactants are expected to defend or save their faces when they are threatened. Here, face refers to a person's sense of favorable self-worth or self-image experienced in communication. The various ways to deal with conflict and face are called facework or facework strategies. There are three general types of facework strategies used in intercultural conflict. Below are the three types and the specific behaviors displayed when employing a strategy.

Facework Strategies	Facework Behaviors
A. Dominating: an effort to control the conflict situation	A1. Assault the other verbally
	A2. Be firm in one's demands and do not give in
B. Avoiding: an attempt to save the other person's face	B1. Dismiss the conflict that threatens the other's face
	B2. Rely on a third party to manage the conflict
C. Integrating: an endeavor for closure of the conflict	C1. Offer an apology for the conflict
	C2. Mutually acknowledge each other's good points

| B |

Scenario 1

Michael and Ken are students from different countries taking the same class at an Australian university. They are partners for an assignment and decide to meet twice a week. However, Michael is always late for the meetings. Ken feels frustrated because in his culture, punctuality is highly important and making others wait is regarded inconsiderate. Ken finally tells Michael how he feels. Hearing Ken's complaints, Michael is upset at first. He thinks Ken is fussing over nothing because in Michael's culture, people are more flexible with time. After consideration, he comes to understand Ken's position and admits his fault. Then, expressing his regret, he promises to be on time.

Scenario 2

Maria and Sue are students rooming together at a US university. They are from different countries. Maria loves hanging out with her friends and invites them to the room to talk and eat. They almost always leave after midnight. However, Sue is irritated because in her culture, staying late at someone's place is not normally acceptable. In contrast, Maria doesn't mind her friends staying late since in her culture, getting along well with other people is a high priority. Sue considers directly telling Maria that her friends should not outstay their welcome. Not wanting to create an unpleasant situation, however, she instead decides to go to the library when her roommate's friends visit.

Based on <A>, identify ONE facework behavior that Michael and Sue each display to deal with their intercultural conflicts in <B>, respectively. Then, explain your answers with evidence from <B>.

Your Answer

_____

_____

_____

_____

_____

_____

문항분석

1. Topic : Teaching culture

2. Focus

서로 다른 문화권에서의 소통은 여러 가지 갈등을 야기하게 되는데, 이와 같은 문화 간 갈등을 해소하기 위해 다양한 facework strategies들이 사용된다.

3. The types of facework strategies & Facework behavior

Facework Strategies	Facework Behaviors
A. Dominating : an effort to control the conflict situation	A1. Assault the other verbally
	A2. Be firm in one's demands and do not give in
B. Avoiding : an attempt to save the other person's face	B1. Dismiss the conflict that threatens the other's face
	B2. Rely on a third party to manage the conflict
C. Integrating : an endeavor for closure of the conflict	C1. Offer an apology for the conflict
	C2. Mutually acknowledge each other's good points

4. Keyword list

intercultural conflict, dominating, avoiding, integrating

모범답안

Michael displays C1 while Sue shows B1. Michael apologizes by admitting his fault and promising to be on time. As for Sue, she dismisses the conflict by going to the library rather than confronting Maria.

06 **Read the passage in <A> and the examples in <B>, and follow the directions.** [4 points] 2022 전공B 11번

| | A | |

Focus on form is one of the approaches to L2 instruction that has been proposed to develop learners' fluency and accuracy. It occurs when learners briefly pay attention to linguistic items within a larger meaning-focused context. Focus on form can be accomplished in various ways. A basic distinction is drawn between 'reactive focus on form' (where attention to form arises out of some problem in a participant's production as in A1 and A2 below) and 'pre-emptive focus on form' (where the participants make a particular form the topic of the conversation even though no actual problem has arisen as in B1 and B2 below).

	Options	Description
Reactive	A1. Implicit feedback	The teacher or another student responds to a student's error without directly indicating an error has been made, e.g., by means of a recast or a clarification request.
	A2. Explicit feedback	The teacher or another student responds to a student's error by directly indicating that an error has been made, e.g., by formally correcting the error or by using metalanguage.
Pre-emptive	B1. Student-initiated focus on form	A student asks a question about a linguistic form.
	B2. Teacher-initiated focus on form	The teacher gives advice about a linguistic form he/she thinks might be problematic or asks the students a question about the form.

B

Example 1

(It is Monday morning and a group of students have just arrived for their English class. The teacher starts the class by asking the students about their weekend.)

T : So what did you do this weekend?

S1 : I ran my first marathon!

T : Wow! Did you finish?

S1 : Yes, eventually.... It was actually a half-course marathon, but really challenging.

T : Way to go! *(turning to S2)* How about you?

S2 : I had gone to the park...

T : You need to use the past simple when you say the things you did over the weekend.

S2 : I has b..., I had?

T : Past simple. For example, I saw, I did, or I played ...

S2 : Ah! I went to the park with my family last weekend.

T : Great! How was it? Did you and your family enjoy it?

S2 : Very much.

Example 2

(Students are doing a communicative task with their conversation partner in their English class. The students are asked to set a date when they can do a project together. While students are checking the date, the teacher shuttles back and forth among the groups.)

S1 : Teacher, is it okay to just say December eighteen?

T : December eighteen?

S1 : Yeah, like December eighteen or January seventeen.

S2 : You know, we need to fix the date we meet together, and we want to make sure the right way of saying dates.

T : Mmm. It's okay but it sounds a little casual. Usually December THE eighteen*th* or THE eighteen*th* of December.

S1 : Aha! December THE eighteen*th*.

T : Yeah, good.

T=teacher, S=student

Among the options A1, A2, B1, and B2 in <A>, identify the option of focus on form used in each example in <B>, respectively. Then, support your answers with evidence from <B>.

Your Answer	

문항분석

1. Topic : Focus on form approach

2. Focus

목표언어의 정확성과 유창성은 성공적인 언어 학습을 위해 상호보완적인 원리이다. 따라서, 의사소통 접근법의 언어 학습을 교실에서 진행할 경우에도 언어 형태에 대한 초점을 간과해서는 안 된다. 즉, 교사는 meaning-focused context 안에서 학습자의 부정확한 언어 형태가 출현할 경우 적절하게 수정할 수 있는 기회를 제공할 필요가 있다.

3. Negative evidence

학습자의 발화의 부정확성에 대하여 언급하는 정보 유형(information that is provided to learners concerning the incorrectness of an utterance)

(1) **Pre-emptive**: occurring before an actual error-as in a classroom context. 오류가 실제로 발생하기 이전에 제공되는 오류에 대한 정보를 가리킨다.

(2) **Reactive**: 실제 일어난 오류에 대한 교정적 정보로서 명시적인 형태와 묵시적인 형태가 있다.

▶ Explicit correction

The teacher directly tells a student what the mistake was and provides the correct answer. For example, she might say, "oh you mean...," or "you should say...," or "the correct form of this verb form is..." An alternative of this strategy is to ask a peer student, other than the one who committed the error, to provide the correct answer.

T: Where did you go after class yesterday?

S: I go home.

T: 'Go' is not the correct past tense form. You need to say, "I went home."

▶ Recast

Recasts are complex discourse structures that have been said to contain positive evidence (a model of the correct form), and negative feedback (since the correct form is juxtaposed with the non-target like form) in an environment where the positive evidence is enhanced (because of juxtaposition). If learners do not selectively attend to and recognize the negative feedback contained in recasts, then the documented contribution of recasts to learning might be attributed to the positive evidence they contain, or to the enhanced salience of the positive evidence.

T: Where did you do yesterday?

S: I go shopping

T: Oh, you went shopping. Where did you go?

S: I went to IFC mall.

4. Keyword list

focus on form, focus on forms, reactive, pre-emptive, explicit feedback, implicit feedback, positive evidence, negative evidence

---

모범답안

Example 1 represents Option A2 since the teacher gives explicit feedback on S2's error saying "You need to use past simple" with metalanguage. On the other hand, Example 2 shows Option B1 in that S1 asks a question about how to say dates before an actual problem.

07 **Read the passage in <A> and the interaction in <B>, and follow the directions.** [4 points] 2021 전공B 7번

| A |

> Some studies claim that there is a predictable language development. For instance, the following is one way of understanding developmental stages for question formation, which posits six stages, each with some prominent features.

Stage	Key Feature	Example
1	• Rising intonation on word or phrase	*Airplane?*
2	• Rising intonation with a declarative word order	*You like this?*
3	• Fronting (e.g., *do*-fronting, *wh*-fronting, other fronting)	*Where the train is going?* *Is the boy has a dog?*
4	• Inversion in *wh*-questions with a copula *be* • No inversion in *wh*-questions with auxiliaries • Yes/no questions with auxiliaries such as *can* and *will*	*Where is the book?* *Where I can draw them?* *Can he catch the ball?*
5	• Inversion in *wh*-questions with both an auxiliary and a copula *be*	*How can she solve it?*
6	• Complex questions (e.g., tag questions, embedded questions)	*She's pretty, isn't she?* *Can you tell me where he is?*

> The information about the sequences in English language acquisition like the above is mostly from child native speakers. Familiarity with them can help EFL teachers estimate their students' level of development, which in turn can help determine realistic goals for language instruction.

B

(Two students are doing an information-gap activity where they are supposed to spot the differences between two pictures.)

S1 : I see a dog in the middle.

S2 : Me, too.

S1 : Is the girl kicks a ball?

S2 : The boy kicks a ball in my picture. Where you can see the duck?

S1 : In the pond.

S2 : I can see the duck in the pond, too.

S1 : Is the boy flies kite?

S2 : No, the girl flies kite. Where are the birds?

S1 : In the trees.

S2 : I find birds on the tree, too.

                                                              S=student

Based on <A>, identify the developmental stages where S1 and S2 are, respectively, with evidence from <B>.

| Your Answer |

_____

_____

_____

_____

_____

_____

문항분석

1. Topic : Interlanguage

2. Focus

학습자가 목표어를 습득하는 과정 중 발생하는 중간언어는 모국어와 목표언어의 중간에 있는 불완전한 언어 체계로, 학습 과정 중 체계적으로 변화·발전하는 특징을 가지고 있다.

3. Characteristics of interlanguage

⑴ **Learner language is systematic**: 중간언어는 나름의 일정한 체계를 가진다. 그러나 모든 학습자가 똑같은 중간언어 체계를 갖는 것은 아니다.

At any particular stage of development, the IL is governed by rules which constitute the learner's internal grammar.

> Ex 부정문에 관한 규칙에 대해서 문두에 No나 Not을 사용하는 경우
>
> No speak English. (= I don't speak English.)
>
> No come. (= I'm not coming.)

⑵ **Learner language is variable**: 중간언어의 불완전한 특성으로 인한 것으로, 변이성이란 어떤 의미를 나타내기 위해 맥락에 따라 중간언어가 다른 형태로 나타나는 특징을 말한다.

Although the IL is systematic, differences in context result in different patterns of language use.

> Ex I don't know anything.
>
> I don't know nothing.

⑶ **Learner language is dynamic**: 중간언어의 규칙 체계는 끊임없이 수정되고 자체적으로 변화하고 발전한다.

The Learners' system changes frequently, resulting in a succession of interim grammars. This change is not a steady progression, but discontinuous progression from stable to stable plateau.

4. Keyword list

interlanguage, systematic, variable, dynamic, presystematic stage, emergent stage, systematic stage, stabilization stage, backsliding, fossilization

모범답안

S1 belongs to the developmental stage 3, while S2 has key features of stage 4. In the conversation in <B>, S1 shows fronting saying "Is the girl kicks a ball?" and "Is the boy flies kite?". On the other hand, S2 says "Where you can see the duck?" and "Where are the birds?" in <B>, which reflects no inversion in wh-questions with auxiliaries, and inversion in wh-questions with copular be, respectively.

08 Read the teacher's note in <A> and the lesson plan in <B>, and follow the directions. [4 points] 2021 전공B 8번

A

Teacher's Note

Last week, I attended a teacher training workshop on intercultural education. In the workshop, the trainer defined culture as the beliefs, way of life, art, and customs that are shared and accepted by people in a particular society. She also explained that understanding another culture involves constructing a new frame of reference in terms of the people who created it. I totally agree with her. I believe that in order to help my students develop intercultural competence, I need to have them understand their own frame of reference as well as the target culture's. I also think that it is necessary to utilize various materials to arouse students' interests. Below is the list of instructional techniques that the trainer taught us in the workshop.

• **Artifact study** : It is designed to help students discern the cultural significance of certain unfamiliar objects from the target culture. The activity involves students in giving descriptions and forming hypotheses about the function of the unknown object.

• **Culture capsule** : It is a brief description, usually one or two paragraphs, of some aspect of the target culture, followed by or incorporated with contrasting information about the students' native culture. Culture capsules can be written by teachers or students.

• **Culture island** : A culture island is an area in the classroom where posters, maps, objects, and pictures of people, lifestyles, or customs of other cultures are displayed to attract learners' attention, evoke comments, and help students develop a mental image.

• **Native informant** : Native informants can be valuable resources to the classroom teacher, both as sources of current information about the target culture and as linguistic models for students. Students can develop a set of questions they would like to ask before native speakers come to the class.

| B |

Lesson Plan

Unit 7 Hello From Around The World

Period 10th out of 12 sessions

Topic Greeting customs in the UK

Goal To teach about the ways in which people greet each other in the UK and how they are different from those in Korea

Preparation

Decorate the culture board in the English classroom with pictures and posters which illustrate the greeting customs of the UK.

Lesson Steps

1. Have the students check out the culture board and tell what they think about the pictures and posters.
2. Read aloud a short passage about greeting customs in the UK, which is prepared in advance, and have the students take notes.
3. Divide the students into small groups to compare their notes. Then, have them discuss and write the similarities and differences between Korea and the UK regarding the greeting customs.
4. Have the students imagine situations in which people from the two cultures meet. Ask them to write a conversation script based on the situation and to perform role-plays.

Based on <A>, identify TWO instructional techniques that the teacher implements in the lesson plan, with corresponding evidence from <B>.

Your Answer _____

_____

_____

_____

_____

_____

1. Topic : Teaching culture

2. Focus

실질적인 의사소통 장애는 언어 자체의 문제보다 상이한 문화적 차이로 인해 발생하는 경우가 많다. 따라서, 실질적 의사소통 능력을 신장시키기 위해 교실 수업에서 다양한 목표 문화지도가 필요하다.

3. Instructional techniques

(1) E-mail survey

Students communicate with their target language counterparts and investigate information about their daily routines, school, and interests and compare these data to their own responses.

(2) Culture capsules

Students hear a brief description that illustrates a difference between Korean culture and the target culture, discuss the difference, perform role plays based on the ideas, and integrate this information into activities that incorporate other skills.

(3) Culture assimilators

Students listen to a description or watch an incident of cross-cultural interaction in which miscommunication occurs between a Korean and a member of the target culture. They choose from a list of alternatives an explanation of the episode and finally they read feedback paragraphs that explain whether each alternative is likely and why.

(4) Cultural minidramas

Students listen to, watch, or read a series of episodes in which miscommunication is taking place; each successive episode reveals additional information, with the exact problem in understanding revealed in the last part. Students are led in discussion in order to understand how misunderstandings arise when wrong conclusions are reached about the target culture on the basis of one's own cultural understanding.

4. Keyword list

culture shock, culture stress, acculturation, culture capsule, culture assimilators

모범답안

As the first instructional technique, she/he uses 'Culture island' by decorating the culture board with pictures and posters. Then, she/he chooses the second instructional technique, 'Culture capsule', where students are required to discuss and write similarities and differences of greeting customs between Korea and the UK.

09 Read the passage in <A> and the interaction in <B>, and follow the directions. [4 points] 2021 전공A 10번

A

In language directed toward linguistically nonproficient second language speakers, native speakers tend to show foreigner-talk adjustments in the flow of conversation. These include slow speech rate, loud speech, long pauses, simple vocabulary (e.g., few idioms, high-frequency words), and paucity of slang. They also tend to make adjustments to their speech in the area of grammar. They often move topics to the front of the sentence, put new information at the end of the sentence, use fewer contractions and pronouns, grammatically repeat non-native speakers' incorrect utterances, and fill in the blank for their incomplete utterances.

B

NS : So what did you have for lunch today?
NNS : I was busy. I eated cookies.
NS : Oh, did you? I see.
NNS : You want cookies?
NS : No, thanks.
NNS : You don't like cookies?
NS : Well... these days I'm on a diet and I rarely eat them.
NNS : Sorry... I don't understand.
NS : These days I am on a diet and I rarely eat cookies.
NNS : Oh, I see. You diet. You don't eat cookies.
NS : Well, I do. But only sometimes.
NNS : Mm.... Sometime. You eat cookies only sometimes.
NS : Right, because they have too much sugar.

NS=native speaker, NNS=non-native speaker

Based on <A>, locate ONE utterance in <B> that reflects NS's grammatical adjustment to his speech and identify its adjustment type. Then, explain how it functions in the given dialogue.

Your Answer

_____

_____

_____

_____

_____

_____

1. Topic : Foreigner-talk adjustment

2. Focus

Native speaker(NS)와 Non-native speaker(NNS) 간 대화는 기존의 NS 간의 대화와 차이가 있다. 즉, NS와 NNS 간 대화는 NS가 목표언어능력이 부족한 NNS를 배려하는 담화가 진행된다. 예컨대, 더 이해하기 쉬운 어휘를 사용하거나 명확한 발음을 위해 축약 등을 하지 않으며 단순한 문장 구조를 사용하는 특징을 보인다.

3. The characteristics of foreigner talk

* slower rate of delivery * increased loudness * clearer articulation * exaggerated pronunciation * more pauses * more emphatic stress * shorter utterances * lower syntactic complexity * more avoidance of low frequency items and idiomatic expressions

(1) **NS-NS speech**

NS : When did you finish?
NS : Ten.

(2) **Foreigner talk-modification in form only (input modification)**

NS : What time you finish? (uninverted *wh*-question, deletion of do, and lack of verb inflection)
NNS : Ten o'clock.

(3) **Foreigner talk-modification in function only (interactional modification)**

NS : When did you finish?
NNS : Urn?
NS : When did you finish? (self-repetition)
NNS : Ten clock.
NS : Ten o'clock? (a confirmation check)
NNS : Yeah.

4. Keyword list

foreigner talk, input modification, interactional modification, confirmation check

모범답안

As grammatical adjustment, NS says "These days I am on a diet and I rarely eat cookies". As shown in the previous utterance, she/he uses fewer contractions and pronouns, which thus makes the incomprehensible utterance more comprehensible to NNS.

10 Read the interaction between a teacher and a student, and follow the directions. [2 points] 2014 전공A 기입형 8번

> (*The teacher asks her student, Dongho, what he did over the weekend.*)
>
> T : Hi, Dongho, how was your weekend?
> S : Hello, uh, have, had fun.
> T : You had fun, oh, good. Did you go anywhere?
> S : Yeah, uh, I go, go, went to uncle, uncle's home.
> T : What did you do there? Did you do something interesting?
> S : I play, played with childs. Uncle have childs, three childs.
> T : Your uncle has three children?
> S : Yeah, uh, one boy and two girls. So three childs.
> T : Do you like them?
> S : Yeah. They're fun. They're good to me.
>
> T=teacher, S=student

Complete the comments on the interaction by filling in the blank with ONE word.

> Language errors may occur as a result of discrepancies between the learner's interlanguage and the target language. One main source of such errors is called _____, one example of which is seen in the student's use of *childs* in the given interaction.

Your Answer _____

문항분석

1. Topic : Error analysis – Interlanguage

2. Focus

학습자의 중간언어를 형성하는 과정 중에 목표언어 규칙 간의 간섭 현상에 의해 오류가 발생하는데 이와 같은 과정에 대한 이해를 하고 있는가? 그렇다면 어떤 유형의 오류가 발생하는가?

3. Analysis of the given conversation

학습자는 목표어를 발달시켜 나가는 과정에서 미완성 단계의 언어 체계를 갖게 되는데, 이를 중간언어 또는 학습자 언어라고 명한다. 이와 같은 언어 체계는 여러 가지 불완전한 언어 형태를 취하게 되는데, 그 대표적인 원인으로 모국어의 간섭 현상 또는 목표언어 자체의 간섭 현상을 들 수 있다. 주어진 대화에서 학습자 오류의 원인은 후자로 intralingual transfer로 간주된다. 예컨대, 교사와 대화 중에 학생이 'three childs'라고 대답하는 부분에서 셀 수 있는 명사를 복수로 만들 때 plural marker '-s'를 붙여야 한다는 규칙을 불규칙 명사에도 과도하게 적용한 것을 볼 수 있다. 이러한 상황에서 발생한 intralingual error의 예를 overgeneralization이라고 부른다.

4. Keyword list

interlanguage, overgeneralization, interlingual errors, intralingual errors

---

| Answer | overgeneralization |

11 Read the passage in <A> and the teacher's log in <B>, and follow the directions. [4 points] 2019 전공A 11번

| A |

Language transfer refers to the effects of the learner's previous language knowledge or performance on subsequent language learning. Transfer can be categorized into positive and negative transfer. Negative transfer can be further divided into two types overgeneralization and interference.

| B |

(Following is a teacher's reflection on a task for her Korean students.)

Teacher's log

I conducted a task that required students in pairs to ask and answer questions in class yesterday. At the beginning of the task, I heard a student asking, "Don't you like bananas?" His partner answered, "No, I eat them everyday. They are good for my health." And another student said, "Yes, I never eat them. But I like mangos," when responding to "Don't you like oranges?" I noticed many other students make such errors later in the course of the task. So I decided to tap into the errors and explained them to students after the task. I gave them further question-and-answer exercises to provide opportunities to practice what I explained before the class was over.

Identify the type of negative transfer in <B> based on <A>. Then, provide TWO examples of the identified type from <B> and explain why they exemplify the identified type in terms of whether transfer occurs intralingually or interlingually.

Your Answer

_____

_____

_____

_____

_____

1. Topic : Error analysis

2. Focus

2언어 학습자의 완벽하지 않은 언어 체계인 중간언어(interlanguage)를 인식하고 학습자의 오류를 관찰하여 분석하고자 한 오류 분석에서, 대표적 오류의 원인을 언어 간 전이와 언어 내 전이로 구분하고있다.

3. 오류의 원인

(1) 언어 간 전이(interlingual transfer)

Mother-tongue influence causes interlingual errors. They are very frequent at the initial stages of L2 learning since the L1 is the only language system the learner knows and can draw on and therefore negative transfer takes place.

Ex *see an exam, pig meat*

(2) 언어 내 전이(intralingual transfer)

Errors that result from L2 itself. Their negative counterpart, more commonly referred to overgeneralization, is an ever-present source of difficulty.

Ex *goed, childs*

(3) 학습 환경(context of learning)

'Context' refers to a number of possibilities. For classroom learning, contextual issues arise in teacher talk, materials, focus on forms, and etc. The classroom context can lead the learner to make faulty hypotheses about the language, what is often called "false concepts" and termed "induced errors". Such errors could stem from *a misleading explanation from the teacher, faulty presentation in a textbook, or simply the juxtaposition of forms.*

(4) 의사소통 전략(communication strategies)

Communication strategies such as *word coinage, circumlocution, and prefabricated patterns* can all be sources of error. As learners employ a variety of strategies either for production or comprehension, they may draw on their L1, previous L2 knowledge, general knowledge, or simply make spur-of-the-moment intuitive guesses.

4. Others

(1) Positive transfer

When the relevant unit or structure of both languages is the same, linguistic interference can result in correct language production called positive transfer : here, the "correct" meaning is in line with most native speakers' notions of acceptability. An example is the use of cognates.

(2) Negative transfer

However, language interference is most often discussed as a source of errors known as negative transfer, which occurs when speakers and writers transfer items and structures that are not the same in both languages.

Within the theory of contrastive analysis, the systematic study of a pair of languages with a view to identifying their structural differences and similarities, the greater the differences between the two languages, the more negative transfer can be expected.

5. Keyword list

interlanguage, interlingual transfer, intralingual transfer, overgeneraliation, error analysis, L1 interference, linguistic interference, crosslinguistic influence

---

모범답안

In <B>, 'interference' as the negative transfer occurs as students incorrectly apply (interlingually transferred) Korean rule for answering negative questions in English. For example, Korean students respond to the negative question like "Don't you like bananas?" and "Don't you like oranges?" as follows: "No, I eat them everyday." and "Yes, I never eat them."

12 Read the passage in <A> and the conversation in <B>, and follow the directions. [3 points] 2014 전공A 서술형 2번

A

A typical conversation organized around making requests has a common overarching sequence of interactional moves:

• A greeting exchange
• Preliminary moves toward a forthcoming request
• Making the request
• Short negotiation about the request
• Acceptance/Rejection of the request
• Closing/Thanking

B

(A low-proficiency English learner asks her roommate, a native speaker of English, to go buy some bread for her.)

Jisu : Hi, Kelly.
Kelly : Hi, Jisu.
Jisu : Buy me bread, OK?
Kelly : Do you want bread?
Jisu : Yeah.
Kelly : So, there's no bread in the fridge?
Jisu : Sorry?
Kelly : You don't have bread?
Jisu : No.
Kelly : So, do you want me to go to the supermarket and get some bread for you?
Jisu : What was that?
Kelly : Do you want me to get bread for you?
Jisu : Yeah.
Kelly : Do you want it right now?
Jisu : Tomorrow morning.
Kelly : OK. I'll get it for you later tonight.
Jisu : OK. Thank you.

Jisu=low-proficiency learner, Kelly=native speaker of English

Explain how the conversation in <B> deviates from the sequence of interactional moves in <A>. Then identify the strategy that Jisu uses when she does not understand Kelly.

Your Answer

_____

_____

_____

_____

_____

_____

1. Topic : Conversation analysis

2. Focus

주어진 대화에서 각 conversation turn이 수행하는 기능을 이해하고 대화를 분석할 수 있어야 한다.

3. Conversation analysis

전형적인 making request를 위한 대화의 진행 순서는 greeting → request에 대한 준비 작업 → making request → request에 대한 협의 → acceptance/ rejection → 대화 종료 등이다. 그러나 Jisu와 Kelly의 대화 순서는 greeting 후 preliminary moves toward a forthcoming request 없이 바로 request로 이어져 있다.

(1) A greeting exchange

　Jisu와 Kelly는 대화를 시작하기에 앞서 인사를 주고받는다.

(2) Preliminary moves toward a forthcoming request

　주어진 대화에서는 찾아볼 수 없다.

(3) **Making the request**

Jisu는 "Buy me bread, OK?"라고 말하며 빵을 달라는 요청을 한다.

(4) **Short negotiation about the request**

요청한 내용이 정확히 전달되지 않아 서로 의미 협상(negotiation for meaning)을 하게 되고, 그 과정에서 clarification request가 사용된다(e.g., "Sorry?" / "What was that?").

(5) **Acceptance/Rejection of the request**

Kelly가 "Okay. I'll get it for you later tonight."이라고 말하며 요청에 대한 수락을 한다.

(6) **Closing/Thanking**

Jisu가 "OK. Thank you."라고 이야기하며 대화를 마무리 짓는다.

4. Keyword list

clarification request

모범답안

The conversation in <B> omitted "preliminary moves toward a forthcoming request" among the sequence of interactional move in <A>. That is, in <B> Jisu exchanges a greeting with Kelly and then directly makes the request of buying some bread for her. During the conversation, also, Jisu uses a clarification request when she does not understand what Kelly says.

Plus+

Managing Interaction

If a conversation is to open, progress, and close smoothly and productively, the speakers need to manage it by following the 'rules' that seem to govern normal interactions. The cultural conventions will need to be learned as well as the appropriate formality in style of speech and the level of politeness that is appropriate to the relationship between the participants.

1. Openings and closings

There are conventional ways of opening a conversation in English: some of these are contextually facilitated, as in the British 'It's a nice day, isn't it?' where the tag ending invites a response. In fact, many openings are ritualized as statement followed by response or question followed by answer, for example, 'These buses get later, don't they?' or "Buy here today, isn't it?" These openings are all the attention-getting and can lead to further conversation. Closings need to be carefully negotiated as there is usually a pre-closing signal, for example, 'Well, I must think about going....' or 'I don't want to keep you....' before the actual closing.

2. Responding appropriately in fixed routines

The term 'adjacency pairs' has been given to exchanges where a turn by one speaker requires an immediate response, as in greetings, invitations, compliments, inquiries about health, and complaints.

3. Taking turns

Students often report that one of their greatest difficulties is entering a conversation. This is not surprising given that this requires a rapid sequence; watching for indications that the current speaker is coming to a close (e.g., falling intonation), giving signals of a desire to come in (e.g., raised eyebrows, leaning forward) formulating a turn which fits the flow of the conversation and which picks up on what has already been said; and finding the language to express it.

4. Topic management

The kind of topics chosen, how these are introduced, and how speakers move from one topic to another are further aspects of managing interaction. Another is to know how to change the topic, as in 'By the way....' or 'That reminds me of....'

13 Read the passages and follow the directions. [4 points] 2017 전공B 4번

| A |

Meaning-negotiation strategies such as comprehension checks, clarification requests, and confirmation checks may aid comprehension during conversational interaction. First, comprehension checks are defined as the moves by which one interlocutor seeks to make sure that the other has understood correctly. Second, clarification requests are the moves by which one interlocutor requests assistance in understanding the other's preceding utterance. Finally, confirmation checks refer to the moves used by one interlocutor to confirm whether he or she correctly has understood what the other has said.

| B |

Miss Jeong has been instructing her students to actively utilize meaning-negotiation strategies stated in <A> during speaking activities. One day, she interviewed two of her students, Mijin and Haerim, about the strategies that they had used during previous speaking activities. The following are excerpts from the interview :

Mijin : When I didn't understand what my friends said during speaking activities, I usually said, "Could you repeat what you said?" or "I am sorry?" Sometimes I tried to check whether my friends clearly understood what I said by saying, "You know what I mean?"

Haerim : Well, during speaking activities, when I had difficulties comprehending what my friends said, I didn't say anything and pretended to understand what they said. I felt it embarrassing to show my lack of understanding to my friends. However, when I talked about something during speaking activities, I often said, "Do you understand?" in order to see if my utterances were understood well by my friends.

Based on the passage in <A>, write down all the meaning-negotiation strategies that Mijin and Haerim used respectively, along with their corresponding utterances from each student in <B>.

Your Answer _____

_____

_____

_____

_____

_____

1. Topic：Negotiation strategies

2. Focus

Mijin과 Haerim이 수업 중에 진행되는 speaking 활동 중에 어떠한 방식의 의미 협상 전략을 사용하였는지 묻는 문제이다. 〈A〉에서 주어진 개념들에 대한 정의를 기반으로 하여 각각의 학생이 사용한 의미 협상 전략을 파악하고, 〈B〉에 있는 evidence를 연관지어 답안에 기술하면 된다.

3. Examples of negotiation for meaning

(1) Comprehension check

발화자가 자신의 발화에 대한 청자의 이해 여부를 확인하는 경우

One speaker attempts to determine whether the other speaker has understood a preceding message.

Ex Do you understand?

(2) Confirmation check

앞선 발화에 대해서 청자가 자신의 이해의 정도를 확인하는 경우

One speaker seeks confirmation of the other's preceding utterance through repetition, with rising intonation, of what was perceived to be all or part of the preceding utterance.

Ex You mean...?

(3) Clarification request

앞선 발화에 대해서 청자가 추가적인 설명이나 정보를 요구하는 경우

One speaker seeks assistance in understanding the other speaker's preceding utterance through questions, statements or imperatives.

Ex Pardon?

4. Keyword list

comprehension check, confirmation check, clarification request

모범답안

Mijin uses a clarification request saying "Could you repeat what you said?" or "I am sorry?" and employs a comprehension check such as "You know what I mean?" In the case of Haerim as she says "Do you understand?" she uses a comprehension check only.

Plus⁺

Interaction Hypothesis

The Interaction Hypothesis suggests a number of ways in which interactions can contribute to language acquisition. More specifically, it suggests that when interaction modifications lead to comprehensible input via the decomposition and segmenting of input, acquisition is facilitated: that when learners receive feedback, acquisition is facilitated, and that when learners are pushed to reformulated their own utterances, acquisition is promoted.

Pushed output & Modified output
A : *I go cinema.*
B : *You what?*
C : *I went to the cinema.*

In the example, A is led to reformulate her initial utterance, producing a more grammatical version of it, as a result of B's clarification request. Thus this kind of exchange provides an opportunity for what Swain has called pushed output, i.e. output that reflects what learners can produce when they are pushed to use the target language accurately and concisely.

NNS : *I go cinema.*
NS : *Uh?*
NNS : *I go cinema last night.*
NS : *Oh, last night.*

The above dialogue shows that the interaction has lead to successful communication, but that it does not contribute to the acquisition of the past tense, a morphological feature. Thus, successful communication takes place without the learner needing to modify his or her output by incorporating the past marker, showing that not all pushed output is in fact modified.

14 Read the passage in <A> and the interaction in <B>, and follow the directions. [4 points] 2020 전공B 4번

A

When problems in conveying meaning occur in conversational interactions, interlocutors need to interrupt the flow and negotiate meaning in order to overcome communication breakdowns and to understand what the conversation is about. A negotiation routine may have a sequence of four components:

• A *trigger* is an utterance that causes communication difficulty.
• An *indicator* alerts the speaker of the trigger that a problem exists.
• A *response* is the component through which the speaker of the trigger attempts to resolve the communication difficulty.
• A *reaction to response* can tell the speaker of the trigger whether or not the problem has been resolved.

B

(The following is a student-student talk occurring in the morning.)

S1: You didn't come to the baseball practice yesterday. What happened?
S2: Nothing serious. I had to study for an exam.
S1: I am sorry you missed the practice. Have you taken the exam yet?
S2: Yes. I took it a little while ago.
S1: How did you do?
S2: Hopefully I did OK. I didn't get any sleep last night.
S1: I guess you must be drained.
S2: Drained? What do you mean?
S1: It's similar to 'tired.'
S2: Oh, I see. Yeah, I am very tired.
S1: You need to take a break.
S2: I sure do, but I think I am going to eat something first.

S=student

Identify an utterance from <B> that is a *response* mentioned in <A>, and explain how the speaker attempts to resolve the communication difficulty with the identified utterance. Then, identify an utterance from <B> that is a *reaction to response* mentioned in <A>, and explain whether the communication difficulty is resolved with the identified utterance.

Your Answer

_____

_____

_____

_____

_____

1. Topic : Conversation analysis

2. Focus

담화 분석(discourse analysis) 중 학생들의 의사소통 능력을 보다 효과적으로 분석할 수 있는 유형이 대화 분석(conversation analysis)으로, 특히 대화 담화자 간의 의사소통 장애(communication breakdown)가 생겼을 경우 무엇 때문에 생겼는지, 어떻게 장애를 극복해 가는지에 대한 negotiation routine에 대해 다루고 있다.

3. Negotiation routine to overcome communication breakdowns

A Trigger (T), is an utterance that causes non-understanding for the hearer. Then, the hearer signals non-understanding through an Indicator (I). A Response (R) phase is when the speaker fixes the non-understanding. Finally, the hearer makes a Reaction to the Response (RR).

A negotiation routine consists of two parts: a trigger and a resolution. The trigger (T) is "an utterance or portion of an utterance on the part of the speaker which results in some indication of non-understanding on the part of the hearer." The second part of the routine, the resolution, consists of two primes: an indicator (I), by which one of the conversational partners lets the other know that something was not clear, and a response (R), which acknowledges the request for information. An optional prime, the reaction to the response (RR), may tie up the routine.

> Ex S1: My father now is retire. (T)
> S2: Retire? (I)
> S1: Yes. (R)
> S2: Oh, yeah. (RR)

The above classroom talk shows an example of one of the routines used by two students to negotiate a non-understanding.

4. Keyword list

negotiation of meaning, trigger, response, indicator, reaction to the response

---

모범답안

As a response mentioned in <A>, S1 says "It's similar to 'tired.'" in <B>. That is, she lexically modifies 'drained' previously used into an easy synonym, 'tired', leading to successful communication. Also, by saying "Oh, I see. Yeah, I am very tired." as a reaction to response, S2 verifies his clear understanding.

15 **Read the dialogue and follow the directions.** [2 points] 2018 전공A 7번

> *(A teacher and a student are talking after seeing a video-clip of a baseball game.)*
>
> T: What was happening in the video?
> S: A ball, uh, a ball.
> T: A ball was thrown.
> S: Thrown?
> T: Yes, thrown. A ball was thrown.
> S: A ball thrown.
> T: And who threw the ball?
> S: Pitcher. Thrown pitcher.
> T: Thrown by the pitcher.
> S: By pitcher.
> T: Yes, by the pitcher. A ball was thrown by the pitcher.
> S: Ball thrown by pitcher.
>
> T=teacher, S=student

Fill in the blank with the FOUR most appropriate words.

> From a socio-cultural perspective, effective learning takes place when what a student attempts to learn is within his or her _____.
> This is the distance between what a student can do alone and what he or she can do with scaffolded help from more knowledgeable others like teachers or more capable peers. For learning to be effective, such help should be provided to a student through interaction like the teacher's utterances offered to aid the student in the above dialogue.

Your Answer _____

문항분석

1. Topic: 비고츠키의 sociocultural theory

2. Focus

Vygotsky의 sociocultural theory 중, 핵심 개념인 ZPD와 scaffolding에 대해 이해하고 해당 이론이 교사와 학생의 상호작용 속에서 어떻게 적용되는지를 알고 있는지 확인하는 문제이다.

3. Vygotsky's sociocultural theory

Vygotsky's sociocultural theory of human learning describes learning as a social process and the origination of human intelligence in society or culture. The major theme of Vygotsky's theoretical framework is that social interaction plays a fundamental role in the development of cognition. Vygotsky believed everything is learned on two levels.

First, through interaction with others, and then integrated into the individual's mental structure. Every function in the child's cultural development appears twice: first, on the social level, and later, on the individual level; first, between people (interpsychological) and then inside the child (intrapsychological). This applies equally to voluntary attention, to logical memory, and to the formation of concepts. All the higher functions originate as actual relationships between individuals.

A second aspect of Vygotsky's theory is the idea that the potential for cognitive development is limited to a "zone of proximal development" (ZPD). This "zone" is the area of exploration for which the student is cognitively prepared, but requires help and social interaction to fully develop (Briner, 1999). A teacher or more experienced peer is able to provide the learner with "scaffolding" to support the student's evolving understanding of knowledge domains or development of complex skills. Collaborative learning, discourse, modelling, and scaffolding are strategies for supporting the intellectual knowledge and skills of learners and facilitating intentional learning.

4. Keyword list

socio-cultural perspective, zone of proximal development, scaffolding, interaction

---

Answer   zone of proximal development

16 **Read the passage and follow the directions.** [2 points] 2018 전공A 1번

Learning a second language (L2) may be viewed as the gradual transformation of performance from controlled to less controlled. This transformation has been called proceduralization or automatization and entails the conversion of declarative knowledge into procedural knowledge. According to this argument, the learning of skills is assumed to start with the explicit provision of relevant declarative knowledge and, through practice, this knowledge can hopefully convert into ability for use. At the same time, it is important to understand that learning an L2 may proceed in a different way. For example, some have wondered if incidental L2 learning is possible as a consequence of doing something else in the L2. Simply put, the question is about the possibility of learning without intention. The answer is still open, but, at present, it appears that people learn faster, more and better when they deliberately apply themselves to learning.

Read Mr. Lee's teaching log below and fill in the blank with the ONE most appropriate word from the passage above.

   Through my teaching experience, I've learned that different students learn in different ways. Considering the current trend in teaching and learning, I believe that students should be provided with more opportunities to be exposed to the _____ learning condition. Minsu's case may illustrate that point. At the beginning of the semester, Minsu introduced himself as a book lover. He wanted to read novels in English but was not sure if he could. I suggested that he didn't have to try to comprehend all the details. Indeed, Minsu has benefitted a lot from reading novels. He said he learned many words and expressions even though he did not make attempts to memorize them. I will continue observing his progress as his way of learning is of great interest.

Your Answer   _____

문항분석

1. Topic : How to teach linguistic knowledge

2. Focus

성공적인 2언어 학습을 위한 두 가지 접근 방법으로 incidental learning과 intentional learning에 대한 차이를 명확히 파악하고 보다 효과적인 학습 과정에 대한 이해를 하고 있는지 묻고 있다.

3. Incidental vs. Intentional learning

(1) Incidental learning

Incidental learning is the process of learning something without the intention of doing so. It is also learning one thing while intending to learn another. In terms of language acquisition, incidental learning is said to be an effective way of learning vocabulary from context. Incidental vocabulary learning motivates learners for extensive reading. It involves learners' ability to guess the meaning of new words from the contextual clues. Incidental learning occurs more particularly through extensive reading in input-rich environments. Extensive reading is a pleasurable reading situation where a teacher encourages students to choose what they want to read for themselves from reading materials at a level they can understand.

Incidental vocabulary promotes deeper mental processing and better retention. The learners get themselves fully involved in the process of deciphering the meaning through the clues available in the text. They think and rethink about the new words involving cognitive process which helps the learners retain the words for a longer period of time.

(2) Intentional learning

Whereas, intentional learning is described as the having the intention to learn the material and to commit it to ones memory. In terms of vocabulary learning, intentional learning based on synonyms, antonyms, word substitution, multiple choice, scrambled words and crossword puzzles, regardless of context, is not so effective, because learners are more prone to rote learning. They cram the meaning of the new words <u>without undergoing cognitive process</u>. A very few words learned through this method get transformed into active process. Whereas reading new words and inferring the meaning through context will be more productive because it sharpens the ability for guessing.

By practicing guessing the students can infer the general import and begin to understand the meaning gradually. Hence the process of guessing is of prime importance for vocabulary learning. Guessing is useful for both the proficient learners and low proficiency-level learners.

4. Keyword list

incidental learning, extensive reading, learning without intention, no memorization

---

Answer	incidental

Plus⁺

Vocabulary from Context

The ability to determine the meaning of vocabulary items from context is one of the most important aspects of successful reading. When bringing reading passages into the classroom, instructors can introduce new vocabulary through use of teacher-developed vocabulary from context formats. Three characteristics qualify a vocabulary item for inclusion in such exercises: If the meaning is not available from the context provided, if the item is likely to impede comprehension, and if the word is frequent enough to be worth teaching, it is a candidate for a vocabulary from context activity.

Successful vocabulary from context items provide adequate context to suggest meaning without providing a format definition.

Although vocabulary from context activities are strengthened by examination of the full discourse context, those exercises designed to teach particular items tend to be written on the sentence level. It is important to remember that each sentence need not perfectly delineate the meaning of the word or phrase in question. Instructors can generate several sentences for a single item to ensure that students will gain a general sense of the term.

17 Read the dialogue and follow the directions. [2 points] 2018 전공A 3번

> T1: There's no doubt that young children beginning school need the basics of reading, writing, and math.
>
> T2: I agree, but the big problem is determining the best way for them to get it. I think the classic mode of a teacher at the chalkboard, and books and homework is outdated.
>
> T1: True. That's why I have been looking at some teaching literature based on the ideas Jonathan Bergman and Aaron Sams came up with.
>
> T2: What do they suggest?
>
> T1: Well, they have reconsidered the role of the traditional classroom and home. So home becomes a classroom, and vice versa in this way of learning. Students view lecture materials, usually in the form of videos, as homework before class.
>
> T2: That's interesting. What's the focus in class?
>
> T1: That's the best part. Class time is reserved for activities such as interactive discussions or collaborative work supervised by the teacher.
>
> T2: I like it. But how does it benefit the students?
>
> T1: They can study the lectures at home at their own pace, or re-watch the videos, if needed, or even skip parts they already understand.
>
> T2: Right. And then, in class the teacher is present when they apply new knowledge. What about traditional homework?
>
> T1: That can be done in class, too. So, the teacher can gain insights into whatever concepts, if any, their students are struggling with and adjust the class accordingly.
>
> T2: What does the literature say about its effectiveness?
>
> T1: Amazingly, according to one study, 71% of teachers who have tried this approach in their classes noticed improved grades, and 80% reported improved student attitudes, as well.
>
> T2: That's fantastic. Let me read that when you're done. I want to look further into this.
>
> T=teacher

Fill in the blank with the ONE most appropriate word.

> The teaching approach discussed by the two teachers is known technically as _____ learning in educational settings.

Your Answer _____

문항분석

1. Topic: Learner-centered instruction

2. Focus

전통적인 교사 중심의 교실수업에서 벗어나 학생 중심의 교실수업 형태에 대해 묻는 문제이다. 즉, 학생 개개인의 수준에 맞춰 가정에서의 동영상 강의 및 학습 자료에 대한 준비를 토대로, 교실 내에서 협동학습 및 토론 위주의 학습자 중심 수업인 flipped learning(거꾸로 수업)에 대해 묻고 있다. (Blended learning: A mixture of online and face-to-face course delivery)

3. Flipped learning(거꾸로 수업)

The traditional classroom is frequently organized as a place where the teacher presents and explains content whilst students listen to and note down all the information provided. The class is usually teacher centered, though one can have a more dialogic approach with the students, depending on one's own perspective. Routinely, in the classroom, all students have to do the same activities, based on the resources available in the classroom and following the same pace and the one established by the teacher. Sometimes, the teacher provides some homework tasks, or asks for exercises to be completed outside the classroom, to reinforce knowledge or elicit further questions. In the Flipped Classroom model, the teacher provides in advance materials created or selected by him/herself (short videos, screencasts or podcasts), for the students self learning activities, out of the classroom. These activities can be performed when and where the student feels most comfortable, taking into account his/her <u>own learning rhythm</u>. In this model, the student studies the materials and the resources pointed out by the teacher, he/she also identifies his/her difficulties and topics he/she wishes to be cleared. Students also <u>look for extra</u> information and follow their own learning rhythm and can review the learning materials <u>whenever they need to</u>. <u>Classroom</u> time is used for <u>questioning and to deepen the knowledge, in a more personalized learning environment where students can learn side-by-side, in small groups, and the teacher helps them to clear misunderstanding</u>. Instead of using classroom time to present information, the teacher has time to clarify doubts, provide extra resources, create activities in the classroom that might be felt as necessary and <u>evaluate immediately the students' performance within the classroom</u>. This way, it promotes <u>the improvement of the quality of learning</u>. This classroom organization model inverts the traditional lecturing classroom concept, creating classes where students are highly engaged in an active and participatory learning.

The relation of the concept Flipped Classroom to online availability of resources and educational contents, defines it commonly as a model of blended learning (b-Learning).

4. Keyword list

blended learning, flipped learning, flipped classroom, learner-centered instruction

---

| Answer | flipped |

Plus⁺

2015년 개정 교육과정

1. 과업 중심 학습(Task-based learning)

실제적인 의사소통 과업을 중심으로 교과를 구성하고 교과 목표를 일차적으로 언어 학습에 두며, 학습의 궁극적인 초점은 ① 과정 중심, ② 의사소통과 의미 강조, ③ 상호작용 극대화이다. 따라서 과업을 중심으로 영어 수업을 타 교과와 통합적으로 설계할 경우 학생들에게 진정한 의사소통의 목적을 갖고 영어를 사용할 수 있는 기회를 제공하고, 문제해결능력을 신장하여 탈분과적인 형태의 내용을 종합적으로 경험하게 하고 다양한 사고를 할 수 있는 기회를 제공한다.

2. Digital literacy learning

Digital literacy란 컴퓨터, 인터넷과 같은 사이버상에서 찾아낸 정보의 가치를 평가할 수 있는 비판적인 사고력 및 다양한 출처에서 나온 여러 정보를 이해하고 자신의 목적에 맞게 새롭게 조합하여 사용할 수 있는 능력을 의미한다. Computer literacy, information literacy, knowledge literacy를 포함하며, ICT 접근 능력, 활용 능력, 정보 생산 능력을 말한다.
➡ 인터넷 활용학습으로 인한 멀티미디어 자료 이용, 자기 주도식 학습, on-line learning, 동기 유발

3. Project-based learning

연구 주제를 정하여 비교적 장기간에 걸쳐 결과물을 창출하는 과업을 통해 직접적인 경험과 능동적인 학습을 유도하는 방법이다. 소집단 중심으로 역할과 책임을 분배하고 활동하여 프로젝트 결과물을 완성하도록 하고, 교과 내용 학습과 언어 사용을 동시에 목표로 두며, 교과목 간의 통합적 접근을 통한 다양한 학습 경험을 제공할 수 있다.

4. Subject-integrated class

영어 교과를 타 교과와 통합하여 가르칠 경우 각 교과나 주제에 관련한 다양한 분야의 어휘와 표현을 자연스러운 맥락 속에서 풍부하게 제공받을 수 있어 의미 있는 담화 맥락 안에서 언어를 학습할 수 있다. 대표적 수업 모델로 theme-based instruction을 제시할 수 있다. 주제 중심의 교육은 학생의 흥미를 고려하여 주제를 선정하고 이와 관련된 활동을 바탕으로 지도하는 방법이다.

5. Genre-based approach

장르 중심의 쓰기 교육에서는 글이 사용되는 사회적 맥락 및 기능뿐 아니라, 언어의 형태와의 관계, 텍스트의 전개 방법, 언어 재료에 대한 연습을 강조한다. 각 장르에 따른 텍스트의 타입은 고유의 rhetorical structure를 가지고 있으며, 이러한 텍스트 성격의 차이가 학생이 텍스트를 processing하는 데 있어 학생의 인지, 기억, 학습 방법, 태도에 미치는 영향이 매우 크다.

18 Read the online discussion about Hyun's opinion and fill in the blank with TWO words from the passage. [2 points] 2016 전공A 7번

Hyun
As an international language, English has many varieties used and taught around the world. Have you ever thought about English varieties?

🖉 like it 28 | recommend it 15

Sarah
Yes! There are many varieties of English. Americans, Australians, Brits and Canadians have many variations in how they use English. Naturally, this exists between non-native speakers, too. I think we should be aware of this reality. Many English teachers in the world today are non-native speakers of English. We need to consider this issue for teacher training and language instruction.

Bill
I agree. Although I am a native English teacher, like many of you, we need to recognize the validity of a variety of Englishes, or better known as, _____.
These include established outer-circle varieties such as Indian English, Singaporean English, and Nigerian English.

Min
Perhaps, but what about standardization? Shouldn't we focus on one clearly understood form of the language for consistency and intelligibility?

Jun
I don't think that is applicable in all cases, Min. The needs and attitudes of students, teachers, and administrators have an influence on the norm or standard adopted for instruction; it is thus best that local norms be respected whenever possible.

Your Answer _____

1. Topic : World Englishes

2. Focus

International language로서 English의 급부상으로 인해 다양한 유형의 English에 대한 논의가 뜨겁게 일어나고 있다. native와 nonnative 간의 전통적 이분화는 더 이상 의미가 없다. 따라서 다양한 언어를 사용하는 나라 간의 소통 수단으로서의 World Englishes에 주목해야 할 것이다.

3. World Englishes

(1) **Definition** : The status of English in its varieties

The study of World Englishes consists of identifying varieties of English used in diverse sociolinguistic contexts globally and analyzing how sociolinguistic histories, multicultural backgrounds and contexts of function influence the use of English in different regions of the world.

(2) **Inner circle vs. Outer circle**

The process of nativization of English has spread from the inner circle of countries (such as the United Kingdom, United States, Australia, New Zealand) to an outer circle of countries that includes India, Singapore, the Philippines, Nigeria, Ghana and others.

4. Others : Classification of Englishes

Perhaps the most common classification of Englishes, especially in the language teaching world, has been to distinguish between English as a native language(ENL), English as a second language(ESL) and English as a foreign language(EFL). In this classification, ENL is spoken in countries where English is the primary language of the great majority of the population. Australia, Canada, New Zealand, the United Kingdom and the United States are countries in which English is said to be spoken and used as a native language. In contrast, ESL is spoken in countries where English is an important and usually official language, but not the main language of the country. These countries are typically ex-colonies of the United Kingdom or the United States. Nigeria, India, Malaysia and the Philippines are examples of countries in which English is said to be spoken and used as a second language. The final classification of this model is EFL. EFL occurs in countries where English is not actually used or spoken very much in the normal course of daily life. In these countries, English is typically learned at school, but students have little opportunity to use English outside the classroom and therefore little motivation to learn English. China, Indonesia, Japan and many countries in the Middle East are countries in which English is said to operate as an EFL.

5. Keyword list

world Englishes, inner circle, outer circle, ENL, EFL, ESL, sociolinguistic context, varieties of Englishes

---

| Answer | World Englishes

Plus⁺

How to Learn English: Improving Your English

1. Speak a little English every day.

The absolute best way to learn any new language is just to speak it. It doesn't matter if you only know five English words or if you're practically fluent—speaking English with another person is the fastest, most effective method of improving.

Don't wait until you "feel more comfortable" speaking in English—you probably won't reach that level for a long time, so push yourself outside of your comfort zone and start speaking English today. You'll be amazed at how quickly your language skills improve.

2. Work on your pronunciation.

Even if you have an acceptable grasp of the English language, with good grammar and an extensive vocabulary, native English speakers may find you very difficult to understand if you don't work on your pronunciation.

• Correct, clear pronunciation is essential if you really want to improve your level of English. Listen closely to how native English speakers pronounce certain words and sounds and do your best to copy them.

- Pay particular attention to any sounds that you are unfamiliar with or that do not exist in your native tongue. For example, some people have difficulty pronouncing the "r" sound, as it does not exist in their native language, while other people have difficulty with certain consonant clusters, such as the "th" sound.
- Be aware that the pronunciation of certain English words varies greatly depending on the part of the world it's spoken in. For example, American English is very different from British English. If you intend to travel to or live in an English-speaking country, this is something you should take into account when learning how to pronounce certain words.

3. Expand your vocabulary and use idiomatic phrases.

The wider your vocabulary and the more English phrases you learn, the easier speaking English will become.

- Again, spending time with native English speakers will help you to pick up on common vocabulary and phrases in a natural way. Although reading, watching English TV and listening to the news is also beneficial.
- Once you have learned a new word or phrase, you should make an effort to use it in a sentence—this is the best way to commit it to memory.
- Another easy way to commit new words to memory is to make labels for everyday household items and stick them around your house or apartment. Then every time you use the kettle or look in the mirror, you will see the English word for these items staring back at you.
- You should also start a notebook of idiomatic phrases that English speakers use all the time. Some examples include "it's raining cats and dogs" (raining heavily), to be on "cloud nine" (to be very happy) or saying something is a "piece of cake" (when something is very easy). Sprinkling these kinds of phrases into your conversation will bring your level of English up several notches.

Chapter

02 Learner Variables and Teacher's Roles

01 Read the passage in <A> and the lesson plan in <B>, and follow the directions. [4 points] 2023 전공A 12번

A

In designing activities for cultural instruction, it is important to consider the purpose of the activity, as well as its usefulness for teaching language and culture in an integrative fashion. The most basic issue in cross-cultural education is increasing the degree to which language and culture are integrated. Several suggestions for dealing with this issue are as follows:

1. Use cultural information when teaching vocabulary. Teach students about the cultural connotations of new words.
2. Present cultural topics in conjunction with closely related grammatical features whenever possible. Use cultural contexts for language-practice activities, including those that focus on particular grammatical forms.
3. Make good use of textbook illustrations or photos. Use probing questions to help students describe the cultural features of the illustrations or photos.
4. In group activities, use communication techniques for cultural instruction, such as discussions and role-plays.
5. Teach culture while involving the integration of the four language skills. Do not limit cultural instruction to lecture or anecdotal formats.

B

	Lesson 4. World-famous Holidays	
Objectives	Students will be able to 1. introduce world-famous holidays using *-er than* and 2. perform activities related to the holidays to deepen their understanding of diverse cultures.	
Development	Step 1	• T asks Ss to speak out about anything related to the pictures in the textbook on p. 78. • T asks Ss some questions to elicit their ideas about what cultural features they see in the pictures of world-famous holidays. • Ss tell each other about the cultural differences among the holidays based on the pictures.
	Step 2	• T tells Ss about the origins of the world-famous holidays in detail. • T explains the cultural characteristics of those holidays. • T shares his experiences related to the holidays, and Ss listen to T's stories.
	Step 3	• T has Ss listen to a story about the world-famous holidays, and underline the expressions of comparative forms in the story on p. 79. • T talks with Ss about the meanings and functions of the expressions based on the cultural characteristics of the holidays. • T asks Ss, in pairs, to search the Internet for more information about cultural differences among the holidays and to describe the differences using comparative forms.
	Step 4	• T introduces new words in the story on the screen. • T explains the meanings of the words (traditional, adapting, polite, etc.), comparing them with their synonyms and/or antonyms. • Ss note the words and memorize them using mnemonic devices.

Step 5	• T has Ss sit in groups of four, and choose one distinct aspect of the world-famous holidays, such as costume, food, and festivals. • Ss write a culture capsule in groups about the differences. • T gives preparation time, and each group performs a role-play based on the culture capsule in front of their classmates.

T=teacher, Ss=students

Identify the TWO steps from <B> that do NOT correspond to the suggestions in <A>. Then, support your answers, respectively, with evidence from <A> and <B>.

Your Answer _____

_____

_____

_____

_____

_____

1. Topic : Cultural instruction

2. Focus

언어와 문화를 효과적으로 통합하기 위한 지침들을 토대로 "World-famous Holidays"로 진행된 수업과정 중 어느 단계에서 지침준수가 일어나지 않았는가에 대한 문항이다.

3. Some activities for cultural instruction

(1) **Culture capsules** : Students hear a brief description that illustrates a difference between Korean culture and the target culture, discuss the difference, perform role plays based on the ideas.

(2) **Culture assimilators** : Students listen to a description or watch an incident of cross-cultural interaction in which miscommunication occurs between a Korean and a member of the target culture.

(3) **Cultural minidramas** : Students listen to, watch, or read a series of episodes in which miscommunication is taking place; each successive episode reveals additional information, with the exact problem in understanding revealed in the last part.

4. Keyword list

culture capsules, culture assimilators, cultural minidramas, cross-cultural education

---

모범답안

Steps 2 and 4 do not follow suggestions 5 and 1, respectively. In Step 2 the teacher asks students to just listen to his experiences (anecdotes) and explanation (lecture) about world-famous holidays, not facilitating integrated skills. Also, in Step 4, without mentioning the cultural connotations of new words, the teacher just explains their meanings with synonyms and/or antonyms.

02 Read the teacher log and follow the directions. [2 points] 2023 전공B 1번

Teacher Log

Skill-integration is considered more and more important in modern language learning, but I found that at any one time I was almost always teaching just one skill in isolation. As part of my development as a teacher, I wanted to integrate multiple language skills and pursue a more real-life style of communication. To do this, I first investigated my own class practices. I video-recorded eight lessons. After reviewing the video files, I found that in six lessons I taught only one skill. In the other two, I was only able to integrate listening and speaking but never reading or writing. I drew up a plan to integrate language skills more often. What I did was implement the project-based learning approach so that students could collaborate in groups to advance their projects. I conducted the experiments over the second half of the semester and gathered the data. Then, I video-recorded another eight lessons toward the end of the semester to test the effectiveness of the measure I had implemented. After I analyzed the videos and the data, the results were as follows: two of the lessons showed the integration of speaking and reading skills, two other lessons integrated reading and writing skills, and one lesson integrated all four skills! Based on these results, I feel the approach really improved my teaching practice and my ability to teach students with the four skills in an integrated fashion.

Fill in the blank with the TWO most appropriate words.

The log above describes how the teacher addresses a problem in the classroom and resolves it through a systematic process of inquiry. Sometimes referred to as teacher research or classroom research, _____ is considered an important part of self-reflective teacher development. It usually involves four steps: planning, acting, observing, and reflecting. Its major goal is to improve both student learning and teaching effectiveness.

Your Answer

문항분석

1. Topic: Action research

2. Focus

주어진 data에 따르면 통합수업을 위하여 교사는 자신의 여덟 번의 수업을 녹화하여 문제점이 무엇인지 체계적으로 찾아 개선하고자 한다. 이와 같이 교사는 자신의 수업에 대한 연구 또는 교사연구를 통하여 스스로의 수업을 성찰하여 더 나은 수업을 만들어 갈 수 있다.

3. Rationale for the use of action research in foreign and second language classroom

Increasingly language teachers are required not only to teach in the classroom but also to do research. While teachers are knowledgeable about teaching, many of them may not be as knowledgeable about doing research. Action research is becoming a tool for school reform; as its very individual focus allows for a new engagement in educational change. Some of the most beneficial aspects about teacher action research are that it is small scale, contextualized, localized, and aimed at discovering, developing, or monitoring changes to practice, evaluate the results. However, language teachers who engage in action research are developing their professional judgment and autonomy and encourage new teaching strategies and implies a different way of generating knowledge.

4. Keyword list

project-based learning approach, integrated skills, skill-integration, systematic process of inquiry, action research(teacher research, classroom research), self-reflective teacher

Answer   action research

03 Read the passage in <A> and the dialogue in <B>, and follow the directions. [4 points] 2022 전공A 9번

A

While styles are preferred ways of processing information, strategies are conscious mental and behavioural procedures that people engage in with the aim to gain control over their learning process. Although the definitions and boundaries of learning strategies can be varied, there are several categories of strategies that have generally been agreed upon, as shown below.

Strategy	Definition	Examples
Metacognitive	Learners being consciously aware of their thought processes and cognition	• Planning • Monitoring • Evaluating
Cognitive	Learners using their brains to manipulate or transform L2 input in order to retain it	• Keyword technique • Repetition • Inferencing • Visualization
Social	Learners involving others in their L2 learning processes	• Having conversations in L2 with other speakers • Practicing L2 with other classmates
Affective	Learners engaging their own emotions to facilitate L2 learning	• Rewarding oneself for studying • Intentionally reducing anxiety

B

Mina : Hi, Junho. Is everything going well?

Junho : Hey, Mina! Good to see you here. Can I ask you something?

Mina : Sure. What's up?

Junho : I know you are a good English learner and I'd like to get some tips.

Mina : Sure. Will you tell me how you study?

Junho : I try to set schedules for learning. For example, I decide what I should study first and what I can study at a later time.

Mina : That's a good way. Anything else you do?

Junho : While studying, I sometimes stop to check my comprehension.

Mina : Okay. In my case, I usually create pictures in my mind to remember the things I've studied.

Junho : Oh, you do? I've never tried to create mental images when I study.

Mina : Actually, it helps me remember things a lot longer.

Junho : That makes sense. I think I need to try it.

Mina : And, whenever I find some difficult English expressions I'm not familiar with, I talk in English with native speakers to find out exactly what those expressions mean.

Junho : I usually use my online dictionary. But I often find the dictionary explanation is rather difficult for me.

Mina : That happens a lot. I think asking questions to others is one of the best ways to clarify the meaning.

Junho : I quite agree. I'll apply your advice to my English learning immediately. Thanks for your tips!

Identify TWO strategies in <A> that Mina recommended to Junho in <B>. Then, support your answers with evidence from <B>.

Your Answer
_____
_____
_____
_____
_____
_____

문항분석

1. Topic : Learning strategies

2. Focus

성공적인 학습을 위해 학습자 개개인들은 학습 전략을 키울 필요가 있으며, 특정한 과업에 효과적인 전략을 선별적으로 사용할 필요가 있다. 예컨대, 학습자들이 학습 전략을 가지고 있을지라도 특정한 과업에 맞게 선택적으로 사용하지 않고 무작위로 사용할 경우 학습의 효율성은 떨어진다.

3. How to manage strategies-based instruction

Developing a strategies-based training workshop involves different phases: preparation, presentation, practice, evaluation, and expansion.

(1) The preparation phase lays the foundation or groundwork for creating a learner-centered environment that is ready for strategy instruction.

(2) In the presentation phase, language learning strategies are explicitly modeled, named and explained.

(3) The practice phase builds the real construction of independent learning and involves students in developing strategic thinking about the strategies themselves and their strategic use.

(4) The fourth phase, evaluation engages students in reflective sessions and focuses on evaluating the new learning strategies, thus developing their metacognitive abilities.

(5) The last phase, expansion allows learners to transfer the application of a strategy from a familiar context to an unfamiliar one effectively. This match of familiar strategies to new contexts or new tasks (real classroom practice) adds appropriateness and real ownership to learners to choose the best strategies to complete classroom tasks successfully. More importantly, this phase completes the cycle of strategy instruction and fosters a climate of sharing information of strategy use with peers where learners teach others how to use the strategies.

4. Keyword list

metacognitive strategies, cognitive strategies, social strategies, affective strategies, strategies-based instruction

---

모범답안

Mina recommends each of cognitive and social strategies to Junho. First, she advises visualizing what he has studied in his mind. Second, she suggests that he should have a conversation (talk) with native speakers of English to work out its exact meaning whenever encountering a(n) unfamiliar (difficult) expression.

04 **Read the questionnaire in <A> and the teacher's note in <B>, and follow the directions.** [2 points] 2019 전공A 1번

A

This questionnaire is designed to identify students' learning styles. Each category (A, B, C, D) has 10 items. Students are asked to read each item and check their preferences.

	Learning Style Questionnaire	4	3	2	1
A	1. I understand better when I hear instructions.				
	2. I remember information better when I listen to lectures than when I read books.				
	3. I like to listen to radio shows and discussions more than reading the newspaper.				
	⋮				
B	1. I like to look at graphs, images, and pictures when I study.				
	2. I follow directions better when the teacher writes them on the board.				
	3. I can easily understand information on a map.				
	⋮				
C	1. I enjoy working with my hands or making things.				
	2. I remember things better when I build models or do projects.				
	3. I like to 'finger spell' when I learn words.				
	⋮				
D	1. I like activities that involve moving around.				
	2. I prefer to learn by doing something active.				
	3. I learn the best when I go on field trips.				
	⋮				

4=strongly agree, 3=agree, 2=disagree, 1=strongly disagree

| B |

Based on the findings of the questionnaire conducted in my class, I have noticed that four students each have a major learning style.

Scores of the four students

Youngmi	Minsu	Taeho	Suji
A = 38	A = 18	A = 15	A = 13
B = 11	B = 36	B = 12	B = 14
C = 10	C = 10	C = 40	C = 12
D = 12	D = 12	D = 11	D = 36

This week, I am going to teach names of wild animals, like 'ostrich' and 'rhinoceros,' by trying different activities to address these students' different learning styles. Youngmi scored the highest in category A, showing that she is an auditory learner. So I will let her listen to a recording and say the names of animals out loud. Minsu's high score in category B shows that he is a visual learner. I will let him look at images of animals and read the corresponding names. The person who had the highest score in C was Taeho, who is a tactile learner. I am going to use origami so he can use his hands to fold papers into animal shapes. This will help him learn their names better. Lastly, Suji's score in category D shows that she is a(n) _____ learner. For her, I am planning to do an animal charade activity where she acts like different animals and others guess the names of them. I think she will enjoy moving around the classroom. In these ways, I want to maximize students' learning outcomes in my class.

Based on the information in <A> and <B>, fill in the blank in <B> with the ONE most appropriate word.

Your Answer _____

1. Topic : Learning style

2. Focus

개인에 따라 방식이 달라지는 학습 양식(learning style)의 종류에 대해 인지하고 있어야 하며 정확한 term을 찾아 쓰는 것이 관건인 문제이다.

3. Learning style taxonomy for the L2 classroom

  ⑴ **Type 1** : **Cognitive styles**

    ① A field dependent student learns best when information is presented in context. They are often more fluent language learners.

    ② A field independent student learns most effectively step-by-step and with sequential instruction. They are often more accurate language learners.

    ③ A reflective student learns more effectively when they have time to consider new information before responding.

    ④ An impulsive student learns more effectively when they can respond to new information immediately; as language learners, they are risk takers.

  ⑵ **Type 2** : **Sensory styles**

    ① A visual student learns best when there is visual reinforcement such as charts, pictures, graphs, etc.

    ② An auditory student learns more effectively by listening to information.

    ③ A tactile student learns more effectively when there is an opportunity to use manipulative resources.

    ④ A kinesthetic student learns more effectively when there is movement associated with learning.

  ⑶ **Type 3** : **Personality styles**

    ① Tolerance of ambiguity refers to how comfortable a learner is with uncertainty; some students do well in situations where there are several possible answers; others prefer one correct answer.

    ② Left-brain dominant learners tend to be more visual, analytical, reflective, and self-reliant.

③ Right-brain dominant learners tend to be more auditory, global, impulsive, and interactive.

4. Keyword list

learning styles, visual learners, auditory learners, tactile learners, kinesthetic learners

---

Answer   kinesthetic

05 Read the passages and follow the directions. [4 points] 2019 전공B 4번

| | A | |

(Below is a student's writing and a conversation with his teacher about the writing.)

Student writing

    Someone first showed the bicycle to the public in the late 18th century. People first thought it was not safe or comfortable. But many creative people improved it. So, many people use the bicycle widely as a form of transportation or for exercise today. Bicycle makers manufacture lighter, faster and stronger bicycles now than before. Because of that, more people ride the bicycle around the world these days than any time in the past. But they used some unique types of cycles in the old days like the four-cycle.

Teacher-student one-on-one conference

T : What is this writing about?

S : It's about the bicycle. Do you ride a bicycle?

T : Yes, I sometimes do. So your writing is not about people who produce or use the bicycle.

S : That's right.

T : OK, the main theme is the bicycle. But none of the sentences has the bicycle as its subject.

S : I know. But if the bicycle becomes the subject, then I have to use many passives. They are complicated and difficult. So I tried not to use them.

T : But it would be better to use the bicycle as the subject in most sentences. That way, it will become clear that the main focus of your writing is the bicycle.

S : Well, okay. I'll try.

T : You used the word "manufacture." Did you know this word?

S : No, I didn't. At first, I wanted to use "make" but then the sentence looked a bit awkward because the subject is "makers." It would go like "Bicycle makers make."

T : I see.

S : So I looked up a different word in a dictionary that has the same meaning as "make."

T: That works. What about this word "four-cycle?" What do you mean? Are you trying to describe a bicycle but with four wheels?

S: Yes, I am. I added "four" to "cycle" just like "bi" is put before "cycle" in bicycle.

T: Oh, it is called "quadricycle." "Quadri" means four just as "bi" means two.

T=teacher, S=student

B

When writing as well as speaking in a second language, learners who have limited command of the second language may have to use a variety of strategies that can compensate for their lack of knowledge of the target language grammar and vocabulary in order to effectively get their intended meaning or message across to a reader or listener. Strategies employed for this purpose include avoidance, code switching, word coinage, appeal to authority, and using prefabricated patterns. As these strategies constitute a significant part of strategic competence, advances in the learners' ability to effectively use them play a considerable role in promoting their communicative competence.

Based upon the student's writing and his dialogue with the teacher in <A>, identify THREE strategies the student used from those mentioned in <B>. Then, provide corresponding evidence for each identified strategy from <A>.

Your Answer

_____

_____

_____

_____

_____

_____

문항분석

1. Topic : Communication strategies

2. Focus

학생의 쓰기 활동을 바탕으로 교사와 conference를 진행하는 통합수업모형이다. 교사와의 의사소통 과정에서 완벽하지 않은 언어 체계(interlangauge)를 가진 학생이 의사소통을 지속하기 위해 사용하는 전략이 어디에 어떻게 쓰였는지 구분하는 문제이다.

3. Communication strategies

⑴ **Avoidance strategies**

Avoidance is a tactic for preventing a pitfall, a linguistic weakness that could break down communicative flow. Syntactic, phonological, and lexical avoidance are common tactics in successful learners, as is topic avoidance.

⑵ **Prefabricated pattern**

Using memorized stock phrases usually for "survival" purpose.

⑶ **Appeal for help**

Asking for aid from the interlocutor directly.

⑷ **Code-switching**

Using a L1 word with L1 pronunciation or a L3 word with L3 pronunciation while speaking in L2.

⑸ **Circumlocution**

Describing or exemplifying the target object of action.

⑹ **Approximation**

Using an alternative term which expresses the meaning of the target lexical item as closely as possible.

⑺ **Word coinage**

Creating a nonexisting L2 word based on a supposed rule.

4. Keyword list

communication strategies, compensatory strategies, interlanguage, strategic competence, conference

모범답안

The student uses three communication strategies as follows: avoidance, appeal to authority, and word coinage. As corresponding evidence, first, the student does not use 'bicycle' as the subject to avoid the passive voice. Next, to find the synonym of the verb 'make,' the student refers to a dictionary. Finally, instead of 'quadricycle,' he creates a non-existent word 'four-cycle.'

06 Read the lesson procedure and follow the directions. [2 points] 2016 전공A 1번

Lesson Procedure

1. Ss listen to a recorded conversation about the topic of the lesson.
2. T asks Ss to make associations among key words and to guess the meaning of the words from context. Then T teaches new vocabulary.
3. Ss read passages and find semantic clues to get the main idea.
4. Ss reread the passages and scan for specific information.
5. Ss, in groups, do categorizing activities.
6. Ss discuss the topic and write a short comment on it.
7. T hands out the checklist and has Ss keep a daily log after school for one week.

A Daily Learning Log

Name: **Jihae Park**

※ Respond to each of the following statements with a checkmark (✔).

	Day 1			Day 2			Day 3			Day 4			Day 5		
	1	2	3	1	2	3	1	2	3	1	2	3	1	2	3
1. I make guesses to understand unfamiliar words.															
2. I first read over passages quickly, and then go back and reread them.															
3. I make summaries of the text that I read in English.															
19. I ask a friend questions about schoolwork.															
20. I write down my feelings in a language learning diary.															

Note: 1 = Never, 2 = Sometimes, 3 = Always

T=teacher, S=student

Complete the comments by filling in the blanks with the SAME word.

The lesson procedure shows that the students are instructed to practice various kinds of _____ during the class. Also, they are encouraged to be aware of their use of _____ by keeping a daily learning log.

Your Answer _____

문항분석

1. Topic : Strategies-based instruction

2. Focus

자율적인 학습과 효율성을 키워 나가기 위한 목적으로 교실 수업에서 각 기능 지도에 대한 전략과 학습 전략을 훈련시키고자 한다. 가령, 듣기나 읽기 전략 및 daily log를 통한 학습 전략에 대한 점검을 하도록 하여 학습자 개인의 주체성과 책임감을 기르도록 하는 데 목적이 있다.

3. Strategies trained in this lesson

(1) Vocabulary strategies

① **Guessing the meaning of the unknown word in context** : The best internalization of vocabulary comes from encounters with words within the context of surrounding discourse.

② **Word association task** : It is a common word game involving an exchange of words that are associated together.

(2) Reading strategies

① **Skimming** : Quickly running one's eyes across a whole text for its gist predicting the purpose of the passage, the main topic, or message

② **Scanning** : Quickly searching for some particular piece or pieces of information in a text (e.g., looking for names or dates, finding a definition of a key concept, listing a certain number of supporting details, and extracting specific information without reading through the whole text)

(3) Learning strategies

① **Grouping or classifying** : Reordering or reclassifying and perhaps labeling the materials to be learned on common attributes

② **Metacognitive strategies** : Keeping a daily log /Evaluating the work process

4. Keyword list

strategies-based instruction, skimming, scanning, guessing strategies, metacognitive strategies

---

Answer | strategies

Plus +

How to Manage Strategies-based Instruction

Developing a strategies-based training workshop involves different phases: preparation, presentation, practice, evaluation, and expansion.

1. The preparation phase lays the foundation or groundwork for creating a learner-centered environment that is ready for strategy instruction.
2. In the presentation phase, language learning strategies are explicitly modeled, named and explained.
3. The practice phase builds the real construction of independent learning and involves students in developing strategic thinking about the strategies themselves and their strategic use.
4. The fourth phase, evaluation engages students in reflective sessions and focuses on evaluating the new learning strategies, thus developing their metacognitive abilities.
5. The last phase, expansion allows learners to transfer the application of a strategy from a familiar context to an unfamiliar one effectively. This match of familiar strategies to new contexts or new tasks (real classroom practice) adds appropriateness and real ownership to learners to choose the best strategies to complete classroom tasks successfully. More importantly, this phase completes the cycle of strategy instruction and fosters a climate of sharing information of strategy use with peers where learners teach others how to use the strategies.

07 **Read the passage in <A> and the conversation in <B>, and follow the directions.** [5 points] 2015 전공A 서술형 2번

| A |

In negotiation of meaning, "uptake" refers to an interlocutor's immediate response to his or her partner's signal of noncomprehension. In uptake, the interlocutor often uses a variety of communication strategies such as message abandonment, topic change, circumlocution, word coinage, foreignizing, and code switching.

| B |

The following is part of a teacher-student interaction that contains negotiation of meaning.

T: Hi, Sangjee. How was your weekend?

S: Hello. Well, I had a busy weekend.

T: Did you go anywhere?

S: No, I stayed home all weekend.

T: Why were you busy, then?

S: I had to fly ten chickens.

T: Uh, what? What did you do?

S: Uh, you know, put chickens in oil, very hot oil, kind of bake them.

T: Oh, you FRIED them!

S: Yeah, I fried them with my mother.

T: Why did you have to fry that many chickens?

S: We had a big party on Sunday. My grandfather's birthday. Many people came.

T: Oh, so that's why you fried so many. The party must have been a lot of fun.

T=teacher, S=student

Identify where the uptake takes place by writing the specific utterance from <B>, and select the strategy used in the uptake from those in <A>. Then explain how the utterance in the uptake shows the selected strategy.

Your Answer _____

_____

_____

_____

_____

_____

문항분석

1. Topic : Classroom talk

2. Focus

교실 수업에서 일어나는 대화에서 학생이 교사가 제공하는 피드백에 대하여 어느 시점에서, 어떻게 uptake를 취하는지에 대한 과정을 이해할 필요가 있다.

3. Teacher-Student interaction

(1) IRE vs. IRF

① IRE: 대부분의 교실 담화의 구조로 다음과 같다.

- The teacher initiates an assertion or asks a question.
- The student responds.
- The teacher evaluates, by giving an evaluative statement such as "Very good" or by asking the same or similar question of another student.

② IRF

- The teacher initiates an assertion or asks a question.
- The students responds.
- The teacher provides feedback in order to encourage students to think and to perform at higher levels (e.g., "Tell me more! Are you saying that....?)

(2) Uptake

Uptake is what learners report to have learnt from a language lesson. Typically what learners say they have learnt does not necessarily match what the teacher intended to teach. Moreover, uptake can vary from learner to learner. Factors that appear to enhance uptake are salience, i.e., how much emphasis was given to an item or topic.

(3) Communication strategies

① Avoidance strategies: 자신의 제2언어 활용 능력의 부족으로 표현이 떠오르지 않을 때 회피한다(syntactic, lexical, phonological, and topical avoidance).

② Compensatory strategies: 자신의 제2언어 활용 능력의 부족으로 표현이 떠오르지 않을 때 다른 보상 전략을 사용하여 의미를 전달한다.

ⓐ **Prefabricated pattern**: 문장이나 구를 통째로 암기하는 경우

ⓑ **Appeal for help**: 의사소통의 문제가 발생할 때 즉각적으로 도움을 요청하는 경우

ⓒ **Code-switching**: 제2언어로는 표현이 어려운 부분을 자신이 알고 있는 제1언어 혹은 제3언어로 대체하는 경우

ⓓ **Circumlocution**: 학습자가 전하고자 하는 내용을 돌려서 표현

ⓔ **Approximation**: 나타내고자 하는 표현과 유사한 언어를 사용

ⓕ **Word coinage**: 학습자 나름의 규칙에 의해 존재하지 않는 표현을 생성

ⓖ **Literal translation**: 제2언어를 모국어로 그대로 직역하여 표현

4. Keyword list

uptake, IRE, IRF, avoidance strategies, compensatory strategies, prefabricated pattern, appeal for help, code-switching, circumlocution, approximation, word coinage, literal translation

---

모범답안

In this conversation, the uptake takes place in the student's fourth utterance, "put chickens in oil, very hot oil, kind of bake them." Here, s/he uses circumlocution as a communication strategy, which is to describe or exemplify the action for the target verb "fry (fried)."

Chapter

03 Textbook Evaluation and Adaptation

01 Read the passages in <A> and <B>, and follow the directions. [4 points]

A

There are always sound reasons for adapting materials in order to make them as accessible and useful to learners as possible. When adapting materials, having clear objectives is a necessary starting point. The objectives a teacher may hope to achieve by adapting classroom materials can be listed as follows:

- To cater to learners' language proficiency levels: The teacher can modify the difficulty of language features such as grammar and vocabulary in the materials.
- To reinforce learner autonomy: Through materials adaptation, the teacher can give students opportunities to focus on their own learning processes to become more independent learners.
- To enhance higher-level cognitive skills: The teacher can adapt materials in such a way as to require students to hypothesize, predict, or infer.
- To encourage learners to tap into their own lives: Through materials adaptation, the teacher can increase the relevance of the contents or activities in relation to the students' experiences.

B

Ms. Lee is teaching first-year high school students, and she is preparing for her English reading class next semester. Based on the results of a needs analysis, she has decided to adapt two chapters of the textbook materials to meet her students' needs. For Lesson 2, which is about career paths, she will use magazine pictures of various jobs like engineer, baker, and fashion designer, along with some pictures related to jobs in the textbook. She will use these pictures as a springboard to get students in groups to share their dream jobs. She thinks this adaptation will help students think about more varied jobs in the real world. For Lesson 5, there is a reading passage about Simon's adventure in Kenya in the textbook. However, she worries that there are only simple activities to check students' understanding of the story. So, she will edit the story, intentionally deleting a few sentences at the end. This will challenge the students to think about the story's structure and look ahead to possible endings, using the storyline.

Based on <A>, identify the ONE objective that Ms. Lee wants to achieve through adaptation in Lesson 2 and the ONE objective in Lesson 5. Then, explain your answers with evidence from <A> and <B>.

Your Answer

_____

_____

_____

_____

_____

_____

1. Topic : Material analysis/ Material adaptation

2. Focus

교사는 성공적인 언어 학습을 위하여 학습자들의 needs analysis를 토대로 성취목표(achievement objectives)를 결정하며, 그에 따른 교재 분석 및 수정을 진행하고자 한다. 주어진 문항에서도 Ms. Lee는 학생들의 요구분석에 따라 교재를 분석 및 수정하고 있다. 따라서, 주어진 data를 분석하여 Ms. Lee가 왜 교재를 수정 및 보완하는지 찾도록 하는 문항이다.

3. Textbook adaptation

교사나 교과 전문가에 의해 만들어진 텍스트를 학습자에게 보다 적합한 자료로 만들기 위해서는 다음과 같은 방법들이 있다.

Adapting and supplementing the texts we choose can bridge the gaps that exit between a textbook and learner needs. This can be achieved by adding visuals, realia, and authentic materials, by adjusting activities to promote more interaction, or by implementing activities in ways that appeal to multiple intelligences and learning styles.

4. Keyword list

textbook adaptation, material analysis(adaptation), needs analysis, achievement objectives, realia, authentic materials, multiple intelligence, learning styles

모범답안

Lesson 2 encourages learners to tap into their own lives while Lesson 5 enhances higher-level cognitive skills. The former leads students to share their dream jobs based on magazine pictures of real-world jobs for the relevance of content related to students' experiences. The latter challenges students to predict or infer the intentionally deleted endings of a story.

02 Read the passage in <A> and the email in <B>, and follow the directions.
[4 points] 2023 전공B 6번

A

Ms. Hong, a new English teacher, had a hard time getting her students to talk in her English speaking class. She investigated the issue and found a checklist related to the problems that hinder the students' active engagement in speaking. The checklist consisted of seven categories with descriptions: no preparation time, uneven participation, poor listening ability, lack of speaking strategy use, mother-tongue use, nothing to say, and inhibition. Based on her observations, she evaluated how often her students struggled with the problems in the checklist during her English speaking class.

Class Observation Checklist

Descriptions	Scale		
	1	2	3
1. Students need some quiet time before they are engaged in a speaking activity.		✓	
2. In group activities, some of the students free-ride without contributing to the discussion.		✓	
3. Students have listening difficulties when engaged in speaking activities.	✓		
4. Students are not aware of speaking strategies and need to develop their own.			✓
5. When students speak the same mother tongue, they tend to use it in group work, especially when the teacher is far away.			✓
6. Students complain that they cannot think of anything to say.		✓	
7. Students are often inhibited from trying to say things in English in the speaking class.			✓

1=seldom, 2=sometimes, 3=often

Ms. Hong gave careful thought to six, out of the seven problems, that she checked as "sometimes" or "often" in the checklist. She came up with satisfactory solutions to four of the problems; but for the other two, she decided to ask for help. She sent an email about the two problems to Mr. Park, a head teacher, in order to seek some advice. He replied as in <B>.

B

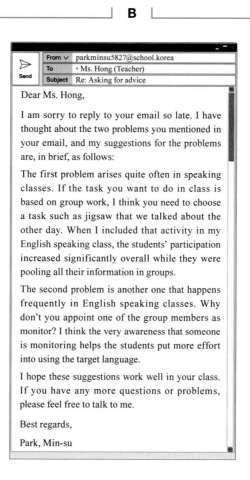

From ∨ parkminsu5827@school.korea
To ◦ Ms. Hong (Teacher)
Subject Re: Asking for advice

Dear Ms. Hong,

I am sorry to reply to your email so late. I have thought about the two problems you mentioned in your email, and my suggestions for the problems are, in brief, as follows:

The first problem arises quite often in speaking classes. If the task you want to do in class is based on group work, I think you need to choose a task such as jigsaw that we talked about the other day. When I included that activity in my English speaking class, the students' participation increased significantly overall while they were pooling all their information in groups.

The second problem is another one that happens frequently in English speaking classes. Why don't you appoint one of the group members as monitor? I think the very awareness that someone is monitoring helps the students put more effort into using the target language.

I hope these suggestions work well in your class. If you have any more questions or problems, please feel free to talk to me.

Best regards,

Park, Min-su

Based on <A> and <B>, identify the TWO problems Ms. Hong asked for Mr. Park's advice about. Then, explain why he made the suggestions for her two problems, respectively. Do NOT copy more than FOUR consecutive words from <A> and <B>.

Your Answer _____

_____

_____

_____

_____

문항분석

1. Topic : Self-observation (Class evaluation)

2. Focus

Ms. Hong은 말하기 수업에 대한 자가 관찰 및 평가를 통하여 자신의 수업에 대한 문제점을 찾아 개선하고자 주임선생님이신 Mr. Park에게 조언을 구하고 있다. 홍 선생님의 수업에 대한 문제점과 박 선생님의 조언에 대한 정확한 분석을 요구하는 문항이다.

3. Encouraging even participation and decreasing mother-tongue use

Discussion-based activities such as case-study analyses, role playing, and jigsaws encourage students to talk with one another and with the instructor. To be effective, however, they typically require clear instructions, including timelines.

In an effort to encourage all students to speak up, the instructors can take several steps such as;

(1) Invite the students to speak up

(2) Affirming or valued their contributions matter

(3) Give marks/grade for every active participation

(4) Be skillful in varieties of teaching techniques

(5) Reinforce that it is ok to speak up regardless of what is said to be true or not

(6) Be approachable and friendly

4. Keyword list

checklist, (un)even participation, preparation time(rehearsal), inhibition, jigsaw, mother tongue

---

모범답안

Ms. Hong asks for Mr. Park's advice about two problems, 'uneven participation' and 'mother-tongue use.' Thus, he is convinced that a jigsaw significantly increases overall students' participation. Also, he thinks that the very awareness that someone is monitoring pushes students to use the target language, instead of their mother tongue.

03 Read the passages in <A> and <B>, and follow the directions. [4 points]

2022 전공A 12번

A

Digital technology provides students with a new battery of tools with which language can be learned effectively. Below are some apps that students can use for their English learning.

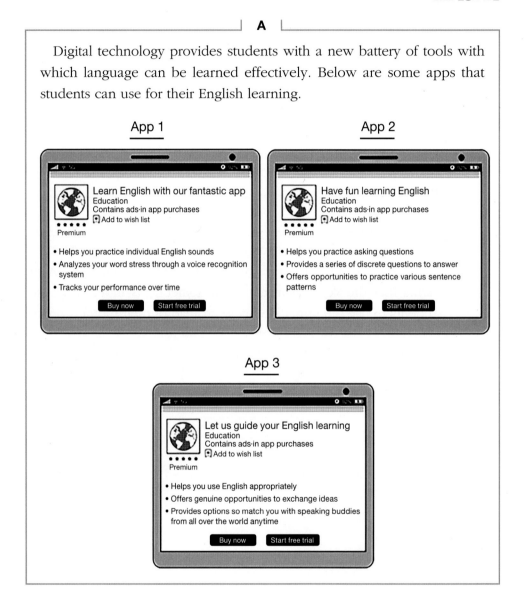

App 1

Learn English with our fantastic app
Education
Contains ads·in app purchases
Add to wish list
Premium

• Helps you practice individual English sounds
• Analyzes your word stress through a voice recognition system
• Tracks your performance over time

Buy now Start free trial

App 2

Have fun learning English
Education
Contains ads·in app purchases
Add to wish list
Premium

• Helps you practice asking questions
• Provides a series of discrete questions to answer
• Offers opportunities to practice various sentence patterns

Buy now Start free trial

App 3

Let us guide your English learning
Education
Contains ads·in app purchases
Add to wish list
Premium

• Helps you use English appropriately
• Offers genuine opportunities to exchange ideas
• Provides options so match you with speaking buddies from all over the world anytime

Buy now Start free trial

B

Minsu's Case

Minsu is very active in English classes and always looks for opportunities to speak English with other people. Since he lives in Korea, where English is not usually used outside the classroom, it is difficult to find English conversation partners. He once tried a conversation program where he spoke with native speakers on the phone. However, the program seemed too rigid in that he could only practice at designated times and with predetermined contents. Now, he wants to find an app where he can talk with partners whenever he wants and apply what he learns in the English class while speaking in a more natural context.

Jieun's Case

Jieun is afraid of speaking in English. But she was not like that before. She used to be outgoing and willing to communicate with people in English whenever she could. However, sometimes people didn't understand her and kept asking her to repeat the words she had just said. When she consulted her English teacher about the issue, the teacher advised her to focus on practicing pronunciation of words. Now, she is looking for an app which could help her practice pronouncing English words accurately.

Based on <A>, identify the ONE most appropriate English learning app for Minsu and Jieun, respectively. Then, explain your answers with evidence from <B>.

Your Answer

_____

_____

_____

_____

_____

_____

1. Topic : Instruction tools (digital technology)

2. Focus

첨단 기술 출현은 학습 시스템뿐 아니라 교육 환경에 큰 변화를 주고 있으며, 컴퓨터·인터넷 등을 활용한 학습은 영어 교육에서도 점차 증가하고 있는 추세다. 인터넷과 다양한 디지털 기술을 활용할 경우, 목표언어 국가의 가상 문화 체험, 원어민 발음, 상호작용적인 대화 등 멀티미디어 학습 자료를 활용한 자연스러운 상호작용을 통해 의사소통 능력을 향상시킬 수 있다. 또한, 여러 방향의 학습을 통해 자기주도 학습이 가능하다. 따라서, 교사들은 학생들의 개별적인 needs와 wants에 따라 자가 학습의 기회를 줄 필요가 있으며, 그런 기회를 mobile-assisted language learning의 일환으로 다양한 APP을 통해 이끌어 볼 수 있을 것이다.

3. Use digital technology for language teaching and learning

By using digital technology, it is expected that the class is more active and they can evolve their knowledge. Technology is changing the ways language teachers teach and that language learners learn and consequently is playing an increasingly central role in curriculum implementation.

(1) The physical level, with tools such as mobile phones, digital cameras, laptops and tablets.

(2) The management level, which includes learning management systems (LMSs) that enable the administration, delivery, tracking, reporting etc. of a language course.

(3) The applications level, including word processing software, email and chat clients, social networking sites and blogs.

(4) The resource level, which includes access to authentic materials, such as online newspapers, magazines, language tutors and dedicated websites for learners.

(5) The component technology level, such as spelling checkers, grammar checkers, electronic dictionaries and other support tools.

In this case, technology gives much richer information that now easily provided for students. Thus, technology will lead the students to take part more in learning.

PART

01

4. Keyword list

digital technology, digital literacy, information literacy, computer literacy, knowledge literacy, mobile-assisted language learning

---

모범답안

App 3 can help Minsu have a real and natural conversation with speaking buddies about the contents he learns in the English lesson whenever he wants. On the other hand, App 1 can help Jieun have the accurate pronunciation of English words based on the practice of individual sounds and word stress.

04 **Read the conversation and follow the directions.** [2 points] 2021 전공A 1번

> T : Today, we are going to read a text about cooking. Are you interested in cooking?
>
> Ss : Yeah.
>
> T : Great. Let's study today's key words first. *(The teacher brings out kitchen utensils from a box.)* I brought some cooking utensils.
>
> S1 : Wow! Are those yours?
>
> T : Yes, they are. I use them when I cook. *(showing a saucepan)* You've seen this before, right?
>
> S2 : Yes. My mom uses that when she makes jam.
>
> T : Good. Do you know what it's called in English?
>
> S3 : It's a saucepan.
>
> T : Excellent, it's a saucepan. Everyone, repeat after me. Saucepan.
>
> Ss : Saucepan.
>
> T : And, *(showing a cutting board)* what's this in English?
>
> S4 : A board?
>
> T : Right, it's a cutting board. Good job. I also brought a couple of things from my refrigerator. This is one of my favorite vegetables. *(The teacher holds up an eggplant.)*
>
> S5 : Umm.... It's an egg...
>
> T : Nice try! It's an eggplant.
>
> T=teacher, S=student

Fill in the blank with the ONE most appropriate word.

> In this lesson, the teacher is using a type of supplementary materials called _____ to teach key vocabulary. Along with other visuals, these materials are expected to attract students' attention and to aid understanding and retention of vocabulary.

문항분석

1. Topic : Instruction tools

2. Focus

Realia는 실제 물건들을 의미하는 것으로, 언어 학습 시 사용할 경우, 학습자가 학습 경험을 잘 기억할 수 있도록 도와준다. 따라서, 교실의 역동성과 학생들의 적극적 참여를 위해 교사들은 다양한 실물 교재(realia)를 사용해 교실 지도하도록 한다.

3. Using realia in class

If you are going to teach vocabulary of fruits and vegetables, it can be much more affective for students if they can touch, smell and see the objects at the same time as hearing the new word. This would appeal to a wider range of learner styles than a simple flashcard picture of the fruit or vegetable.

Suppose that you are going to teach some functional language for asking for the timetable for a train. You could use a fictitious timetable or you could use a real one from the local train station or the internet. This way you expose students to more language than simply the times and destinations. They will see information about prices, discounts, bank holidays, etc.

4. Keyword list

realia

Answer	realia

05 Read the teacher's reflection and follow the directions. [4 points] 2021 전공B 6번

Teacher's Reflection

This semester I have been using a checklist in my English writing class to help my students revise their drafts by themselves. The checklist I provide for my students covers the following areas: content, organization, grammar, vocabulary, and mechanics. Below is a part of the checklist.

Areas	Indicators	Yes	No
(1) _____	I use correct subject and verb agreement.		
	I use verb tense correctly.		
(2) _____	I put a period at the end of every sentence.		
	I use capital letters correctly.		
	I spell the words correctly.		

At first, the checklist didn't seem feasible because there was little improvement, especially in organization in writing. To find the reason, I held group conferences with the students and discovered that the indicators for organization were too complicated for them to understand. Some of them included more than one aspect to check simultaneously. So, I divided those indicators into two or three separate sentences so that one indicator assesses only one aspect. Since the revision of the indicators, the students' organization has gotten much better.

However, some students still had problems using the checklist appropriately. So, I ran a couple of training sessions to teach the students what the indicators meant and how they should be utilized. First, we read the indicators and I asked if they made sense. Then, I had them practice checking particular errors with a sample paragraph I had prepared. Since the training sessions, the students have been making significantly fewer errors. Overall, the use of the checklist has worked well in the revision process.

Fill in the blanks (1) and (2) with the ONE most appropriate word from the teacher's reflection, respectively. Then, explain how the teacher solved the problems encountered while using the checklist. Do NOT copy more than FIVE consecutive words from the passage.

Your Answer _____

_____

_____

_____

_____

_____

1. Topic : Coursework evaluation

2. Focus

교사는 더 나은 수업을 계획하기 위해 자신의 수업에 대한 성찰(reflection)이 필요하다. 따라서 성찰의 수단으로 학생들에게 checklist를 제공하고 학생들과의 group conference, 자가 장학(self-observation) 또는 동료 장학(peer observation)을 진행하여 coursework에 대한 자신의 teaching skill이나, 학생들의 기능 향상 및 개선점 등을 파악할 수 있다.

3. Example

The table below lists the self-assessment results of 19 students in a writing class. The teacher has decided to give them a follow-up lesson on writing skills about which more than half of them show dissatisfaction.

Self-assessment Items	SD	D	A	SA
1. I'm getting better at generating interesting and original ideas.	8	7	4	0
2. I'm gaining skills at organizing my ideas and putting them together logically.	4	10	3	2
3. My final draft has fewer grammatical errors than they did before this course.	4	2	7	6
4. My use of vocabulary has expanded in my writing over the course of this semester.	0	4	9	6
5. My papers now contain fewer errors in spelling and punctuation than they did previously.	7	8	2	2

*unit: number of the respondents

SD: strongly disagree, D: disagree, A: agree, SA: strongly agree

➡ a. peer-reviewing centering on mechanics
  b. re-sequencing the sentences of a fractured paragraph back into their original order
  c. brainstorming and sharing ideas in a small group

4. Keyword list

checklist, group conference, reflection, self-observation, peer observation

모범답안

(1) Grammar (2) Mechanics
When the checklist is not feasible, the teacher provides two solutions. Firstly, by revising rather complicated indicators for organization into simplified several sentences, she/he targets that each indicator assesses a single aspect. Also, with some training sessions, she/he instructs all students to figure out the meaning of the indicator and to utilize it correctly.

06 Read the passage in <A> and the teaching procedure in <B>, and follow the directions. [4 points] 2021 전공A 9번

┤ **A** ├

Mr. Yang, a middle school English teacher, believes that his lessons should help students meet the achievement standards which are specified in the school curriculum. He selects a group of standards for each semester and tries to incorporate them into his lessons. The following are the achievement standards for this semester.

Achievement Standards

[Oral Language Skills]

Students can
- use strategies to open and close conversations.
- explain their likes and dislikes.
- describe their dreams and future jobs.
- talk about their worries and problems.

[Written Language Skills]

Students can
- read a book or watch a film and write their feelings and impressions.
- read a short text about a familiar topic and write a conclusion.
- read a short text about a familiar topic and organize the content.
- view an object or picture and write their thoughts or feelings about it.

B

Teaching Procedure

Mr. Yang designed a reading lesson for his 2nd year students based on two of the achievement standards that he set out to accomplish this semester.

<Reading text>

What Should I Do?

Everyone has worries. When you have things you worry about, what do you do?

Sumi's Worries

Sumi thought Kate was her best friend, but now, she feels that Kate has changed and that she is avoiding her. A few days ago, Sumi met Kate in the hallway at school, but Kate turned around and walked away from her. Sumi tried to find the reason, but she couldn't think of anything wrong she had done to Kate. So, Sumi asked for her older sister's advice. Sumi's sister suggested that she simply ask Kate what's wrong.

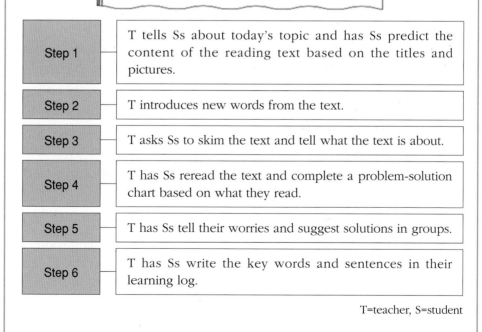

Step 1	T tells Ss about today's topic and has Ss predict the content of the reading text based on the titles and pictures.
Step 2	T introduces new words from the text.
Step 3	T asks Ss to skim the text and tell what the text is about.
Step 4	T has Ss reread the text and complete a problem-solution chart based on what they read.
Step 5	T has Ss tell their worries and suggest solutions in groups.
Step 6	T has Ss write the key words and sentences in their learning log.

T=teacher, S=student

Identify ONE oral language achievement standard and ONE written language achievement standard from <A> that the teaching procedure in <B> targets. Then, explain how each achievement standard is addressed with evidence from <B>.

Your Answer _____

_____

_____

_____

_____

_____

문항분석

1. Topic : Lesson plan

2. Focus

모든 교사들은 수업 설계를 할 경우, 각 수업에 대한 정확한 성취 기준(achievement standard)을 우선적으로 파악하고 각 수업의 objectives를 세운 뒤 해당 목표를 이룰 수 있는 교실 활동을 계획해야 한다.

3. Achievement standards and related activities

(1) Oral Language Skills

① Standard 1 : Use strategies to open and close conversations
Students use some gambits used for opening and closing conversations.

② Standard 2 : Explain their likes and dislikes
Students say about their likes and dislikes regarding sports or movies and explain why.

(2) Written Language Skills

① **Standard 1 :** Read a book or watch a film and write their feelings and impressions

Students write a book review or write in reponse to a movie after reading or watching their favorites.

② **Standard 2 :** Read a short text about a familiar topic and write a conclusion

Students read a story whose ending is intentionally omitted by the teacher and write the ending based on the storyline.

4. Keyword list

achievement standard, lesson objectives, lesson plan, syllabus, curriculum

---

모범답안

In the lesson in <B>, students can achieve one oral language achievement standard "talk about their worries and problems" by sharing their own worries and solutions in groups. Also, by filling in a problem-solution chart after reading the text, they accomplish one written language standard "read a short text about a familiar topic and organize the content".

07 Read the passage in \<A\> and the word entries in \<B\>, and follow the directions. [4 points] 2021·전공A 12번

A

    A corpus is a collection of texts of written or spoken language from various sources presented in electronic form. It provides evidence of how language is used in real situations, from which lexicographers can analyze millions of examples of each word to see how real language behaves. Many contemporary dictionaries, therefore, incorporate the features derived from the analyses of corpus data, some of which are shown below.

1) Frequency : statistical data on how often words are used in the language

2) Collocation : information on what other words commonly occur with the word in focus

3) Context : information on which particular field (e.g., law, engineering, medicine) or social situation (e.g., formal vs. informal) a word is used in

4) Authentic example sentences : sentences from what users of the language actually write or say in books, newspapers, speeches, or recorded conversations, etc.

| B |

Both Dictionary X and Dictionary Y are developed in part by incorporating data from corpora.

Dictionary X

Shed [ʃed] UK ◀) US ◀)

        verb *(past tense and past participle* **shed**,
        present participle **shedding***)*
        [transitive]

1. GET RID OF   to get rid of something that you no longer need or want
2. DROP/FALL   to drop something of allow it to fall

Word Partners

♦ *shed jobs/workers/staff*
♦ *shed weight/pounds/kilos*
♦ *shed an image*
♦ *shed your inhibition*
♦ *shed a load*
♦ *shed tears*

Dictionary Y

Shed UK ◀) US ◀) [ʃed]

        verb [shedding], [shed], [shed]

1. transitive to get rid of something you do not need or want

USAGE BOX

Shed is mainly used in journalism. In everyday English, people usually say that one **gets rid of** something.

2. transitive to lose a covering, such as leaves, hair, or skin, because it falls off naturally, or to drop something in a natural way or by accident

With regard to the word 'shed,' identify ONE corpus-based feature described in <A> for each dictionary in <B>, respectively. Then, provide evidence from <B> for each feature that you choose.

| Your Answer |

---

1. Topic : Instruction tools (Corpus-based learning)

2. Focus

교사와 학습자는 교실에서 다양한 방식으로 corpus를 활용할 수 있다. 실생활에 사용되는 어휘의 유형 및 맥락에서의 의미를 살펴보기 위해 electronic dictionary를 활용하여 다의어에 접근할 수 있고, concordancing program을 통해 해당 어휘의 collocation 및 frequency, authentic use 등을 살펴 볼 수 있어 목표어휘에 대한 지식을 키워 나가는 데 용이하다.

3. Corpus linguistics

By showing how corpus can influence the preparation of tests, textbooks, grammar books, dictionaries, classroom activities. Johansson(2009) is strongly arguing for the effective relevance of corpora in language teaching. Actually, corpus tools have contributed in discovering the behavior of various lexical and grammatical features.

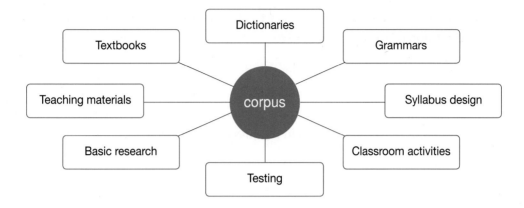

4. Keyword list

corpus, concordancing, frequency, authentic use, context, collocation

---

Dictionary X describes the collocation by showing word partners of 'shed' such as 'jobs' and 'workers' and so on. On the other hand, Dictionary Y offers the context of where the verb 'shed' is mainly used by pointing out 'journalism' in the usage box.

08 Read the passage in <A> and a teacher's note in <B>, and follow the directions. [2 points] 2020 전공A 2번

A

Curriculum design is a series of systematic efforts to develop a curriculum that satisfies the target learners as well as teachers. Researchers suggest that there are five main stages in the process of designing a curriculum.

————————

⇓

Goal Specifications

⇓

Materials Development

⇓

Language Teaching & Learning

⇓

Curriculum Evaluation

B

Teacher's Note

I am planning to develop a new English course for winter session, so I wanted to establish the basis for developing the curriculum. The first step of this process requires me to systematically collect and analyze areas of necessity for my students in order to satisfy their language learning requirements. So, I created a survey which asked students questions about their English deficiencies and the difficulties they face in performing certain language tasks in their current classes. It also asked them about the methods they enjoy learning through as well as the types of English skills that they want to improve. For the second step of this process, I wanted to get more information about the students' preferred learning styles and interests, so I referred to my classroom observation notes to learn about them. I then asked my school's principal to show me the results of their placement tests to gain an understanding of their levels of linguistic proficiency and background experience. Furthermore, I interviewed students both in groups and individually to get more detailed information. In short, I conducted _____ by collecting all these data.

Based on the information in <A> and <B>, fill in the blanks in <A> and <B> with the TWO most appropriate words. Use the SAME words in both blanks.

Your Answer _____

1. Topic : Curriculum design

2. Focus

구성주의 관점에서 영어 학습의 방향은 교실에서 학습자가 주체가 되는 learner-centered instruction을 지향하고 있다. 학생이 주체가 되는 수업에서 가장 중요하게 다뤄지는 것이 학생들의 적극적인 참여를 이끌어 나가는 것이다. 따라서, 학생들의 적극적 참여를 위해 학생들의 필요와 요구분석(needs analysis)을 토대로 curriculum을 구성해야 한다는 제안을 하고 있다.

3. How to develop the curriculum

(1) **Step 1** : Needs Analysis

To systematically collect and analyse areas of necessity of students based on the survey results

(2) **Step 2** : Goal Specifications

(3) **Step 3** : Materials Development

(4) **Step 4** : Language Teaching & Learning

(5) **Step 5** : Curriculum Evaluation

4. Keyword list

needs analysis, syllabus design, product-oriented view of needs (by the experts), process-oriented view of needs (learner motivation and learning styles)

Answer   needs analysis

Plus +

Product-Oriented Syllabus and Process-Oriented Syllabus

A product-oriented syllabus focuses on things learned at the end of the learning process (outcomes) while a process-oriented syllabus focuses on the skills and processes involved in learning language. Thus, process-oriented syllabi are developed as a result of a sense of failure in product-oriented syllabi to enhance communicative language skills.

Product-oriented Syllabus vs. Process-oriented Syllabus

CASE 1

Students work with grammatical structures in their English course and they will show their progress at the end of the term by answering a grammar test.

CASE 2

A writing lesson would focus on the processes writers use to complete their tasks, such as collecting information, organizing ideas, drafting and revising, rather than just the features of the products of writing, such as letters, compositions, notes, reports etc.

1. Examples of product-oriented syllabi
   ① Structural syllabus
   ② Situational syllabus
   ③ Notional-Functional syllabus

2. Examples of process-oriented syllabi
   ① Procedural/Task-based syllabus
   ② Learner-centered syllabus
   ③ Content syllabus

09 Read the passages and follow the directions. [4 points] 2018 전공A 10번

---| **A** |---

Task-based language teaching (TBLT) holds a central place in current second language acquisition research and also in language pedagogy. Some suggest there are six main steps in designing, implementing, and evaluating a TBLT program.

〈1〉
Target tasks are identified through a needs analysis.

➡️

〈2〉
The target tasks are grouped into target task-types.

➡️

〈3〉
Pedagogic tasks are derived.

➡️

〈4〉
A task syllabus is developed with its primary focus on communication not on linguistic forms.

➡️

〈5〉
The task syllabus is implemented in classrooms via various techniques of focus on form.

➡️

〈6〉
Student achievement is assessed using task-based tests.

---| **B** |---

Mr. Kim designed and implemented a TBLT program based on the six steps described in <A>.

- **Step 1.** He did some questionnaire surveys with his students and interviewed fellow teachers to identify what his students would really want to do in everyday life.

- **Step 2.** He grouped the identified real-world tasks (e.g., purchasing a train ticket, booking a room, renting a car) into more general categories (e.g., planning a trip).

- **Step 3.** He developed tasks that his students would perform in the classroom. Those tasks were expected to elicit communicative language use in the classroom.

- **Step 4.** He designed a syllabus with a central aim of presenting different grammatical items one at a time and teaching them separately.

- **Step 5.** He drew student attention to linguistic forms when needed, while the primary focus of the lessons was still on communication during task performance.

- **Step 6.** He assessed the student outcomes, focusing on whether and how much they accomplished each given task.

Identify the step in <B> that does not match with its corresponding suggestion in <A>. Then, explain how that identified step deviates from its suggestion in <A>. Do NOT copy more than FOUR consecutive words from the passage.

Your Answer

_____

_____

_____

_____

_____

_____

1. Topic : Task-based syllabus (Syllabus design)

2. Focus

Task-based syllabus의 각 단계의 특성에 대해 이해하고, 각 단계에 해당하는 활동 유형이 수업 상황에서 어떻게 적용되는지 알고 있어야 한다. 특히, 최근 경향에 가장 적합한 수업 형태로서 task-based syllabus의 최우선적인 목표가 문법 학습이 아니라 의사소통 능력의 습득임을 인지하고 교실 상황에 적절하게 반영되었는지를 확인하는 문제이다.

3. Task-based instruction

Task-based language teaching(TBLT), also known as task-based instruction(TBI), focuses on the use of authentic language and on asking students to do meaningful tasks using the target language. Such tasks can include visiting a doctor, conducting an interview, or calling customer service for help. Assessment is primarily based on task outcome (in other words the appropriate completion of real world tasks) rather than on accuracy of prescribed language forms. This makes TBLT especially popular for developing target language fluency and student confidence. As such TBLT can be considered a branch of communicative language teaching(CLT).

Step 4 from TBLT	Step 4 from \<B>
A task syllabus is developed with its primary focus on communication not on linguistic forms.	He designed a syllabus with a central aim of presenting different grammatical items one at a time and teaching them separately.

4. Keyword list

task-based instruction, needs analysis, communication, linguistic forms, focus on form, task-based tests, task outcome, communicative language teaching(CLT)

PART
01

모범답안

Step 4 in <B> deviates from the suggestion of TBLT in <A> because the syllabus mainly focuses on grammatical forms separately, not communication.

Plus⁺

Jigsaw Listening or Jigsaw Reading Activity

A jigsaw listening or reading activity is an information gap exercise. Learners hear or read different parts of a text, then exchange information with others in order to complete a task.

Ex 1   Learners in three groups hear different versions of an encounter with aliens. Together with other learners, they complete comprehension questions based on all three descriptions of the encounter.

Ex 2   One student could have a timetable for train travel in Canada. Another could have a map of Canada. Without showing each other the visual information, they must speak English to plan a one-week trip.

In the classroom, jigsaw tasks are an excellent way to integrate the skills, as learners read or listen to a text, and speak and listen to others to reconstruct the information in the text. Most written texts can be made into a jigsaw activity easily. Managing a jigsaw listening exercise is more challenging as it requires multiple tape recorders, enough space to listen without disturbing other groups, and time.

10 **Read the conversation between two teachers and follow the directions.**
[2 points] 2020 전공B 2번

(Two teachers are evaluating two textbooks, Textbook A and Textbook B, in order to select the one that their students are going to use next year. This is part of their conversation.)

T1 : So, why don't we start with the first criterion? I went with Textbook A.

T2 : May I ask you why?

T1 : I think that the illustrations and graphics in Textbook A portray people in the target culture more realistically.

T2 : Yeah! Textbook A contains very realistic visuals that can provide our students with cultural information more accurately.

T1 : Good! Then, what about the second criterion?

T2 : Well, I think Textbook B is the better of the two. I couldn't give Textbook A a good score, because it appears to aim at explicit learning with many contrived examples of the language.

T1 : Hmm... could you clarify your point a bit more?

T2 : Well, I mean the texts and dialogues in Textbook A are oversimplified.

T1 : I had the same impression, but don't you think that they may help our students by focusing their attention on the target features?

T2 : You may be right, but I think that such texts might deprive them of the opportunities for acquisition provided by rich texts.

T1 : Oh, I see. That's a pretty good point.

T2 : So, in my opinion, Textbook B can provide more exposure to language as it is actually used in the real world outside the classroom.

T1 : Yeah! From that point of view, Textbook B will be intrinsically more interesting and motivating to our students.

T2 : I agree. Okay, then, I think we are ready to move on to the next evaluation criterion.

T=teacher

Fill in the blank with the ONE most appropriate word.

> There are many criteria that can be used in textbook evaluation. The teachers, T1 and T2, are mainly focusing on, first, the criterion of reality of visuals and then, the other criterion of _____. In the dialogue, the latter is specifically related to language use shown in the textbooks.

Your Answer _____

문항분석

1. Topic : Textbook evaluation

2. Focus

학생들의 요구분석(needs analysis)과 의사소통 능력을 향상하기 위한 teaching materials의 선택 기준으로 authenticity를 제시하고 있다.

3. Authentic text & Simplified text

Authentic texts have been generally defined as texts "originally created by a real speaker or writer for a real audience and designed to convey a real message", whereas simplified texts generally refer to texts created "to illustrate a specific language feature … to modify the amount of new lexical input introduced to learners; or to control for propositional input, or a combination thereof."

4. Positive and negative aspects of authentic materials

(1) Positive aspects

One of the main ideas of using authentic materials in the classroom is to "expose" the learner to as much real language as possible.

① Giving authentic cultural information
② Having a positive effect on student motivation
③ Relating more closely to students' needs
④ Supporting a more creative approach to teaching

(2) Negative aspects

In authentic texts, the vocabulary may not be relevant to the learners' needs and too many structures can create difficulty. This can have the opposite effect: rather than motivate the learner, it can demotivate—it means "...put up the affective filter."

① Being too culturally biased (often a good knowledge of cultural background is required when reading)
② Having too many structures being mixed, causing lower levels problems when decoding the texts
③ Containing difficult language, unneeded vocabulary items and complex language structures

5. Keyword list

authenticity, adding, deletion, personalizing, modifying, simplifying

Answer | authenticity

Plus⁺

1. Comprehensible input

Krashen's input hypothesis has been advocated by suggesting rich sources of comprehensible input in second language acquisition such as modified input, interactionally modified input and modified output by a few researchers (Doughty & Williams, 1998; Ellis & He, 1999; Long, 1983b; Long, 1996; Mackey, 1999). It is also claimed that when 'i+1' is provided in the classroom environment, it means a semantic based input arrangement in tuning down the challenge to the students' level of understanding. This can be done by helping students to understand the input by shortening of sentences, using concrete vocabulary etc. but not deliberately calibrating the syntactic level of the comprehensible input. Linguistic, conversational, strategic and visual adjustments are some ways to make input comprehensible. Also, choosing the materials according to students' background knowledge and interest areas will help teachers to prepare better lessons according to students' level of understanding.

2. Precautions on text adaptation

① 수업 시작 전 학생들의 삶, 흥미와 관련이 있는지 평가한다.

Evaluate a chapter ahead of time in terms of relevance to learners' lives and interests, and prepare visuals and realia that will make the material more meaningful to your students.

② 수업 시작 전 난이도에 대해 미리 평가한다.

Could the vocabulary, grammar, or functional language be more challenging? If so, brainstorm other words, forms, or phrases around the same theme that you want to present and practice. Are there many words that you anticipate will be particularly difficult in this lesson? If so, be prepared to demonstrate those words through multiple means, both visual and aural/oral.

③ 다중 지능(multiple intelligences)을 고려한다.

A common activity in ESL books is to place information in a sequence, either a dialogue, or information from a listening or reading passage. For someone who has a strong spatial intelligence, this task can be made easier by copying the sentences from the book, cutting them into strips, and having learners sequence information on a table.

11 Read Mr. Han's materials for his level-differentiated classes, and follow the directions. [2 points] 2015 전공A 기입형 2번

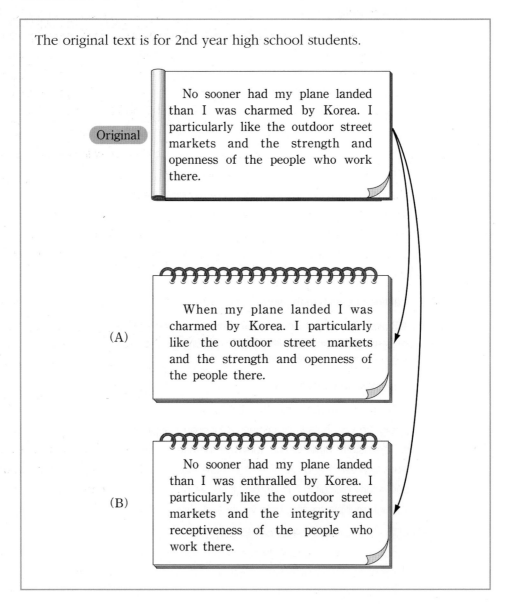

The original text is for 2nd year high school students.

Original

No sooner had my plane landed than I was charmed by Korea. I particularly like the outdoor street markets and the strength and openness of the people who work there.

(A)

When my plane landed I was charmed by Korea. I particularly like the outdoor street markets and the strength and openness of the people there.

(B)

No sooner had my plane landed than I was enthralled by Korea. I particularly like the outdoor street markets and the integrity and receptiveness of the people who work there.

Complete the comments by filling in each blank with ONE word. Write your answers in the correct order.

The original text has been adapted to suit the students' English proficiency levels. (A) shows how input is simplified through (1) _____ modification to make the original text easier for the lower level students. (B) shows how input is adapted through (2) _____ modification to make the original text more challenging for the upper level students.

Your Answer (1) _____

(2) _____

문항분석

1. Topic : Text modification

2. Focus

학습자의 수준에 맞게 입력을 조정하기 위하여 어떠한 방식으로 텍스트를 수정하는지에 대하여 이해할 필요가 있다.

3. Input modifications

(1) Lexical modification

Original text에서 Text (B)로 수정되는 과정에서 좀 더 어려운 어휘들이 사용되면서 난이도가 상향 조절된다.

(2) Syntactic modification

Original text에서 Text (A)로 수정되는 과정에서 문장 구조가 단순화되면서 텍스트의 난이도가 낮아졌다.

(3) Elaboration

앞서 말한 것에 대하여 좀 더 상세하게 설명하는 전략이다.

4. Keyword list

lexical modification, syntactic modification, elaboration, simplified

Answer   (1) syntactic (2) lexical

12 Read Mr. Park's comments in <A> and examine the results of a textbook evaluation by a review committee in <B>. Then follow the directions. [3 points]

2014 전공A 서술형 3번

| A |

Mr. Park: The goal of my class is to help students use the language to communicate and perform authentic tasks. So I want to spend most of my class time letting students rehearse tasks they need to perform outside the classroom. I also want my students to have a lot of opportunities to work together so that they can use their linguistic knowledge to convey meaning rather than just practice form.

| B |

Evaluation Criteria	Textbook A			Textbook B			Textbook C		
	1	2	3	1	2	3	1	2	3
pattern drill activities		✓		✓					✓
role-play based on real-life situations		✓				✓		✓	
pronunciation tips			✓	✓					✓
regular grammar review			✓	✓			✓		
group projects	✓					✓		✓	

1=poor, 2=average, 3=good

Considering the information in <A> and <B>, identify the textbook you would recommend for Mr. Park and provide TWO reasons for recommending it based on its characteristics.

Your Answer

_____

_____

_____

_____

_____

문항분석

1. Topic : Textbook analysis

2. Focus

주어진 세 가지 textbooks에 대한 평가 결과를 기반으로 하여 Mr. Park의 수업에 적합한 교재를 선택할 수 있어야 한다.

3. Mr. Park의 수업 목표

- Use language for communication within authentic tasks.
- Provide opportunities to work together.

4. Characteristics of three textbooks

Textbook A	• (average) pattern drill activities • (average) role-play based on real-life situations • (good) pronunciation tips • (good) regular grammar review • (poor) group projects
Textbook B	• (poor) pattern drill activities • (good) role-play based on real-life situations • (average) pronunciation tips • (average) regular grammar review • (good) group projects
Textbook C	• (good) pattern drill activities • (average) role-play based on real-life situations • (good) pronunciation tips • (poor) regular grammar review • (average) group projects

5. Keyword list

pattern drill activities, role-play, cooperative learning

모범답안

Since "role-play based on real-life situations" and "group projects" on Evaluation Criterion are highly marked, Textbook B could be recommended for Mr. Park. First, it enables students to use language for communication within real tasks as Mr. Park wishes. Second, group projects provide lots of opportunities to work together, in which students are encouraged to convey their own meaning, unlike pattern drill activities.

13 Read the passages and follow the directions. [4 points] 2017 전공B 2번

| A |

Materials can be adapted for many reasons, for example, to localize, to modernize, or to personalize. We can localize materials to make them more applicable to our local context. We can modernize materials when they are outdated in terms of English usage or content. We can also personalize materials by making them more relevant to learner needs and interests. Materials adaptation can be carried out by using a number of different techniques, as shown in the figure.

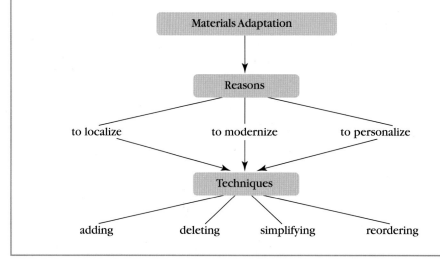

B

Mr. Lee is teaching first-year middle school students whose proficiency levels are very low. After conducting a needs analysis, he has learned that the students find the writing sections of the textbook difficult and that they are interested in sports. While he is planning a writing lesson for next week, he realizes that there is only one pre-writing activity in Unit 1 of the textbook. He thinks that one activity is not enough for his students to develop ideas for writing. Thus, he is going to increase the number of the pre-writing activities from one to three. In addition, thinking that the reading passage on sports in Unit 3 will better suit learner interests than the reading text in Unit 1, he decides to switch the two reading texts. He believes that this change will help his students become better prepared for writing and more engaged in English language learning.

Referring to the terms in <A>, explain the reason why Mr. Lee wants to adapt the materials, and identify which techniques he is going to use for materials adaptation. Do NOT copy more than FOUR consecutive words from the passage.

Your Answer

_____

_____

_____

_____

_____

1. Topic: Textbook (Materials) adaptation

2. Focus

Mr. Lee가 수업에 사용하는 자료를 수정하려는 목적을 이해하고, 그에 따라 어떤 technique을 사용하려고 하는지에 대하여, 〈A〉에서 주어진 개념에 충실해 설명하여야 한다.

3. How to modify a textbook

(1) **Purpose**

① **To localize**: localize materials to make them more applicable to our local context.

② **To modernize**: modernize materials when they are outdated in terms of English usage or content.

③ **To personalize**: personalize materials by making them more relevant to learner needs and interests.

(2) **Techniques**

① **Adding**: 기존의 텍스트에 양 혹은 질적으로 자료를 추가함으로써 텍스트를 보완한다.

Materials are supplemented by putting more into them. The teacher can do this by either extending or expanding.

ⓐ **Extending**: 같은 학습 내용, 같은 수준의 연습 활동 등을 추가함으로써 양적으로만 자료를 추가하는 방법이다.

The teacher supplies more of the same type of material, thus making a quantitative change in the material. This means that the techniques are being applied within the methodological framework of the original materials.

ⓑ **Expanding**: 기존의 자료와는 다른 기능을 다룬 연습 활동, 다른 차원의 언어 접근법을 적용한 연습 활동을 추가함으로써 텍스트를 질적으로 추가하는 것을 의미한다.

Expanding adds something different to the materials; the change is qualitative. The expanding goes further than extending by putting in a different language skill or a new component.

② **Deleting** : 기존 텍스트에서 불필요한 부분을 생략하는 방법이다. Adding 과 마찬가지로 양적인 방법과 질적인 방법이 있다.

Deletion is the opposite process to that of addition by omitting materials from the original.

ⓐ **Subtracting** : 동일한 언어 기능 내에서 지나치게 많은 연습 활동을 생략 하는 등 양적으로 텍스트를 줄이는 것을 의미한다.

Subtracting refers to reducing the length of materials in quantitative way. It does not have a significant impact on the overall methodology.

ⓑ **Abridging** : 여러 기능을 다룬 연습 활동 중 질적으로 다른, 불필요한 활동을 생략하는 것을 말한다.

Abridging means omitting materials qualitatively, making the changes greater than subtracting.

③ **Modifying** : 학습자의 요구나 언어 접근법에 보다 적절하게 텍스트의 내용 이나 수업의 형식적인 면을 수정하는 것을 말한다.

Modifying refers to a change in the nature or focus of an exercise, or text, or classroom activity. Currently the most frequently stated requirement for a change is for materials to be made more communicative. Therefore, modifying may relate activities more closely to learners' own backgrounds and interests, introducing models of authentic language.

ⓐ **Rewriting** : 학습자의 요구나 특정 교수법(특히 CLT)에 맞게 텍스트의 내용을 수정하는 기법을 말한다.

Rewriting means an internal change that can be applied to any aspect of content.

ⓑ **Restructuring** : 학습 상황에 보다 적합하게 학생들의 활동이나 교실 (혹은 그룹) 배치를 조정하는 방법을 말한다.

Restructuring can be applied to classroom management.

④ **Simplifying**: 학습자들의 이해를 높이기 위해서 단어, 문법, 문장 길이 등 언어의 수준을 조절하는 방법을 말한다.

When simplifying, the teacher could be rewording instructions or text in order to make them more accessible to learners, or simplifying a complete activity to make it more manageable for learners and teachers. There is a distinct danger of distorting language when attempting to simplify a text and thus making the text inauthentic.

ⓐ **Sentence structure** : Sentence length is reduced or a complex sentence is rewritten as a number of simpler ones, for example by the replacement of relative pronouns by nouns and pronouns followed by a main verb.

ⓑ **Lexical content** : The number of new vocabulary items is controlled by reference to what students have already learned.

ⓒ **Grammatical structur** : For example, passives are converted to actives; simple past tense to simple present; reported into direct speech.

⑤ **Reordering** : 연습 활동이나 자료의 제시 순서를 교육적인 관점에서 좀 더 적합한 순서로 변경하는 방법을 말한다.

The teacher makes materials more pedagogic sense by sequencing activities in a different order.

4. Keyword list

adding, deleting, modifying, simplifying, reordering

모범답안

Mr. Lee wants to personalize the textbook materials to meet his students' needs for easier writing sections and their interests in sports. Accordingly, he, first, decides to add two pre-writing activities. Moreover, he tries to reorder some reading texts according to students' interests.

Plus⁺

Material Evaluation

1. External evaluation

자료의 목차나 표지에 나와 있는 객관적인 사실을 바탕으로 교재를 분석하는 방법으로, analysis level 1이 해당된다.

2. Internal evaluation

표면적으로 드러난 사실 이외에 자료가 담고 있는 의미까지 분석하는 것으로, analysis level 2와 3이 이에 가깝다고 볼 수 있다.

✐ Analysis Level

Level	Focus of analysis	Examples of features to be considered
1	What is there	publication date, intended users, type of material, classroom time required, intended context of use, physical aspects (durability, components, use of colour), the way the materials is divided up across components, how the student's book is organized, how learners and teachers are helped to find their way around
2	What is required of users	Tasks: what the learner has to do whether their focus will be on form, meaning or both what cognitive operations will be required what form of classroom organization will be involved (e.g. individual work, whole class) what medium will be involved who will be the source of language or information
3	What is implied	selection and sequencing of content(syllabus) and tasks, distribution of information across teacher and student components, reconsideration of information collected at levels 1 and 2

14 Examine the survey results in <A> and part of the interview with the teacher who taught Practical English II in <B>, and follow the directions. [4 points] 2016 전공B 1번

A

A school administrator conducted a survey with 60 students from two classes of Ms. Lee's Practical English II in order to improve the course in the future.

Evaluation of Practical English II

Content	Number of respondents per category			
	1	2	3	4
(1) I feel I achieved my learning objectives as a result of taking this course.	4	9	25	22
(2) I feel more confident in my self-expression in English as a result of taking this course.	5	9	24	22
(3) I feel the supplementary material used in this course was helpful.	5	6	25	24
(4) I feel my speaking performance was assessed effectively based on the tests and assignments given.	29	22	8	1

1=strongly disagree, 2=disagree, 3=agree, 4=strongly agree

B

A: Your Practical English II was very satisfying for students. What do you think made it so successful?

T: Well, I thought it was necessary to make decisions about what would be taught and how it would be taught before designing a course, so I did a survey and interviews.

A： You mean you chose the teaching materials, contents, and activities based on what your students wanted to learn?

T： That's right. The results also provided me with a lot of information about what my students needed to learn or change, their learning styles, interests, proficiency levels, etc. Based on that information, I decided on the course objectives, contents, and activities.

A： You must have been very busy working on designing the course before it started. What about assessment?

T： Students just took one major test at the end of the semester. I regret that I evaluated only their learning product.

A： You mean just once over the semester?

T： Yes, I thought it was impossible to assess their speaking performance regularly by myself and I gave one major test to the students. So I was actually unable to gather information on the developmental process of their speaking abilities.

. . .

A： Okay. Thank you for your time.

A=administrator, T=teacher

Describe ONE strong point with evidence of what the teacher did for the success of the Practical English II course. Then describe ONE weak point of what the teacher did in the course, and suggest ONE possible solution from the teacher's standpoint.

Your Answer _____

_____

_____

_____

_____

1. Topic : How to plan and manage a successful lesson

2. Focus

성공적인 교실 수업을 계획하고자 할 경우 우선 학생들의 여러 가지 기호와 관심 및 수준을 맞추어 준비할 필요가 있으며, 동기를 유발하기 위한 자료 준비 학습 활동뿐만 아니라 평가까지도 고려해 보아야 할 것이다.

3. Successful lesson plan and management

(1) Needs analysis

학생들의 흥미와 관심을 유발할 수 있는 자료를 선택·구성하기 위하여, 지도하고자 하는 학생들의 needs 파악이 우선적으로 필요하다. 학생들에게 relevant to students' real lives/preference/interest 등의 checklist를 제공하거나, interview 및 learning log을 통해 학생들의 needs를 파악할 수 있다.

(2) Summative vs. Formative assessment

교실 활동에 학생들을 적극적으로 임하게 하고, 학생들의 동기를 끊임없이 유지하기 위해서 교사는 평가 방향을 정확하게 잡아야 한다. 학생들의 적극적인 참여와 동기는 평가에 의해 많은 부분 영향을 받을 수 있기 때문이다. 따라서 학생들의 학습 목적에 맞게 평가를 준비하되, 학생들의 실력을 점검하여 학생 간의 비교를 할 수 있는 총괄평가(summative assessment)와 학습 과정 중에 있는 언어적 능력을 단계별로 성취해 나가도록 개인 안에서 성취 기준을 세워 이전 학습의 결과를 토대로 새로운 학습에 대한 방향 및 진행을 할 수 있도록 하는 형성평가(formative assessment) 등을 고려해 평가를 진행한다. 가급적 교실 안에서의 평가는 formative assessment의 속성을 갖고 진행한다.

(3) Portfolios as an alternative assessment

교실에서 진행되는 formative assessment의 formal type으로 portfolios를 제안할 수 있다. Portfolios는 학습 과정 중에 나온 결과물을 누적하여 진행하는 평가 방식으로 학생들의 성취 기준 정도를 단계별로 확인해 볼 수 있으며, 학습자들을 평가 방식에 참여시켜 보다 학습 과정에 참여를 높이고 동기 유발을 극대화시킬 수 있다는 점에서 매우 효과적인 평가 방식으로 간주된다. 이와 같은 portfolios 평가는 현재 진행되는 대단위 학습 안에서 학생들의 수준별 학습을 운영하고자 할 때 가장 바람직하고 효과적으로 진행되는 평가로 제시된다.

4. Keyword list

needs analysis, summative/formative assessment, portfolios

모범답안

One strong point is the designing of the course based upon students' needs as gathered through a survey and interviews. A weak point in this course is the use of one major test at the end of the semester without considering their progress in speaking ability. Thus, as an alternative assessment, the teacher can use portfolios, which are to collect performance samples in class and assess students' ongoing progress in learning.

15 Read the passage in <A> and the table in <B>, and follow the directions.
[5 points] 2015 전공B 서술형 1번

A

   As part of an effort to maximize opportunities for her students to interact with others in English, Ms. Park, a high school English teacher, plans to design her lessons from a blended learning perspective. She is considering having the students interact with each other and her both online and offline. She designs lessons as follows: Online activities are based on a synchronous computer-mediated communication (CMC) interaction, and the transcripts of the online interaction are used a couple of days later for offline discussion.

   Realizing that many of her students seem shy, frustrated, and uncomfortable with face-to-face discussion, she would like to use a CMC tool to help students get ready for an offline discussion. By examining their online production with peers and the teacher, she believes that CMC activities will guarantee more equalized opportunities for participation and make students' errors more salient and thus open to feedback and correction.

B

Evaluation of Three CMC Tools

Criteria \ Tools	Tool A	Tool B	Tool C
Easy to Use	Y	Y	Y
Saving and Archiving	Y	N	Y
Real-Time Interaction	N	Y	Y
Video Chatting	N	Y	N
Online Dictionary	Y	N	N

Y=Yes, N=No

Based on the information in <A> and <B>, identify the tool you would recommend for Ms. Park, and provide TWO reasons for your recommendation.

Your Answer _____

_____

_____

_____

_____

1. Topic : Computer-mediated communication(CMC)

2. Focus

주어진 세 가지 CMC tools의 특징들을 비교하여, Ms. Park의 수업에 가장 적합한 tool을 고르는 문제이다.

3. Types

(1) Asynchronous

학습자들이 동시에 인터넷에 접속할 필요 없이 컴퓨터를 매개체로 하여 이루어진다. 따라서 학생들 간의 의사소통에서는 시간차가 존재한다. e-mail이나 bulletin board 등이 이에 해당한다(e.g., keypal project).

(2) Synchronous

학습자들이 컴퓨터와 인터넷을 매개로 의사소통하기 위해서는 동시간대에 인터넷 접속을 해야 한다. 즉각적인 상호작용과 피드백이 이루어진다는 장점이 있지만 시간과 공간의 제약을 받는다는 단점도 있다(e.g., chat programs, video conferencing).

(3) Tools

Tool A	Tool B	Tool C
• Easy to Use • Saving and Archiving • Online Dictionary	• Easy to Use • Real-time Interaction • Video Chatting	• Easy to Use • Saving and Archiving • Real-time Interaction

4. Keyword list

asynchronous mode, synchronous mode

Tool C is recommendable for Ms. Park for the following two reasons. First, as a real-time interaction tool, it enables students to get ready for offline discussion. Second, since it can save and archive students' online production(transcripts of online interaction), the teacher can easily provide feedback and correction on students' errors.

Plus⁺

Computer-mediated Communication

1. Mobile-Assisted Language Learning

The ready availability of mobile devices and easy access to WiFi connections multiply the possibilities for language learning "on the move", or what we now call Mobile-Assisted Language Learning. It has provided educators greater freedom for extending learning outside traditional learning environment. Mobile devices offer immediate access to the Internet and, thus, to an abundance of "apps" that for language learners may be more attractive alternatives compared to structured learning such as playing language games, watching movies in the L2, or listening to a radio.

2. Benefits of technology integration

① **Opportunities for interaction**: Language learners can be exposed to various forms of interaction while using technology. Networking in online environments has become an increasingly popular form of social interaction. It allows users to express themselves, build profiles, form online communities of shared interests, and interact socially with others.

② **Access to authentic linguistic data and use**: While engaging in meaningful social interaction, students naturally tend to use their target language and gain access to authentic linguistic materials.

③ **Opportunities for cross-cultural learning**: Digital learning environments can foster cross-cultural awareness and understanding through online videos, blogs, visual images, and photos, offering a rich storehouse of world history and cultural information.

3. Classroom application

The Internet offers a huge amount of reading material that can be used for class materials as well as for individual or collaborative work. A variety of computer-assisted communication can encourage students to use the target language for authentic and meaningful purposes.

① **Reading and writing**: e-mail, e-book readers, Wikis and blogs, social networking

② **Listening and speaking**: video clips and audio podcasts, audio and video conferencing, portable internet devices with video cameras

③ **Grammar and vocabulary practice**: online grammar exercises, corpus and concordance, mobile devices

Chapter
04 Four Skills, Vocabulary and Grammar Teaching

01 Read the worksheet in <A> and the class observation note in <B>, and follow the directions. [4 points] 2023 전공A 9번

A

Worksheet

Family History

Group Name:_____
Student Number & Name:_____

Role	Assignment	Student Assigned
Discussion Leader	Keeping the conversation going if it falters	
Passage Chooser	Choosing three passages that are important to the story to discuss	
Word Master	Showing the meanings of new words	
Grammar Checker	Using syntactic clues to interpret the meanings of sentences	
Story Summarizer	Summing up the story briefly	
Online Manager	Posting the activity outcome to the web or social network service	

• Before Reading

Can you guess who will mention the following statements? Match the pictures of the characters in the story with their corresponding statements.

• While Reading

Based on the text about the Brown and the Garcia families, complete the following figure.

Family History

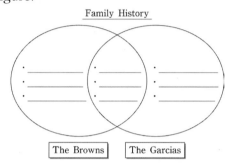

The Browns   The Garcias

• After Reading

What do you think about the characters in the story? Complete the sentences.

1. I feel sorry for _____ because _____.

2. I think _____ is a nice person, but _____.

B

Mr. Han's Class Observation Note

2. How did the teacher use teaching aids?	I set up a Reader's Club using a metaverse platform. While doing the reading activity in an online environment, each student took a specific role. I checked students' comprehension of the passage using the worksheet.
3. Did all the students participate actively?	The students looked absorbed in reading the three paragraphs of the text. After the reading activity, they actively participated in the discussion, carrying out their assigned roles. S1 managed the discussion and controlled each student's speaking time. S2 used an online dictionary when one student asked the meaning of a word, 'crane', and shared a picture of a crane with its meaning. S3 selected one linguistically complex sentence and explained its structure to the other students. S4 uploaded the summary that S5 wrote to the cloud and posted it on the class blog. Lastly, S6 selected another three paragraphs that they would read in the next class.
4. Did the students use suitable reading strategies?	During the discussion, students used various reading strategies such as activating schema, allocating attention, previewing, skimming, scanning, and criticizing. My students were pretty good at making guesses based on the pictures. I also noticed that using a graphic organizer helped students comprehend the story. By comparing and contrasting the two families, they extracted information from the text. My students understood the text very well based on the figure.

S=student

Identify the role that S2 performed in the group activity with the TWO most appropriate words from <A>, and identify the tool that Mr. Han used at the 'While Reading' stage in <A> with the TWO most appropriate words from <B>. Then, explain your answers, respectively, with evidence from <A> and <B>. Do NOT copy more than FOUR consecutive words from <A> and <B>.

Your Answer

_____

_____

_____

_____

_____

_____

문항분석

1. Topic : Collaborative reading in online

2. Focus

온라인상 metaverse platform을 토대로 그룹별 학생들의 적극적 읽기를 도모하기 위하여 그룹 내 각각의 역할을 부여함으로써 협력적인 읽기를 진행하고 있다. 따라서 수업을 관찰하여 각 학생들의 역할과 읽기 중 활동에 대한 명확한 구분을 하고 있는가를 묻고 있다.

3. Graphic organizer

Graphic organizers are visual aids that help students organize, understand, and share information. They can be used with any type of text, from fiction to non-fiction, and can be adapted for students of all ages. In fact, graphic organizers can even be used as a formative assessment tool!

Some common graphic organizers that are familiar to most learners include:

(1) Venn diagrams for comparing and contrasting information
(2) Story webs for outlining the plot of a story
(3) Timelines for tracking chronological events
(4) Concept maps for illustrating relationships between ideas

4. Keyword list

discussion leader, passage chooser, word master, grammar checker, story summarizer, online manager, schema, skimming, scanning, criticizing, making guesses, graphic organizer

모범답안

As a group role, S2 performs a word master who shows the meaning of the new word 'crane' with its picture. In the 'While Reading' stage, Mr. Han uses a graphic organizer in which students complete the figure by comparing/contrasting the extracted information about the two families.

02 Read the conversation in <A> and the two writing drafts in <B>, and follow the directions. [4 points] 2023 전공B 7번

A

(Mr. Min, a middle school English teacher, is talking with his student, Jinhee, about her writing.)

T: Jinhee, I think you put a lot of effort into this first draft.

S: Yeah. But I think I made many mistakes.

T: Don't worry. I'll give you some comments on the categories you need to improve so that you can revise your draft. Can you do that?

S: Yes.

T: Great. Let's begin with content. I like your story, but it'll be better if you add more details here. Do you remember that we discussed how to use supporting details last week?

S: Yes, I do.

T: Good. I also saw that you had problems with organization.

S: You're right. Many events are popping up in my mind, but I can't put them logically.

T: One way to solve the problem is to use linking words such as *and, so, but, however, then, thus,* and so on, in order to show a logical sequence of events.

S: I see.

T: Two more categories are vocabulary and grammar. These two expressions here need to be changed. Look up the appropriate expressions in a dictionary. In addition, swimed here and very not much here are not correct. Think about how you can correct them.

S: Okay.

T: If you have any questions, just let me know. I'm looking forward to reading your second draft.

S: Thank you.

T=teacher, S=student

B

<First draft>

> I went to a game park with my family last weekend. When we arrived, we ate delicious snacks. I swimed in the pool. My father did not swim. My mother did it very not much. We went on the rides. It was very funny and smily. We were very tired. We took a taxi to come home.

<Second draft>

> I went to a game park with my family last weekend. When we arrived, we ate delicious snacks. Both my brother and I love sweets. My brother got three cups of ice cream and I got strawberry cake. I swimed in the pool, but my father did not swim. My mother did it very not much. Then, we went on the rides. It was very funny and smily. We were very tired, so we took a taxi to come home.

Identify the TWO categories Jinhee revised in the second draft based on Mr. Min's comments in <A>. Then, explain how she revised the categories, respectively, with evidence from <B>.

Your Answer

_____

_____

_____

_____

_____

1. Topic : Writing conference

2. Focus

중학교 교사인 Mr. Min이 Jinhee의 first draft에 대해 내용과 구성 측면에서 피드백을 제시하고 있다. 따라서, Jinhee의 first draft가 second draft로 나가도록 Mr. Min이 제공한 구체적인 피드백을 규명하고, Jinhee가 어떻게 자신의 first draft를 개선했는지에 대한 답을 묻는 문항이다.

3. Teacher's feedback (conferencing)

Conferencing (using teacher's feedback) : As the class writes, the teacher can talk with individual students about work in progress. Through careful questioning, the teacher can support a student writer in getting ideas together, organizing them, and finding appropriate language. Also, in a one-to-one conference, the teacher can ask the student to read a section aloud. Frequently the students will then spot errors like an unfinished sentence, a confused sentence, or an omitted word. Some teachers, during a discussion about a topic with a student, make notes of what the student says. The teacher's written notes then form the basis for further prewriting activities.

Ex T: Your first sentence tells the reader one of the reasons why you like puppies. It is a good beginning. Why else do you like puppies?

S: Well. Um. They're cute.

T: Do you know any puppies?

S: Yeah.

T: Can you tell me anything else about the puppy that you know?

S: Well. Um. My puppy is happy when I come home.

T: What is your puppy's name?

S: Argos.

T: You have a really good beginning. Why don't you write about Argos and how Argos feels when you come home?

S: OK.

4. Keyword list

conferencing, content, organization, supporting details, linking words(cohesive devices), logical sequence

---

모범답안

Jinhee revises the second draft in terms of content and organization. First, she provides supporting details about who gets which snacks. Also, she puts a logical sequence of events by linking words such as 'but', 'then', and 'so' between sentences.

03 Read the passage in <A> and the teaching procedures in <B>, and follow the directions. [4 points] 2023 전공B 10번

| A | |

The basic aspects the students need to know about a lexical item are its written and spoken forms, and its denotational meaning. However, there are additional aspects which also need to be learned, as are described in the following table.

Aspects	Descriptions
Grammar	A grammatical structure may be lexically bound, and lexical items also have grammatical features.
Collocation	Collocation refers to the way words tend to co-occur with other words or expressions.
Connotation	The connotations of a word are the emotional or positive-negative associations that it implies.
Appropriateness	Students need to know if a particular lexical item is usually used in writing or in speech; or in formal or informal discourse.
Word formation	Words can be broken down into morphemes. Exactly how these components are put together is another piece of useful information.

B

Teaching Procedure 1

1. Present the following expressions in the table. Ask students to choose which expressions are possible.

do my homework	(O/X)	make my homework	(O/X)
do some coffee	(O/X)	make some coffee	(O/X)
do the laundry	(O/X)	make the laundry	(O/X)

2. Ask students to find more examples using *do* and *make*, referencing an online concordancer.

Teaching Procedure 2

1. Ask students to identify countable and uncountable nouns.

advice	employee	equipment	facility
information	money	proposal	result

2. Tell students to choose the expression of quantity that does NOT fit with the noun in each sentence.

(a) The researchers found [*a significant proportion of / some of / most of*] the results were not corroborated by other sources.

Identify ONE aspect in <A> that each teaching procedure in <B> focuses on, respectively. Then, explain your answers with evidence from <B>.

Your Answer _____

_____

_____

_____

_____

1. Topic : Vocabulary instruction

2. Focus

학습자들의 성공적인 언어 학습을 위해 어휘가 가지고 있는 맥락적 특성에 대한 학습 필요성을 언급하며, 실제 교실에서 진행되는 어휘지도의 구체적 활동에 대하여 규명하는 문항이다.

3. Lexicogrammatical approach

Lexicogrammar, also called lexical grammar, is a term used in systemic functional linguistics(SFL) to emphasize the interdependence of vocabulary (lexis) and syntax (grammar).

(1) How words and grammar are interdependent

The flexibility of verbs, Michael Pearce suggests, proves that grammar and vocabulary are mutually dependent. "Vocabulary and grammatical structures are interdependent; so much so that it is possible to say with some justification that words have their own grammar. This interdependency of lexis and grammar is evident everywhere in language. For example, lexical verbs have valency patterns: some verbs can be used with a direct object (I made some oven gloves), or with both a direct object and an indirect object (The government awarded them a pay rise), others need no object at all (The Colonel was laughing)."

(2) The ability of the same form to appear in many meanings (polysemy)

Core words에 대한 정보를 많이 알면 알수록 어휘력은 더욱 높아질 것이다. 가령, 'rich'라는 단어를 'having a lot of money'로 우선적으로 익히고 배우지만, 이것이 여러 맥락에서 상이한 의미로 사용됨을 알 수 있다. 'rich food, rich soil, rich in resources, a rich color' 등은 'money'와 그 어떤 관련 없이 다른 의미로 사용됨을 알게 된다. 이와 같은 core words의 다양한 의미에 대한 이해는 깊이 있는 어휘 습득을 이끌어 준다.

(3) The ability of the same form to combine with other forms to make new meaning (collocation)

Delexical verbs (have, take, do, etc.)는 동사 자체의 의미는 거의 가지고 있지 않으나, 다른 어휘 형태와 결합하여 특정한 의미를 만들어 주며, 실제 빈번한 사용으로 이어진다. 가령, 'do'는 특별한 의미는 없으나, 특정한 명사와 연결되어 'do a favor, do a tour, do a lap, do the dishes, do the school run' 등의 새로운 의미로 사용된다.

4. Keyword list

lexicogrammar, collocation, connotation, appropriateness, word formation, lexical items, denotational meaning

---

모범답안

Teaching procedures 1 and 2 focus on collocation and grammar, respectively. The former presents some words which co-occur with 'do', and 'make'. On the other hand, the latter asks students to identify countable and uncountable nouns and choose expressions of their quantity.

04 **Read the passage in <A> and the sample items in <B>, and follow the directions.** [4 points] 2021 전공B 9번

A

Ms. Kang, a new high school English teacher, was assigned to create questions for the listening section of the semester's final exam. In order to make the most effective test items, she goes over her notes from her college assessment class and finds the following:

<Item Techniques>

✓ information transfer : transferring aural information to a visual representation

✓ partial dictation : writing down parts of what you hear while listening to a passage

✓ sentence paraphrase : choosing the correct paraphrase from 3-5 distractors

✓ sentence repetition : reproducing a stretch of aural language with oral repetition

✓ short answer : answering a question with a word or a short phrase without given choices

Looking at her notes, she remembers that each of these techniques has its own strengths. For example, the sentence paraphrase technique has high practicality because it is easy to grade. Other techniques, such as information transfer, partial dictation, and sentence repetition, work well for assessing students' listening ability in a more integrative way. Ms. Kang thinks that she will utilize some of these techniques because she wants to test her students' listening and other language skills simultaneously. Ms. Kang also thinks her students should be able to understand specific details, which is one of her main goals for the class this semester. So, she wants to test this particular ability in the final exam. While all the techniques in her notes are good for assessing the ability to find specific information, Ms. Kang thinks the sentence repetition technique may not be appropriate since it may only require students to simply repeat what they hear.

B

Below are two sample items made by Ms. Kang.

Sample Item 1

• Listen to the information about Minsu's daily schedule and fill in his schedule with the correct information. The information will be given twice.

Minsu's Schedule

	Monday	Tuesday	Wednesday	Thursday	Friday
9-10am					
10-11am					
11-12am					
12-1pm			Lunch		
1-2pm					
2-3pm					
3-4pm					

> *Audio Script*
>
> Minsu's classes start at nine in the morning and he eats lunch at noon every day. He has math on Monday, Tuesday, and Friday at nine o'clock. English is scheduled on

Sample Item 2

• Fill in the blanks with the words you hear. You will hear the passage three times.

We can find many geographic regions in Korea. The _____ and _____ parts of the country have huge plains. The main rivers flow westward because the mountainous region is mostly on the _____ part of the country.

> *Audio Script*
>
> We can find many geographic regions in Korea. The southern and western parts of the country have huge plains. The main rivers flow westward because the mountainous region is mostly on the eastern part of the country.

Based on <A>, identify the item technique used in Sample Item 1 and Sample Item 2 in <B>, respectively. Then, explain why the teacher used both item techniques with evidence from <A>. Do NOT copy more than FOUR consecutive words from the passage.

Your Answer

1. Topic : How to teach listening skills

2. Focus

학생들의 듣기 능력 향상을 위해 교사는 가급적 reading이나 writing 등 다른 기능 요구가 동반되지 않는 듣기 활동을 구현할 필요가 있다.

3. Listening activities

(1) **Information transfer**

Students reproduce the message they hear in a new form. For example, when they listen and respond by ordering a set of pictures, completing a map, drawing a picture or completing a table.

(2) **Partial dictation(PD)**

Partial Dictation(PD) as an easier variant of full dictation and a plausible activity in enhancing FL/L2 listening ability. Students are provided with an incomplete written text and fill in missing words while listening to an oral version of the text. Some FL/L2 researchers recommended the use of PD as a reliable, valid, and plausible listening test. Especially, they suggested the use of PD for low-level students when dictation proved too difficult for the students. Using PD helps students focus on missing parts, making it easier for them to follow the text and/or to get its main points.

4. Keyword list

listening comprehension, information transfer, partial dictation, cloze, listening difficulties

Ms. Kang uses 'information transfer' and 'partial dictation' in Sample Item 1 and Sample Item 2, respectively. With these techniques, she wants to test students' listening skills and other skills in an integrative way. Also, she wants to assess students' ability to find specific details.

05 Read the passage in <A> and the teacher's log in <B>, and follow the directions. [4 points] 2021 전공A 8번

A

In an attempt to better understand language development, a three-tiered approach has been proposed, encompassing the following components for investigating production changes: complexity, accuracy, and fluency. Complexity generally refers to the lexical variety and syntactic elaborateness of the learner's linguistic system. Accuracy involves the correct use of the target language, while fluency concerns a focus on meaning, automatization, and real-time processing. These three constructs can be applied to appraise written or spoken language skill (i.e., performance) as well as to assess the state of the linguistic knowledge that supports this performance (i.e., proficiency).

B

Teacher's Log

In order to evaluate the progress of their speaking ability, I usually have my students read a story and then tell about it in their own words. It's not easy to measure all aspects of their speech at once. On the part of the students, it's also not easy to focus on more than one aspect simultaneously. So, I usually give my students two presentation opportunities and ask them to pay more attention to one aspect over the others in each presentation session. In the first presentation session, I focus on how naturally and clearly the content is delivered. To that end, I evaluate students' presentations based on the speed of their talk and the number of pauses and false starts. For the second presentation session, I record and transcribe the students' oral performance for a closer look. At this point, the presentation is evaluated especially by calculating the ratio of independent and dependent clauses and tallying the number of different verbs used.

Based on <A>, identify the component that the teacher focuses on in each presentation session mentioned in <B>, respectively. Then, support your answer with evidence from <B>. Do NOT copy more than FOUR consecutive words from <A> and <B>.

Your Answer
_____

_____

_____

_____

_____

_____

1. Topic : Teaching productive skills

2. Focus

언어 수행의 주요 요소는 complexity, accuracy, fluency로 이루어진다. 따라서, 교실에서 학생들의 말하기 및 쓰기 과업 시 수행뿐 아니라, 언어 능력 측면에서도 세 가지 요소를 골고루 평가해야 한다.

3. Speaking ability

(1) **Complexity** : it generally refers to the lexical variety and syntactic elaborateness of the learner's linguistic system.

> **Ex** calculating the ratio of independent and dependent clauses and tallying the number of different verbs used.

(2) **Accuracy** : it involves the correct use of the target language.

> **Ex** accurate articulation and grammatical correctness(form and syntax).

(3) **Fluency** : it concerns a focus on meaning, automatization, and real-time processing.

> **Ex** evaluating students' presentations based on the speed of their talk and the number of pauses and false starts.

4. Keyword list

complexity, fluency, accuracy, variety, syntactic elaborateness, automatization

모범답안

The teacher focuses on fluency and complexity in each presentation session. In the first session, s/he evaluates how students deliver the content naturally and clearly in terms of speed, pauses, and false starts. In the second session, s/he calculates the rate of dependent and independent clauses and counts how many different verbs are used.

06 **Read the passage in <A> and the conversation in <B>, and follow the directions.** [4 points] 2022 전공B 7번

A

One of the reasons we can communicate successfully, especially in writing, is because we have some understanding of genre, socially recognized ways of using language for particular purposes. Genre represents the norms of different kinds of writing shared among people within a particular community. The emphasis on the social dimension of genre is a major characteristic of genre-based approaches to teaching writing.

A genre-based writing instruction involves students in an in-depth analysis of texts in the genre in which they are going to be writing. In particular, students are asked to analyze three essential features of the genre using example texts: 1) the *context*, which includes the situation and audience, 2) the *content*, which indicates the information and message conveyed, and 3) the *construction*, that is, how the texts of the genre are typically constructed in terms of the layout and language. When students are done with this task, they are in a position to create their own writing within the genre.

| B |

Activity 1

(After conducting a reading lesson about volunteering, a middle school English teacher prepares a poster-making activity for recruiting volunteers. He plans to have his students analyze the features of the poster genre before they make their own posters.)

- Ask the students to share their volunteering experiences.
- Have the students examine the poster and answer the questions in the worksheet.

Worksheet

1. Why are some words capitalized?
2. Does the poster use full sentences? If not, why?

Activity 2

(Believing writing reviews is an important skill that her students should be equipped with, a high school English teacher prepares a genre-analyzing kit with which the students figure out the characteristics of the book review genre.)

- Tell the students they are going to read a book review.
- Have the students use the genre-analyzing kit while reading the book review.

Book Review

"I Really Want the Cup Cake"
Written by Philip Kent
Illustrated by Terra Wang
Ages 3-5 | 20 Pages
Publisher: Green Books | ISBN: 978-1-338-95941-2
What to expect: Rhyme, Dessert, Self Control
(or lack thereof)

Honestly, who of us hasn't wanted to dive in, just a teeny, tiny bit, to that delicious-looking cup cake left on the table? Just a bite couldn't hurt, could it? In this hilarious story about a little boy and his dog, that's exactly what they are trying not to do.

Reviewers' Genre-Analyzing Kit

1. Who do you think the review is aimed at?
2. When would people write this kind of text?

Based on <A>, identify ONE essential feature of the target genre that each activity in <B> focuses on, respectively. Then, explain your answers with evidence from <B>.

Your Answer

1. Topic : How to teach writing skills (Genre-based writing approach)

2. Focus

글은 의사소통의 목적과 기능, 효과에 따라 고유한 수사학적 구조를 갖는 상이한 유형의 담론으로 형성되어 있다. 따라서, 효율적인 의사소통 능력을 갖추기 위해 학습자들은 각 담론에 사용되는 고유의 수사학적 구조를 사용할 수 있어야 하며, 상이한 담론의 글을 접할 경우에도 해당 특징에 맞는 수사학적 구조에 따라 글을 이해할 수 있어야 한다.

3. Genre-based language approach

(1) **What is a genre?**

- A genre is primarily recognised by its communicative purpose, which shapes how a text is realised.
- Texts that belong to a genre share similar characteristics, such as target audience, organisation of ideas and language choices.
- For example, a thesis statement is obligatory in an argumentative essay because the communicative purpose of this genre is to argue for or against a position.

(2) **Stages of a genre-based writing approach**

① **Step 1** : Setting the context

exploring the communicative purpose (e.g., to persuade readers to care for the environment) of a particular genre.

> Learners can read a text and discuss its communicative purpose with their classmates.

② **Step 2** : Modelling

guiding learners to identify language features (e.g., tenses, personal pronouns) of a sample text of a particular genre. At this stage, learners should also pay attention to moves (i.e., writers' intentions) in the text.

> Examples of moves in a factual essay can include presenting an argument, supporting an argument, and predicting possible outcomes.

③ **Step 3** : Joint construction

reinforcing features that learners identified at the modelling stage.

④ **Step 4** : Independent construction

writing their essays with support from teachers if necessary. (apply a process approach to writing)

⑤ **Step 5** : Comparing

comparing and contrasting the communicative purpose and language characteristics of the genre they have learned with other genres.

4. Keyword list

genre-based approach, rhetorical structure

모범답안

Activity 1 focuses on the *construction* while Activity 2 the *context*. In the former, students pay attention to capitalized words and incomplete sentences of the poster in terms of layout and language. In the latter, students identify the audience and the situation of the book review by figuring out for whom and when to write the book review.

07 **Read the passage in <A> and the master plan in <B>, and follow the directions.** [4 points] 2022 전공 A 8번

A

  Ms. Yoon is an English teacher at a local middle school. According to her school curriculum, students should be able to use a combination of top-down and bottom-up processing when they practice the receptive skills of English, that is, listening and reading. Bottom-up processing is the processing of individual elements of the target language for the decoding of language input, while top-down processing refers to the use of background knowledge in understanding the meaning of a message. Now, she is developing a master plan for one of the units she will teach next semester. To help her students achieve this curriculum goal, she makes efforts to ensure that both bottom-up and top-down processing are practiced during each lesson period.

| B |

Ms. Yoon's Unit 1 Master Plan

1. **Lesson**: Challenge & Courage

2. **Objectives**

   Students will be able to:
   - listen to a dialogue and explain the content
   - ask for reasons and make decisions
   - read a text and retell the story

3. **Study points**
   - Functions: asking for and giving reasons
   - Forms: passive, subject-verb agreement

4. **Time allotment**: 8 periods, 45 minutes each

Period	Section	Learning Activities
1st	Listen 1	• Listen to a series of phrases for consonant/vowel linking between words • Listen to short sentences to discriminate between rising and falling intonation
2nd	Listen 2	• Listen to a dialogue and find the main idea • Do a sentence dictation activity with the active and passive voice
5th	Read 1	• Read the introductory paragraph and predict what will come next • Distinguish sentences containing subject-verb agreement errors
6th	Read 2	• Recognize whether a sentence is in the active or passive voice • Change base forms of verbs into the past participle by adding '-ed / -en'

Based on <A>, identify TWO periods in <B> in which the teacher focuses on both types of processing. Then, explain your answers with evidence from <B>.

Your Answer	

---

1. Topic: How to teach listening and reading skills(integrated lesson)

2. Focus

Real life에서 사용하는 진정성 있는 언어 능력을 길러 나가기 위해서 교사는 교실에서도 real life 환경과 같은 언어 사용을 계획해야 할 것이다. 따라서, 개별적 언어 기능 사용의 수업이 아니라 최소 2가지 이상의 language skills을 사용할 수 있는 수업을 계획해야 한다.

3. Real life listening and reading

In 'real-life' listening and reading, our students will have to use a combination of the two processes, with more emphasis on 'top-down' or 'bottom-up' listening and reading depending on their reasons for listening and reading.

⑴ **Case 1**

Over lunch, your friend tells you a story about a recent holiday, which was a disaster. You listen with interest and interject at appropriate moments, maybe to express surprise or sympathy. (TOP-DOWN LISTENING)

(2) **Case 2**

That evening, another friend calls to invite you to a party at her house the following Saturday. As you've never been to her house before, she gives you directions. You listen carefully and make notes. (BOTTOM-UP LISTENING)

4. Keyword list

top-down, bottom-up, integrative lesson, predicting

In the 2nd and 5th periods, Ms. Yoon asks students to listen and read based on both top-down and bottom-up processing. In the 2nd period, they find out the main idea after listening and then, dictate some sentences with active and passive voices. In the 5th period, they predict what comes next and then identify some sentences with subject-verb agreement errors.

08 **Read the conversation and follow the directions.** [2 points] 2015 전공A 기입형 4번

> T : The other day we were talking about the Battle of Waterloo. And we've already talked about the two main generals in that war. Does anybody remember who they are?
>
> S1 : Napoleon and Wellington.
>
> T : Correct, but don't forget that Wellington is a title which he received for his military successes. Born Arthur Wesley, he became the Duke of Wellington in 1814. He received that title for ending the Peninsular War by storming what city?
>
> S2 : Toulouse.
>
> T : That's right. Shortly after, Napoleon abdicated and was imprisoned on Elba. And when did the Battle of Waterloo take place?
>
> S3 : 1815.
>
> T : Very good. Napoleon escaped Elba and was attempting to restore his rule. It wasn't until his defeat at Waterloo by Wellington that Napoleon's reign finally came to an end. Now we're going to see...
>
> T=teacher, S=student

Complete the comments on the conversation above by filling in the blank with ONE word.

The conversation above is part of a teacher-student talk in the classroom in which a teacher and students mainly give and receive specific information. Among types of speaking functions, the type shown in the conversation refers to situations where the focus is on information rather than on the participants. The conversation above serves a(n) _____ function in that its priority is not the interpersonal function of speaking but information exchange.

Your Answer _____

1. Topic : Conversation analysis

2. Focus

주어진 대화에서 교사와 학생들이 워털루 전쟁에 대한 정보를 교환하는 담화가 어떤 기능(i.e., interactional, transactional)을 수행하는지 이해할 필요가 있다.

3. Discourse functions

(1) Interpersonal

상호작용을 촉진시키기 위한 대화로, 메시지 그 자체보다 화자와 화자들 간의 관계에 그 목적이 있다.

- Social type talk
- Person oriented
- The establishment and maintenance of cordial social relationship

(2) Transactional

전달하는 내용에 집중을 요하는 사실적 정보, 명제 등을 전달하기 위한 대화로, 실생활에서 언어 행위의 결과를 유도한다.

- Business type talk
- Message oriented
- The focus on content and conveying factual or propositional information

(3) Implications(시사점)

- Teachers need to provide practice experiences in both transactional talk and interactional talk.
- Students need instruction and listening practice to help them recognize when one of the two functions is operating and how they can respond appropriately.

4. Keyword list

interactional, transactional

Answer | transactional

Plus +

1. The aim of conversation analysis

"CA is the study of recorded, naturally occurring talk-in-interaction. But what is the aim of studying these interactions? Principally, it is to discover how participants understand and respond to one another in their turns at talk, with a central focus on how sequences of action are generated. To put it another way, the objective of CA is to uncover the often tacit reasoning procedures and sociolinguistic competencies underlying the production and interpretation of talk in organized sequences of interaction."

2. Adjacency pairs

One of the most common structures to be defined through conversation analysis is the adjacency pair, which is a call and response type of sequential utterances spoken by two different people. Here are some examples:

① Summons/Answer

    A： *Can I please get some help over here?*

    B： *I'll be right there.*

② Offer/Refusal

    Sales clerk： *Do you need someone to carry your packages out?*

    Customer： *No thanks. I've got it.*

③ Compliment/Acceptance

    A： *That's a great tie you've got on.*

    B： *Thanks. It was an anniversary present from my wife.*

09 **Read the conversation between two teachers and follow the directions.**
[2 points] 2019 전공A 2번

T1: My students are having trouble with plural nouns. I'm thinking of trying a new task.

T2: What's your idea?

T1: I'm planning to give a short text where every seventh word is blanked out. Students have to guess the correct word for each blank to make a complete sentence.

T2: Well, that might be a bit difficult for beginning level students. I did a similar activity last semester. I gave a text where I blanked out only plural nouns so that students could focus on them.

T1: Oh, I see.

T2: You can also give students only parts of words in the blanks and ask them to restore each word in the text.

T1: Hmm, that seems interesting. Well, then, for my students, I'll try to use only plural nouns in the written text and ask my students to fill in the blanks. Thanks for the suggestion.

T1=teacher 1, T2=teacher 2

Complete the comments by filling in the blank with the ONE most appropriate word.

In the above dialogue, the two teachers are talking about teaching plural nouns through three types of gap-filling tasks which require students to read the texts and fill in the blanks. The gap-filling described by the teachers here is _____, which can be readily adapted for pedagogical tasks in classrooms.

Your Answer _____

문항분석

1. Topic : 통합 과업(Integrative task)

2. Focus

대표적인 통합 과업인 cloze task의 종류에 대해 알고 있고, cloze의 개념을 알고 있는지 묻는 문제이다.

3. Cloze task

A sentence with a word left out should be filled with a calculated guess, using linguistic expectancies and background knowledge. Cloze tasks are an integrative measure not only of reading ability but also other language abilities.

4. Types of cloze tasks

Typically every seventh word is deleted (known as fixed-ratio deletion), but many cloze task designers instead use a rational deletion procedure of choosing deletions according to the grammatical or discourse functions of the words. Rational deletion also allows the designer to avoid deleting words that would be difficult to predict from the context.

5. C-task

In a C-task, a suggested alternative to the cloze task, the second half of every other word is deleted, leaving the first and the last sentence of the passage intact. This alternative eliminates certain problems associated with cloze, such as choice of deletion rate and starting point, representational sampling of different language elements in the passage, and the inadvertent assessment of written production as well as reading. Within a C-task, a clue (half the word) serves as a stimulus for respondents to find the other half. It is still not clear to what extent it tests more than microlevel processing. Because half the word is given, students who do not understand the macro-context may still be able to mobilize their vocabulary skills adequately to fill in the appropriate word without engaging in higher-level processing.

6. Keyword list

cloze task, fixed-ratio deletion, rational deletion, gap-filling, C-task

Answer | cloze

10 **Read the passage and follow the directions.** [2 points] 2017 전공A 6번

> The following is part of a lesson procedure that aims to facilitate students' comprehension of a text concerning global warming.
>
> **Steps** :
> 1. Before reading the text, T activates Ss' background knowledge concerning global warming and provides other relevant information to help Ss to have a better comprehension of the text.
> 2. T instructs Ss to read the text quickly in order to grasp the main ideas. In doing so, T tells them not to read every word.
> 3. T asks Ss to reread it quickly for specific information, such as the type of disasters caused by global warming.
> 4. T instructs Ss to read the text again at their own pace.
> 5. T checks Ss' overall comprehension by having them write a brief summary of the text.
> 6. T then checks Ss' understanding of the details by using a cloze activity.
>
> T=teacher, S=student

Identify the two kinds of expeditious reading that the teacher instructs students to use in steps 2 and 3 with ONE word, respectively. Write them in the order that they appear.

Your Answer _____

문항분석

1. Topic : How to teach reading skills

2. Focus

주어진 수업 절차에서 훈련에 초점을 두고 있는 읽기 전략들을 파악하는 문제이다. Reading에 관련한 주요 전략들에 대해서 인지하고 있고, 각각의 전략들이 읽기

상황에서 어떻게 학생의 이해를 도울 수 있는지(각 전략의 사용 목적)에 대하여 파악하고 있어야 한다.

3. Reading strategies

(1) How to skim

텍스트의 전반적인 내용, 전체 구조, 중심 내용 등을 알아내기 위해 텍스트 전체를 재빨리 읽는 전략

Skimming means glancing rapidly through the text to get a general idea of what it is about.

- cast your eyes over its surface to get a gist.
- mainly concerned with finding key points, main ideas, overall theme, and basic structure.

(2) How to scan

텍스트에 나와 있는 특정 정보(e.g., names, prices, dates, etc)를 찾기 위해 텍스트를 빨리 읽는 전략

Scanning means glancing rapidly through the text to pick out specific information.

- do not have to read every word and line to scan the text for particular bits of information you are searching for.
- read to find the required answer quickly, by speed-reading through the text without understanding the whole text.

(3) How to make inferencing

명시적인 의미 이외에 숨겨진 의미(intended meaning)를 파악, 추론하는 전략

The students consider what is implied but not explicitly stated. The readers may put together pieces of information that are scattered throughout the text.

4. Keyword list

scanning, skimming, inferencing, guessing, clustering

Answer skimming, scanning

11 Below are an excerpt from a reading text and part of a student's think-aloud data generated while reading it. Based on the think-aloud data, identify the reading strategy that the student is using. Use ONE word. [2 points]

2014 전공A 기입형 10번

Computers have the potential to accomplish great things. With the right software, they could help make science tangible or teach neglected topics like art and music. They could help students form a concrete idea of society by displaying on screen a version of the city in which they live.

In practice, computers make our worst educational nightmares come true. While we bemoan the decline of literacy, computers discount words in favor of pictures or video. While we fret about the decreasing cogency of public debate, computers dismiss linear argument and promote fast, shallow romps across the information landscape. While we worry about basic skills, we allow into the classroom software that will do a student's arithmetic or correct his spelling.

> Well, nightmares? The author thinks computers do harm to education.

> Hmm . . . the author is blaming computer software for a decline in basic skills.

Your Answer _____

문항분석

1. Topic : Reading strategies

2. Focus

다양한 reading 전략들(e.g., skimming, scanning, guessing, inferencing)의 특징들에 대하여 이해하고 있어야 한다.

3. Think-aloud technique

You ask someone to do a task, and to think aloud (vocalize) about what they are doing while they are doing it. Think-aloud technique is also useful for giving insights into whether people are tackling a task using pattern matching or sequential reasoning; it's also useful for identifying which things they bother with, and which things they don't notice.

4. Reading strategy

Think-aloud technique을 통하여 text에서 얻게 된 정보를 토대로 독자 자신의 경험에 비추어 글쓴이의 컴퓨터 사용에 대한 부정적 태도를 추론해낸다는 측면에서 inferencing으로 분류된다.

5. Keyword list

think-aloud technique, inferencing, implied meaning

Answer | inferencing

12 Read the conversation between two high school English teachers, and identify the type of reading that Ms. Kim recommends to Mr. Hong. Use **TWO words.** [2 points] 2015 전공A 기입형 5번

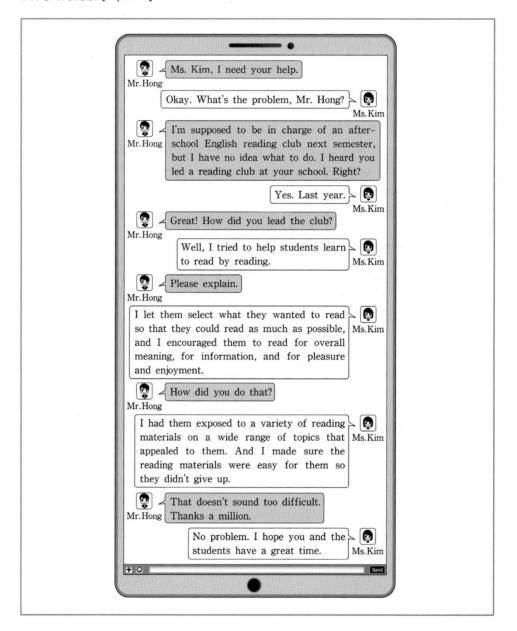

Your Answer _____

문항분석

1. Topic : How to teach reading skills

2. Focus

두 교사의 대화 중 기술되는 extensive reading의 주요 특성들(e.g., read for pleasure, choose what students want to read)에 대하여 이해하고 있어야 한다.

3. Reading types

(1) Intensive reading

특정 텍스트의 정확한 이해 혹은 읽기 기능 연습을 위해 교실 수업에서 행해지는 읽기 활동이다. Reading for information을 목적으로 하고 있어 text에 제시된 언어적 정보부터 함축적인 의미까지 파악하고 필요한 reading strategy training 까지 다루는 교실 내 읽기 활동이다.

(2) Extensive reading

다양한 텍스트 혹은 보다 긴 텍스트를 즐거움과 전반적인 내용의 이해를 위해 읽는 읽기 활동이다. Reading for pleasure의 목적을 갖고 있으며, 학생들은 각자 원하는 텍스트를 개별적으로 선정하여 각기 읽기의 목적대로 진행되는 교실 밖의 실생활 읽기 활동이다.

(3) How to engage in extensive reading

① The reading material is easy.

② A variety of reading material on a wide range of topics must be available.

③ Learners choose what they want to read.

④ Learners read as much as possible.

⑤ The purpose of reading is usually related to pleasure, information and general understanding.

⑥ Reading is its own reward.

⑦ Reading speed is usually faster rather than slower.

⑧ Reading is individual and silent.

⑨ Teachers orient and guide their students.

⑩ The teacher is a role model of a reader.

4. Keyword list

intensive reading, extensive reading

Answer extensive reading

13 Read the passage in <A> and the conversation between two teachers in <B>, and follow the directions. [2 points] 2020 전공A 3번

| A |

The way you speak is affected in many ways. For example, how much attention you are paying to your speech may be one factor. When you are not paying much attention to the way you are speaking, your speech may be more casual. By contrast, if you are conscious about the way you are speaking, your output will be less casual. The social position of the person with whom you are engaging in conversation may also affect your language output. It is natural to use more formal language when you speak to someone whose social position is above yours. The sociolinguistic concept of solidarity should also be considered. If your interlocutor comes from the same speech community or shares a similar social or cultural identity with you, you will feel connected to him or her, and this will affect the way you deliver your message. In addition, where you are affects the formality of your output. When you are in a formal situation, such as a business meeting, you naturally use more formal language, and the opposite is true as well. Lastly, the channel or medium of language, that is, whether you deliver your message through speech or writing, can be another critical factor that affects your speech. All of these things need to be considered carefully, because they constitute what is called pragmatic competence which relies very heavily on conventional, culturally appropriate, and socially acceptable ways of interacting.

B

T1: What are you writing?

T2: Oh, this is a recommendation letter for Miri.

T1: I see. She is very active in school activities, so you must have a lot to write about her.

T2: Yes, she is a good student, but she doesn't know how to adapt her conversational style when making a request.

T1: Hmm... what do you mean by that?

T2: When Miri approached me, she said, "Hi, teacher, can you write me a recommendation letter?"

T1: Haha... I understand what you mean. Some of my students also seem to have trouble making their speech style appropriate to the situation. Miri is just one example.

T2: Exactly! Still, I feel it's my responsibility to show them how speech styles differ across various situations. Hey, why don't we offer a special lecture on this topic?

T1: Definitely! We can invite a guest speaker who can show the importance of selecting the appropriate conversational style to match the _____ of the situation.

T=teacher

Fill in the blank in <B> with the ONE most appropriate word from <A>.

Your Answer _____

1. Topic : Speech styles

2. Focus

의사소통 능력 중 sociolinguistic competence는 사회·문화 규칙과 담화 규칙에 대한 지식을 포함한다. 따라서 언어 사용자의 언어 사용의 적절성이 평가되며, 그 중에 대화 담화자 간의 관계 및 대화 상황에 따른 언어 사용이 중요하며 이 기준인 formality에 대한 중요성을 제기하고자 한다.

3. Main types of speech styles

(1) Frozen

It refers to historic language or communication that is intended to remain unchanged, like a constitution or prayer.

Ex the Bible, the United States Constitution, "Romeo and Juliet"

(2) Formal

Less rigid but still constrained, the formal register is used in professional, academic, or legal settings. Slang is never used, and contractions are rare.

Ex a TED talk, a business presentation, the Encyclopaedia Britannica

(3) Consultative

People use this register often in conversation when they're speaking with someone who has specialized knowledge or who is offering advice.

Ex the local TV news broadcast, an annual physical, a service provider like a plumber

(4) Casual

This is the register people use when they're with friends, close acquaintances and co-workers, and family. Use of slang, contractions, and vernacular grammar is all common.

Ex a birthday party, a backyard barbecue

(5) Intimate

Usually between only two people and often in private. Intimate language may be something as simple as an inside joke between two college friends or a word whispered in a lover's ear.

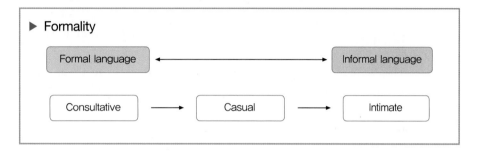

4. Keyword list

formality, consultative, casual, intimate

Answer   formality

14 Read the activity procedure and identify the type of learning activity with ONE word. [2 points] 2016 전공A 3번

	Activity Procedure
Step 1	• T places various information on a different job in each of the four corners in the classroom. (Each corner is labelled with a different letter, A, B, C, or D.) • T assigns individual Ss a letter (A, B, C, or D) in order to create four groups of four Ss, each of which is a base group composed of A to D.
Step 2	• T provides Ss in each base group with handouts. (Each handout has a set of questions about four different jobs.) • T helps Ss understand that they should be interdependent upon one another not only for their own learning but also for the learning of others throughout the activity. • T informs Ss which corner to go to based on their letter in order to form four different expert groups.
Step 3	• Ss move to their expert groups and find out information about different jobs through discussions and answer the questions on the handouts. • T circulates within the groups and makes sure each of the Ss has all the answers.
Step 4	• Ss return to their initial base groups and exchange the information through discussing what they learned in the expert groups. • All the base groups present their findings to the whole class and decide which job they would like most.

T=teacher, S=student

Your Answer _____

문항분석

1. Topic : Communicative tasks

2. Focus

Communicative approach 안에서 학생들의 언어 사용 및 상호작용을 극대화하기 위한 교실 활동을 제안하고자 한다. 가령, Jigsaw 활동은 서로 다른 정보를 토대로 정보를 나누고 과업을 완수하면서 목표언어의 사용과 그룹 안에서 학생 간의 상호작용을 극대화할 수 있다.

3. Task types

(1)

	Interactant relationship	Interaction requirement	Goal Orientation	Outcome options
Jigsaw	Two-way	required	convergent	closed
Information gap	One-way or Two-way	required	convergent	closed
Problem solving	One-way or Two-way	required or optional	convergent	closed
Decision making	One-way or Two-way	required or optional	convergent	open
Opinion exchange	One-way or Two-way	required or optional	divergent	open

Advantages of Jigsaw

① Interdependence: 각각의 정보를 나누고 정보를 취합하여 과업을 완성하는 데 있어 서로의 도움과 의지가 절대적으로 요구된다.

② Accountability: 학습자들의 각자 역할 부여로 인한 학습 활동의 책임감을 키울 수 있다.

③ Social skills: Collaboration을 토대로 과업에 대한 완수를 이루어내야 하므로 학생들 간의 사회적 능력을 자연스럽게 키워 나갈 수 있다.

4. Keyword list

jigsaw, information-gap, split/shared

Answer | jigsaw

15 **Read the dialogue and follow the directions.** [2 points] 2019 전공A 3번

T: What are you going to do this weekend?

S: I will go to a market with my mom.

T: Is there anything you want to buy?

S: Eggs. Many eggs.

T: Is that all you want?

S: No. I will buy many bread and cheese, too.

T: (1) Well, you said you will buy... buy...

S: Buy bread and cheese. Ah, buy a lot of bread. I will buy a lot of bread and cheese.

T: Why will you buy them?

S: I like to make sandwiches. I will make many sandwiches.

T: Do you have any other plans?

S: I have many homework so I will study for many hours.

T: (2) Well, what word do we use with homework?

S: Many homeworks? No, a lot of? Yes, a lot of homework.

T=teacher, S=student

Fill in the blank with the ONE most appropriate word.

_____ refers to a type of the teacher's corrective feedback that directly induces the correct form of an error from the learner. One technique of this is to induce the correct form of an error by prompting the learner to reformulate the error and complete his or her own utterances, which is seen in the teacher's first corrective feedback, (1), in the dialogue. Another technique is to use questions to lead the learner to produce correct forms as shown in the teacher's second corrective feedback, (2), in the dialogue.

Your Answer _____

문항분석

1. Topic : Classroom feedback – Corrective feedback

2. Focus

학생의 오류를 포함한 발화에 대해 교사의 교정적 피드백이 교실 상황에서 구체적으로 어떻게 진행되며 어떤 분류가 있는지 알고 있어야 하는 문제이다.

3. Types of corrective feedback(CF)

Oral CF can be provided through a variety of strategies. Lyster and Ranta (1997) identified six different types of oral CF: request for clarification, recast, repetition, metalinguistic feedback, elicitation, and explicit correction.

(1) Request for clarification elicits a reformulation of the preceding utterance by indicating to students that their utterance has either been misunderstood by the teacher or is ill-formed in some way.

(2) Recast involves the teacher's rephrasing of the student's utterance by changing one or more components without changing the central meaning.

(3) Repetition refers to the teacher's repetition of the student's erroneous utterance highlighting the error mostly through intonation.

(4) Metalinguistic feedback contains comments, information, or questions related to the form of the student's utterance, without explicitly providing the correct form. Metalinguistic comments generally indicate that there is an error somewhere but, through these comments, the teacher attempts to elicit the information from the student.

(5) Elicitation refers to the techniques that teachers use to directly elicit the correct form from the student.

(6) Explicit correction refers to the explicit provision of the correct form. While providing the correct form, the teacher clearly indicates that the student has made an error.

4. Keyword list

corrective feedback, negative feedback, direct/explicit feedback, indirect/implicit feedback, clarification request, recast, repetition, metalinguistic feedback, elicitation, explicit correction, uptake

Answer Elicitation

16 Read the passage in <A> and the conversation in <B>, and follow the directions. [4 points] 2016 전공A 12번

---| **A** |---

Mr. Jeon's Thoughts

There are various types of teacher corrective feedback on learners' grammatical errors, including clarification request, elicitation, metalinguistic feedback and recast. I believe that corrective feedback may not have an immediate impact but it should meet certain requirements in order to facilitate language learning. I think corrective feedback should not explicitly indicate that an error has occurred so that it does not embarrass the learner inadvertently and disrupt the flow of ongoing communication. I also find it important that corrective feedback should contain a targetlike alternative to the learner's ill-formed output. Such an alternative form enables the learner to make a comparison of his or her problematic form and its correct form, which constitutes a cognitive process facilitative of language learning.

---| **B** |---

S: I am very worried.

T: Really? What are you worried about, Minjae?

S: Math exam for tomorrow. I don't studied yesterday.

T: You didn't study yesterday?

S: No, I didn't studied.

T: Please tell me why. What happened?

S: I did volunteering all day long. So I don't had time to study.

T: Well, Minjae, "don't had" is not the right past tense form.

S: Uh, I didn't had time, time to study.

T=teacher, S=student

Identify the teacher's TWO corrective feedback utterances in <B> and select their respective type from those mentioned in <A>. Then explain how only ONE of the utterances meets what Mr. Jeon believes is required for effective corrective feedback in <A>.

Your Answer _____

_____

_____

_____

_____

_____

문항분석

1. Topic : Classroom feedback

2. Focus

영어를 학습하면서 학생들은 영어에 대한 중간언어(학습자 언어) 형태를 취하게 되는데, 중간언어 상태에서 언어를 사용하는 경우, 많은 부분에서 오류가 발생하게 되며, 더 나은 중간언어 단계로 발전하기 위해서는 반복적이거나 중대한 문제가 있는 오류들은 반드시 수정·보완해야 한다. 따라서 보다 정확한 언어 사용을 위한 학습자들의 awareness를 높이기 위해서는 교사가 학습자의 인지적·정의적 수준을 고려하여 적절한 feedback을 상황에 맞게 제공할 필요가 있다.

3. Classroom feedback types

(1) Explicit correction

A clear indication to the student that the form is incorrect and provision of a corrected form

(2) Recast

An implicit type of corrective feedback that reformulates or expands an ill-formed or incomplete utterance in an unobtrusive way

(3) Clarification request

An elicitation of a reformulation or repetition from a student

(4) Elicitation

A corrective technique that prompts the learner to self-correct. Eliciation and other prompts are more overt in their request for a response.

(5) Metalinguistic feedback

Provides comments, information, or questions related to the well-formedness of the student's utterance.

(6) Repetition

The teacher repeats the ill-formed part of the student's utterance, usually with a change in intonation.

4. Others : Responses to feedback

(1) Uptake

A student utterance that immediately follows the teacher's feedback and that constitutes a reaction in some way to the teacher's intention to draw attention to some aspect of the student's initial utterance.

(2) Repair

As a result of teacher feedback, a learner corrects an ill-formed utterance, either through self-repair or as a result of peer-repair.

(3) Repetition

The learner repeats the correct form as a result of teacher feedback, and sometimes incorporates it into a longer utterance.

5. Keyword list

explicit correction, recast, clarification request, elicitation, metalinguistic feedback, repetition, self-repair/peer-repair, uptake

모범답안

As corrective feedback on a student's error, the teacher used a recast type feedback of "you didn't study yesterday?" and the metalinguistic feedback "'don't had' is not the right past tense form." in the classroom conversation. However, Mr. Jeon thinks that the recast type feedback is more effective because it does not explicitly indicate the error but maintains the communicative flow with the target-like form.

Plus⁺

Feedback on Errors

Existing research on corrective feedback supports the importance of feedback for successful acquisition of oral communicative competence. Therefore, we should employ a variety of feedback options such as recasting, self-correction, and metalinguistic explanation. The important point to keep in mind is that we should adhere to principles of maintaining communicative flow, of maximizing student self-correction, and of sensitively considering the affective state and linguistic stage of the learner.

The treatment of grammatical errors in writing is a different matter. In processing writing approaches, overt attention to local grammatical and rhetorical errors is normally delayed until learners have completed one or two drafts of a paper. Global errors that impede meaning must, of course, be attended to earlier in the process.

Overcorrection can create a negative classroom atmosphere, discouraging learners from risk-taking and experimentation. The extent of error correction will depend on the aim of the lesson.

- When the focus is on meaning, it is inappropriate to interrupt the flow of interaction. In these situations, the teacher can make a note of errors for follow-up treatment later.
- When the focus is on form, the teacher might well interrupt before the students have finished their turn.

17 Read the passage and fill in each blank with TWO words. (Use the SAME answer for both blanks.) [2 points] 2017 전공A 7번

S : Could you give me some advice on how I can improve my pronunciation?

T : Yes, of course. Are you having trouble pronouncing a particular word?

S : I can't think of any right now, but there are a lot of sounds in English that I can't pronounce.

T : Can you give me an example?

S : The word *right*. *R* is very difficult for me.

T : Oh, that's because the consonant *r* doesn't exist in the Korean sound system. Then, you should practice pronunciation with a lot of _____. For example, the words *river* and *liver* have only one sound difference in the same position, but it makes a big difference in meaning.

S : Oh, I see. So, I guess *fine* and *pine* would be another example of _____, right?

T : Yes, you're right. If you want to be able to pronounce *right*, you first need to be able to hear the difference between *right* and *light*. There are so many other examples, like *rice* and *lice*, *rode* and *load*, etc.

S : I can't hear the difference between those words, either.

T : I know they are difficult, but with enough practice, you will be able to hear the difference and pronounce them correctly.

T=teacher, S=student

Your Answer _____

문항분석

1. Topic : How to teach pronunciation

2. Focus

주어진 대화에서는 학생이 교사에게 영어 발음의 어려움(i.e., trouble pronouncing a particular word)에 대해서 토로하고 있다. 학생의 문제를 해결하기 위해 교사는 수업 중에 발음의 어떤 부분(segmentals, suprasegmentals)에 초점을 맞추어서 진행해야 하며, 구체적으로 어떠한 활동을 활용할 수 있는지에 대해서 파악할 수 있어야 한다.

3. Two approaches of teaching pronunciation

(1) **Bottom-up approach** : focus on segmentals, clear articulation, practicing minimal pairs

언어의 분절적인 요소, 즉 음소의 정확한 발음에 초점을 두는 접근법은 모국어의 간섭 현상의 영향을 많이 받기 때문에 대조 분석에 의한 최소대립쌍(minimal pairs)을 토대로 발음 지도를 하되, 유의미한 의사소통 안에서 개별 음가의 유의미한 최소대립쌍을 제공하는 것이 좋다(contextualized minimal pairs).

- Segmentals consist of the phonemes of that language, or its smallest meaning units.
- In the past pronunciation instruction usually focused on the articulation of consonants and vowels and the discrimination of minimal pairs.
- The teacher's job is to identify those area that affect intelligibility the most and to find ways to integrate practice of those pronunciation features into the lesson.

(2) **Top-down approach** : focus on suprasegmentals (intonation, rhythm, stress)

억양, 강세 및 리듬의 초분절적인 요소는 의미에 직접적인 영향을 끼치므로 적절한 지도가 이루어지지 않을 경우 의사소통에 장애가 될 뿐 아니라 무례한 듯한 인상을 남길 수 있다.

Suprasegmentals include intonation, rhythm, and stress. These features can have an even greater impact on intelligibility than the mispronunciation of sounds. Thus, the focus has shifted to fluency rather than accuracy encouraging an emphasis on suprasemengtals.

(3) **Balanced view**: focus on intelligibility (bottom-up & top-down)

최근의 발음 지도의 초점은 원어민과 같은 정확한 발음, 강세가 아닌 이해 가능한 발음(intelligibility)에 있으며, 이해 가능한 발음에 영향을 끼치는 분절적인 요소와 초분절적인 요소를 의사소통의 맥락 내에서 조화를 이루게 하여 가르치도록 함에 있다.

In recent years, emphasis on meaning and communicative intent alone will not suffice to achieve grammatical accuracy and teaching pronunciation has emerged from the segmental/suprasegmental debate to a more balanced view, which recognizes that a lack of intelligibility can attributed to both micro and macro features.

4. Keyword list

bottom-up approach, top-down approach, segmentals, suprasegmentals, minimal pairs, contextualized minimal pairs, intelligibility

Answer　minimal pairs

Plus⁺

UNIT 1. —ed endings

A. Listen to the example. Listen again and repeat the utterance.

walked /t/ dreamed /d/ started /ed/

B. Do you hear /t/, /d/, or /ed/? Listen and check [✓].

	/t/	/d/	/ed/
1. listened			
2. stopped			
3. watched			
4. needed			
5. played			
6. checked			
7. exercised			
8. wanted			

Comments:

It is often the case that pronunciation issues interact with grammar issues. As a result, if learners mispronounce key sounds, it can seem like they are producing ungrammatical utterances. One very important grammar point that beginning learners often work on is the past tense and other cases were verbs end in —ed. Depending on the surrounding sounds, the —ed ending can be pronounced in three different ways. Also, particularly for beginning learners in EFL situations, and especially for those who have had mostly reading exposure to English (not much listening exposure), there is sometimes a tendency to pronounce the —ed as if it were a syllable no matter where it occurs. For instance, students may correctly say "hunted" as two syllables, but then also say "roped" as "ro-ped" or "pulled" as "pull-ed" because the spelling suggests that —ed is a syllable to be said. For learners whose native language doesn't use consonant clusters at the end of words, pronouncing the English past tense and other —ed endings can be very difficult. It will take some practice on learners' part and some explanation on yours.

18 Read the passage in <A> and part of a lesson procedure in <B>, and follow the directions. [4 points] 2019 전공A 14번

A

(Below are suggestions from a conference for teaching L2 writing.)

> ### To help students to write effectively...
>
> (a) Start with pre-writing activities with little emphasis on ungrammaticalities and incorrect spelling.
> (b) Have drafting and revising stages in a recursive way.
> (c) Provide meaning-focused feedback.
> (d) Offer students opportunities to think about their own writing.

B

(The following is part of Ms. Song's lesson procedure for teaching how to write an argumentative essay.)

Steps

1. T provides background information about artificial intelligence and Ss watch videos related to the topic.
2. Ss discuss the topic in groups and brainstorm.
3. Ss sketch their ideas and write the first drafts, focusing on content.
4. T reviews Ss' drafts and provides corrective feedback that reformulates ill-formed expressions.
5. Ss revise their drafts once, based on the feedback, and then hand in their final drafts to T.
6. T asks Ss to write reflective journals about their writing.

T=teacher, Ss=students

Identify TWO suggestions from <A> that Ms. Song does NOT implement in <B>. Then, support your answers with evidence from <B>.

Your Answer _____

_____

_____

_____

_____

_____

문항분석

1. Topic : How to teach writing skills

2. Focus

제시된 조건들과 일치하지 않는 수업 상황을 고르는 문제로서 과정 중심의 글쓰기가 진행되는지 확인하고 의미 중심의 피드백이 이루어졌는지 묻는 문제이다.

3. Product-oriented and Process-oriented approaches to the teaching of writing

(1) Product-oriented approach

① emphasizes mechanical aspects of writing, such as focusing on grammatical and syntactical structures and imitating models.

② primarily concerned with "correctness" and form of the final product.

③ fails to recognize that people write for a purpose and that ideas are created and formulated during the process of writing.

(2) Process-oriented approach

① emphasizes that writing itself is a developmental process that creates self-discovery and meaning.

② While the mechanical aspects of writing are important, they should not interfere with the composing process. This composing process requires much revision and rewriting.

③ The teacher intervenes and guides students during the composing process.

④ Instead of worrying about form, students concentrate on conveying a written message. Hence the product of writing will improve with the discovery involved in composing.

▶ Sequence of activities in process writing from White and Arndt, 1991

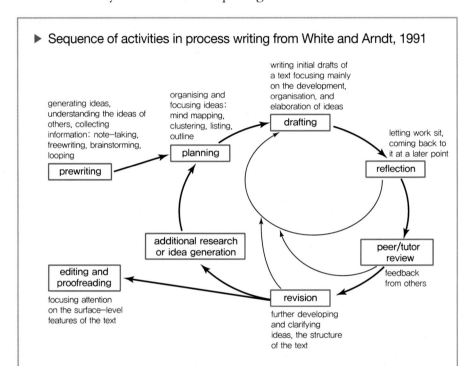

generating ideas, understanding the ideas of others, collecting information: note-taking, freewriting, brainstorming, looping

prewriting

organising and focusing ideas: mind mapping, clustering, listing, outline

planning

writing initial drafts of a text focusing mainly on the development, organisation, and elaboration of ideas

drafting

letting work sit, coming back to it at a later point

reflection

peer/tutor review

feedback from others

additional research or idea generation

editing and proofreading

focusing attention on the surface-level features of the text

revision

further developing and clarifying ideas, the structure of the text

In reality, the writing process is complex like this. The various stages of drafting, reviewing, re-drafting and writing, etc. are done in a recursive way: we loop backwards and move forwards between there various stages. Thus at the editing stage we may feel the need to go back to a pre-writing phrase and think again; we may edit bits of our writing as we draft it. Ron White and Valerie Arndt stress that '... writing is re-writing ... re-vision—see with new eyes—has a central role to play in the act of creating text'.

4. Form-focused or Meaning-focused instructions

(1) Form-focused instruction

Form-focused instruction can be distinguished focus on forms and focus on form. Two types of focus on form instruction can be further distinguished: planned focus on form and incidental focus on form. The former involves the use of focused tasks, that is, communicative tasks that have been designed to elicit the use of specific linguistic form in the context of meaning centered language use. Incidental focus on form involves the use of unfocused tasks, that is, communicative tasks designed to elicit general samples of the language rather than specific forms.

(2) Meaning-focused instruction

Meaning-focused instruction is based on the idea that learners learn the second language if they follow the natural principles of first language learning (Long & Robinson, 1998). For instance in natural approach and direct method learners acquire the second language in a natural way. By the same token, meaning-focused instruction stems from teaching the second language naturally. Errors are tolerated and are rarely corrected by the teacher but this view of meaning-focused approach to reading has been criticized because language produced by the learner without any correction will bring about fossilized errors (Seedhouse, 1997).

5. Keyword list

feedback, process-oriented writing, product-oriented writing, form-focused instruction, meaning-focused instruction

---

모범답안

Ms. Song does not implement suggestions (b) and (c). As for (b), the drafting and revising stages should be repeated but Ms. Song provides only one chance to revise the drafts. Regarding (c), instead of meaning-focused feedback, she gives only form-focused feedback to fix ill-formed expressions.

19 Read part of a lesson plan and follow the directions. [4 points] 2016 전공B 3번

Lesson Procedure

Stage 1	• T shows video clips on environmental campaigns. • T encourages Ss to brainstorm. • T asks Ss to discuss their previous experiences in pairs.

> **<Purposes>**
> ✓ To arouse Ss' interests and motivation
> ✓ To activate Ss' _____

Stage 2

• T shows new words and structures, and then explains how to use them within a sentence.

New Words	Grammatical Structures
transportation, recycle, mayor,	to leave ~, leaving ~, to protect ~, protecting ~,

• Please circle the right form in the sentences.

1. We require you (to leave/leaving) your cars.
2. . . . .

• T has Ss read an article related to environmental problems with the following questions in mind:

• What are the problems?
• What are the causes of the problems?
• How can you solve the problems?

• T asks Ss to write down key words related to the topic.

<Trash Problems in Our City>

Problems	dirty roads, _____, _____
Causes	no trash cans, _____, _____
Solutions	recycling bins, _____, _____

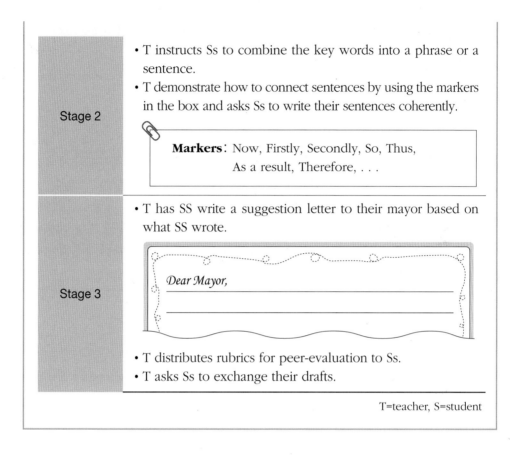

Stage 2	• T instructs Ss to combine the key words into a phrase or a sentence. • T demonstrate how to connect sentences by using the markers in the box and asks Ss to write their sentences coherently. **Markers**: Now, Firstly, Secondly, So, Thus, As a result, Therefore, . . .
Stage 3	• T has SS write a suggestion letter to their mayor based on what SS wrote. *Dear Mayor,* • T distributes rubrics for peer-evaluation to Ss. • T asks Ss to exchange their drafts.

T=teacher, S=student

Fill in the blank in the <Purposes> box in Stage 1 with ONE word. Then identify ONE way the teacher directly prepares students to write a well-organized suggestion letter in Stage 2, and explain it with evidence. Do NOT copy more than FIVE consecutive words from the passage.

Your Answer

1. Topic : How to teach writing skills

2. Focus

EFL 안에서 어떻게 쓰기 지도를 효율적으로 진행해 나갈 것인지에 대한 문제를 반영하고 있다. 일반적으로 쓰기를 '하나의 사고 과정'으로 인식하여 주제에 대한 자신의 생각을 이끌어 내는 활동으로 준비 작업을 하고, 학생들에게 주제에 대한 배경지식을 심어주기 위한 읽기 활동이 쓰기 전 단계로 제시되고 있다. 이와 같은 writing skills를 키우고자 진행하는 교실의 쓰기 수업도 통합수업모형을 토대로 이루어지는 것을 확인할 수 있다. 일반적 글쓰기는 읽기를 통해 genre writing이 특별한 rhetorical structures 등에 대한 awareness와 text의 구성인 cohesion과 coherence에 대한 훈련을 진행한다.

3. Writing stages

(1) Pre-writing stage

① Activate schematic knowledge

Ex video clip watching, brainstorming/discussing Ss' previous experience pre-teaching vocabulary

② Pre-teaching new words and discourse markers

Ex showing some words and structures related to environmental problems

③ Read the materials relating to the topic

Ex questions and answers activities/key words picking-up/cohesion & coherence practice (combining sentences/connecting sentences using discourse markers)

(2) Drafting stages and Revision

① Writing a suggestion letter

② Peer-editing : give and take some feedback on their own writing using evaluation checklist.

4. Keyword list

schematic knowledge, brainstorming, coherently, sentence combining

Schemata. The teacher prepares students to write a well-organized letter by demonstrating how to combine sentences with transitional markers. After his demonstration students are expected to write sentences in a coherent way and construct a well-paragraphed letter.

Plus⁺

How to Respond to Students Writing

Work out your own strategy for handling errors and explain it to your students. If you use any editing symbols, make sure that the students are familiar with all of them and know what to do when they see one.

Decide if you will correct or simply *indicate* where they occur, if you will deal only with the errors you have discussed in class, with errors of a certain type, or with all errors; decide what importance you attach to grammatical errors and, again, let your students know. Provide opportunities for the students to use the symbols, too.

Codes can *indicate* where an error is and what type of error it is. However, they leave the learners to do some work in order to *find the corrections for themselves*.

It often seems inappropriate to point out every error; it can be dispiriting to get back work with a large quantity of marks on it. The teacher probably needs to decide which errors she thinks most important or useful for the student to work on at the moment and then to draw attention to these.

In a conclusion, remember that when you or any other reader responds to a student's piece of writing, your main job is not to pass judgement on its quality, but to help the writer see what to do next. Ask yourself: what should the writer do now to improve this paper?

20 Read the lesson procedure and complete the objectives by filling in each blank with TWO words. Write your answers in the correct order. [2 points]

2014 전공A 기입형 9번

Students : 2nd year middle school students

Approximate time : 45 minutes

Lesson objectives :

Students will be able :

• to describe a daily routine using correct verb forms and (1) _____ from a sample paragraph

• to revise writing through (2) _____ on first drafts

Lesson Procedure

1. The teacher asks students what they do when they get home every day.

2. Students take turns asking and answering questions about their daily routine in pairs. Students take notes on each other's answers.

3. The teacher provides a sample paragraph, and students choose the correct expressions.

> (As soon as/Since) Taebin finishes school, he goes to taekwondo. When he arrives, he puts on his workout clothes, and (first/then) he practices. (After/Before) he finishes, he rides his bike home. (As soon as/After that), he takes a shower. (After/Next), he eats his dinner. (Before/When) he finishes dinner, he does his homework. (Before/While) he goes to bed, he brushes his teeth.

4. Students use their notes to write a short paragraph about their partner's daily routine.

5. Students exchange writings and underline their partner's mistakes using the checklist.
   - Are the present forms of verbs used correctly?
   - Are the events described in time order?
   - Is time order indicated using the expressions focused upon in the sample paragraph?
   - Is punctuation used correctly?

6. Students rewrite their paragraph based on Step 5.

Your Answer	(1) _____
	(2) _____

1. Topic : Process-oriented writing approach

2. Focus

주어진 writing lesson에서 취하고 있는 접근법을 파악하고, 그에 따른 수업 전개 과정에 대해 이해할 수 있는가?

3. Process-oriented writing approach

⑴ **Pre-writing activity**

Step 1~Step 3 : Daily routine에 대한 topic을 이해시키고, 각자 daily routine에 대한 question-answer activity를 진행하여 정보를 모으고, 단락으로 쓰기 위한 활동 간의 연결고리 time order에 대한 연습 활동을 진행하도록 하고 있다.

⑵ **Drafting activity**

Step 4 : 자신의 partner에 대한 daily routine에 대한 짧은 단락 쓰기

⑶ **Revision activity**

• **Step 5** : Checklist를 통하여 서로 쓴 글에 대해 피드백을 주고받기
• **Step 6** : Rewrite

주어진 수업에서는 학생들이 time order를 표현하기 위한 부사나 동사 표현들을 학습할 수 있도록 쓰기 활동을 활용하고 있다. 일단 학생들로 하여금 자신의 짝의 일상생활에 관련한 문단(first draft)을 작성하도록 요구한다. 그리고 나서 writing을 짝과 교환하여 서로 피드백을 주고, writing을 수정한다. 이와 같이 학생들이 작성한 writing에 대하여 피드백을 주고받으며 계속적인 수정을 하는 과정(process)에 초점을 둔 쓰기 수업을 process-oriented writing approach라고 한다.

4. Keyword list

process-oriented writing approach, product-oriented writing approach

---

Answer ⑴ time order ⑵ peer editing

Plus⁺

Process-oriented Writing Approach

글쓰기 활동을 하나의 사고 과정이라 생각하고 작가의 생각을 글로 옮기는 과정을 중시하는 접근법이다. 따라서 무엇을 쓰느냐가 아니라 어떻게 쓰느냐에 초점을 맞추고 글을 수정하는 과정 자체를 중시한다.

1. Process-oriented approaches focus on the steps involved in drafting and redrafting a piece of work.
2. There will never be the perfect text, but one can get closer to perfection through producing, reflecting on, discussing and reworking successive drafts of a text.
3. Teachers focus less on a perfect final product than on the development of successive drafts of a text.
4. The focus is on quantity rather than quality. Thus, writers are encouraged to get their ideas onto paper without worrying too much about formal correctness in the initial stages.
5. Students share their work with others, getting feedback on their ideas and how they are expressed.
6. Higher order choices (for example, discourse context) determine lower order ones such as how to package information within a sentence, and what grammatical forms to use.

21 Read the passage in <A> and the teacher's journal in <B>, and follow the directions. [2 points] 2020 전공A 1번

| A |

Vocabulary is a core component of language knowledge and provides much of the basis for how well learners listen, speak, read, and write. Without extensive knowledge of vocabulary or diverse strategies for acquiring new words, learners are often unable to produce as much language as they would like.

Knowing a word does not simply mean knowing its surface meaning. Rather, it involves knowing diverse aspects of lexical knowledge in depth including phonological and morphological forms and syntactic and semantic structures. Therefore, activities that integrate lexical knowledge of form, meaning, and use should be included in class.

| B |

Teacher's Journal

Ms. Kang and I read an article on teaching vocabulary and discussed how we can improve the way we teach vocabulary. We realized that we have been heavily focused on expanding the size of our students' vocabulary. As a result, they seem to know a lot of words but do not understand or use them properly in context. So, we came up with the following activities that we believe help our students develop _____ of vocabulary knowledge across form, meaning, and use.

Vocabulary activities to be implemented:

• Trying to pronounce the target words by listening to a recorded text
• Analyzing parts of the target words (e.g., prefixes and suffixes)
• Guessing the meanings of the target words using contextual cues
• Studying concordance examples to see various contexts and collocation patterns
• Writing a short story using the target words

Fill in the blank in <B> with the ONE most appropriate word from <A>.

Your Answer _____

문항분석

1. Topic : How to teach vocabulary

2. Focus

의사소통 능력에 있어서 어휘 학습의 중요성을 언급하며, 과거와 달리 현재 어휘 학습을 어떻게 효과적으로 해야 할 것인가에 대한 제시를 하고자 한다.

Vocabulary learning is an indispensable process for ESL learners to acquire proficiency and competence in target language. Word power facilitates fluent speaking and knowledge. It enriches learner's integrated language skills such as listening, speaking, reading and writing.

3. Breadth and depth of vocabulary knowledge

(1) Breadth of vocabulary knowledge

It refers to the number of words the meaning of which a learner has at least some superficial knowledge.

(2) Depth of vocabulary knowledge

It focuses on the idea that for useful high-frequency words learners need to have more than just a superficial understanding of the meaning : it covers such components as pronunciation, spelling, meaning, register, frequency, and morphological, syntactic, and collocational properties.

4. Keyword list

depth of vocabulary knowledge, breadth of vocabulary knowledge, intentional learning, incidental learning

Answer   depth

22 Read the passages and the teaching journals, and follow the directions.
[4 points] 2017 전공B 1번

A

Form-focused instruction (FFI) can be split into two types: focus on formS and focus on form. According to R. Ellis (2001), FFI "includes both traditional approaches to teaching forms based on structural syllabi and more communicative approaches, where attention to form arises out of activities that are primarily meaning-focused" (p.2).

B

Mr. Song

My students often tell me that they feel overwhelmed by the number of grammatical structures they have to learn. While thinking about ways to help students develop grammatical competence, I decided to teach grammar explicitly in class. Today I spent most of the class time on explaining grammatical rules using meta-linguistic terms. Although some of the students initially showed some interest in learning about the rules, many of them got bored, with some dozing off after ten minutes or so.

Miss Oh

Most of my students find grammatical rules difficult and boring. So I decided to implement a new approach. For this approach, I typed up the reading passage in the textbook and deliberately italicized the target structures, hoping that this would help my students notice how the target structures function. After I passed out the reconstructed reading passage, I had my students read it by themselves and then work together in groups, cross-checking their understanding.

Referring to the terms in <A>, identify the type of form-focused instruction exemplified in each of the teachers' teaching journals, and explain with supporting evidence from <B>. Do NOT copy more than FOUR consecutive words from the passage.

| Your Answer | _____ |

_____

_____

_____

_____

문항분석

1. Topic : How to teach grammar

2. Focus

Mr. Song과 Miss Oh의 저널을 통하여 그들이 각각 어떤 방식으로 문법 지도를 진행하는지에 대해서 이해하고, 제공된 form-focused instruction의 두 가지 접근과 관련하여 문법 지도의 특징을 명확하게 설명할 수 있어야 한다.

3. Two approaches of form-focused instruction

(1) Focus on forms approach

과거에 문법 지도가 진행되었던 방식으로, 정확성에만 초점을 두어 문법 지도를 실시한다. 의사소통 상황과 문법 지도를 연계시키지 않고 탈맥락화(decontextualization)된 문법 학습이 일어난다.

(2) Focus on form approach

현재 의사소통 접근법에 가장 부합하는 문법 지도 접근법으로 의미에 제1의 초점(meaning first)을 두고 그 다음으로 정확성에 초점(form second)을 두게 된다. 따라서, focus on form approach는 언어의 의미와 정확성 모두에 초점을 둔다는 점에서 focus on meaning과 focus on forms approach의 문법 지도를 보완할 수 있다.

> ▶ **Meaning-based Approach** : 언어의 의미와 의사소통에 초점을 둔 접근법으로
> 교실 수업 내에서 문법 교육은 중시되지 않는다.

4. Others

(1) **Deductive approach(연역적 접근법)**

The teacher presents the grammar rule and then gives students exercise in which they apply the rule.

(2) **Inductive approach(귀납적 접근법)**

The teacher presents samples of language, and the students have to come to an intuitive understanding of the rule.
- **Advantage** : more meaningful, memorable, and serviceable/actively involved
- **Disadvantage** : to take longer time for the students to arrive at an understanding of a rule/to come to the wrong conclusion about particular grammatical principle

5. Keyword list

form-focused instruction(FFI), focus on form approach, focus on forms approach, meaning-based approach, deductive approach, inductive approach

---

모범답안

Mr. Song's class is based on the focus on forms approach, whereas Miss Oh uses the focus on form approach. To be specific, Mr. Song explicitly provides grammatical explanation through meta-linguistic terms. Miss Oh, on the other hand, helps students to notice the target grammar within the reading text.

Plus +

Another Approach to Obtaining Linguistic Knowledge : Abduction

1. Abduction

Unlike inductive (i.e., data-driven, extracting rules and patterns form examples) and deductive (i.e., rule-driven, from rule-learning to rule application) reasoning, in abductive learning learners come to understand hidden rules of language use through the process of exploring hypothesis and inferences.

2. Abduction in the L2 Classroom

- **Step 1**: Present an authentic text that incorportates some features you want to highlight.
- **Step 2**: Design an activity that focuses on the target points: the target points into an information-gap activity.
- **Step 3**: Ask students work in groups and note the grammatical features or patterns they observe.
- **Step 4**: Students report their findings to the class.

3. Expansion

- **Step 5**: Inductive
- **Step 6**: Deductive

23 Read the passage in <A> and examine the teaching procedures in <B>, and follow the directions. [4 points] 2016 전공B 5번

A

Language learning can be classified into different types in various ways in terms of how learners process linguistic form to acquire rules that govern its use. One way is to distinguish inductive learning from deductive learning. This distinction is made by taking into account how a rule is learned in relation with its specific instances.

B

(Below are parts of two teachers' instruction procedures for teaching past tense verb forms in hypothetical conditionals.)

Teacher A's Class

• T explains to Ss that past tense verb forms should be used in sentences with *if* clauses to describe hypothetical situations.
• T asks Ss to complete sentences with appropriate verb forms to show hypothetical situations.

1. I _____ (can) fly to you, if I _____ (be) a superhero.
2. If he _____ (have) a time machine, he _____ (will) go back in time.

• T asks Ss to read a short text with sentences describing hypothetical situations.

If I had a spaceship, I would fly to Mars. I would also build my own house there and live forever, if there were both oxygen and water. Unfortunately, I don't have lots of money to buy a spaceship. . . .

• T asks Ss to write a paragraph starting with the given expression.

> If I lived on Mars,. . .
> ---
> ---
> ---

Teacher B's Class

• T gives back the written texts about hypothetical situations Ss produced in the previous class and provides their reformulated texts T has produced at the same time. Only incorrect verb forms in Ss' writings are changed in T's reformulation as in the examples below.

> <A student's original writing>
>
> If I have last year to live over again, I will exercise more and eat less junk food because I can be healthier. I will spend more time with my friends and have better grades, if I am more active and watch less TV. . . .

> <The teacher's reformulated text>
>
> *If I had last year to live over again, I would exercise more and eat less junk food because I could be healthier. I would spend more time with my friends and have better grades, if I were more active and watched less TV. . . .*

• T asks Ss to compare T's reformulated sample with their writings and to underline all the words in the sample that are different from those in their writings.

> • T asks Ss to find what the underlined words have in common and in what way they differ from the ones used in their original writings in terms of language form.
> • T asks Ss to work out the rule that applies to all their underlined words based on their findings in the previous step.
>
> T=teacher, S=student

Identify the type of learning applied to each class in <B> based on <A>. Then explain how each class orients students toward its identified type of learning with supporting evidence.

Your Answer

_____

_____

_____

_____

_____

_____

문항분석

1. Topic : How to teach grammar

2. Focus

Communicative competence의 중요 요소 중 하나인 grammatical competence 를 길러 나가도록 하기 위해 교실에서 두 가지 문법 지도 접근이 제시되고 있다. 성공적인 언어 습득을 위해서는 언어의 유창성뿐 아니라 정확성까지 갖추어야 하며, 이를 위해 교실에서 form-focused instruction을 meaning-focused instruction과 함께 병행해야 할 것이다.

3. Two approaches of grammar instruction

(1) Inductive approach

Example을 통해 학습자에게 해당 규칙을 이끌어 내도록 하는 발견 학습의 형태로 진행되는 문법 지도 접근법이다. 따라서 각 규칙에 대한 context를 제공하여 학습을 진행하도록 한다.

(2) Deductive approach

학습자들에게 규칙이나 문법적 지식에 대한 요소를 먼저 제시하고, 관련 규칙과 문법 요소를 실제 예를 토대로 연습시켜 나가도록 하는 문법 지도 접근을 의미한다. 따라서 이와 같은 접근법에서는 학습자가 문법적 규칙을 일방적으로 학습하고 연습하도록 하는 교실 환경이 만들어지며, 맥락이 주어지지 않은 상태에서 문법 규칙에 접근이 이루어질 수 있다.

(3) Techniques

- **Deductive learning**: Drilling
- **Inductive learning**: CR tasks

4. Keyword list

inductive learning, deductive learning, noticing the gap

모범답안

The type of learning that occurs in Teacher A's class is deductive learning since the teacher explains the rule of *if-clause* and then gives students exercises in which they apply the rule. On the other hand, Teacher B's class orients students toward inductive learning because he presents the examples of *if-clause*, and then students have to infer the rule by themselves.

24 Read Ms. Lee's opinions about the grammar lesson in <A> and the sample lesson plan in <B>, and follow the directions. [4 points] 2018 전공B 5번

A

　I think teachers should keep in mind that the ultimate goal of any grammar lesson is to build up communicative ability. In order to achieve this goal, I believe that classroom activities should not focus on practicing structures and patterns in a meaningless way. Instead, they should be designed to involve students in real communication. By doing so, grammar lessons will be able to encourage the students' interest in learning and elicit more active and meaningful interaction with others in the classroom.

B

Subject	High School English	Students	1st-year students
Title	Lesson 9 My Dream	Date	Nov. 24th

Objectives	• Students will familiarize themselves with the expression "If I were … ." • Students will be able to communicate using the expression "If I were … ."

Teaching-Learning Activities		
Introduction	Greeting & Roll-call	• T and Ss exchange greetings. • T checks if all the Ss are present.
	Review	• T reviews materials from the previous lesson.
	Stating the Objectives	• T introduces the objective of the lesson.
Development	Activity 1	• T hands out a text that contains several instances of "If I were … ." • Ss scan the text and highlight all the sentences including "If I were … ." • Ss check the ones they highlighted with T. • T tells Ss to pay attention to the verb form "were."

	Activity 2	• T tells Ss that she is going to read a passage on "My Dream." • T explains difficult words in the passage. • T reads the passage at a normal pace. • Ss jot down the key words in the passage as T reads. • Ss reconstruct the passage individually. • T hands out the original text to Ss.
	Activity 3	• T has Ss form groups of three. • T asks Ss to think of a job that they would like to have in the future. • Ss use "If I were ... " to share their opinions about their future dream jobs. • Assuming that their dreams come true, two Ss take a reporter's role and interview the other S asking how he or she feels about his or her job. • Ss take turns and continue the activity.
	Activity 4	• T hands out a worksheet. • Ss put together sentence fragments to form complete sentences. • T reads out complete sentences and each S checks their own answers. • T writes three more sentences using "If I were ... " on the board. • T asks Ss to read the sentences.
Consolidation	Review	• T reviews what Ss learned.
	Closure	• T hands out homework and announces the next lesson. • T says goodbye to Ss.

T=teacher, S=student

Based on <A>, choose the ONE most appropriate activity in the development stage that reflects Ms. Lee's opinions. Then, support your choice with evidence from <B>. Do NOT copy more than FOUR consecutive words from the passage.

Your Answer
_____

_____
_____
_____
_____
_____

문항분석

1. Topic : Structured output activity

2. Focus

학생들의 의사소통 능력을 극대화하기 위한 교실 내 문법지도 활동으로 의사소통 상황하에서 의미에 초점을 두며 정확한 목표언어 형태를 사용하도록 유도한다.

3. Form-focused instruction(FFI)

Long(1991) elaborated on the differences between Focus on Form and Focus on Forms. Focus on Form(FonF), 'overtly draws students' attention to linguistic elements as they arise incidentally in lessons whose overriding focus is on meaning or communication'. In contrast, Focus on Forms(FonFs) involves traditional language teaching consisting of the presentation and practice of items drawn from a structural syllabus. Later Long(1997) also sought to distinguish 'FonF' from 'focus on meaning(FonM)' —an approach to teaching that emphasized incidental and implicit language learning through content-based instruction or immersion programmes where the learners' focus was more or less entirely on meaning. Long's views about FonF can be characterized as entailing a focus on form that:

① arises in interaction involving the L2 learner.

② is reactive (i.e. occurs in response to a communication problem).

③ is incidental (i.e. it is not pre-planned).

④ is brief (i.e. it does not interfere with the primary focus on meaning).

⑤ is typically implicit (e.g. it does not involve any metalinguistic explanation).

⑥ induces 'noticing.' (i.e. conscious attention to target linguistic forms)

⑦ induces form-function mapping.

⑧ constitutes an 'approach' to teaching (i.e. FonF) that contrasts with a traditional form centered approach (i.e. FonFs).

4. Keyword list

form-focused instruction, focus on form, focus on forms

모범답안

Activity 3 best follows Ms. Lee's opinion about how the grammar lesson should be given. In this activity, students are asked to use the target phrase "If I were..." by exchanging their future jobs in groups. Also, through interviewing in pairs they continue to engage in more active and meaningful interaction.

25 Read the passage in <A> and examine the teaching procedure in <B>. Then follow the directions. [3 points] 2014 전공A 서술형 6번

A

Processing instruction, a type of focus-on-form instruction, is based on the assumption that when processing input, L2 learners have difficulty in attending to form and meaning at the same time due to working memory limitations. Not surprisingly, they tend to give priority to meaning and tend not to notice details of form. Processing instruction uses several principles to explain what learners attend to in the input and why. Below are some of these principles.

The Lexical Preference Principle: In (1), both *-es* and *boy* convey the same information, 'the third person singular'. Yet, learners prefer to focus on the lexical item, *boy*, to arrive at meaning, and often ignore the grammatical item, *-es*, while processing the sentence.

(1) The *boy* stud*ies* in the library, not at home.

The First Noun Principle: Learners tend to process the first noun or pronoun they encounter in a sentence as the agent of action. For example, they may misinterpret (2) as "Jack collected the data for the project."

(2) *Jack* let *Joe* collect the data for the project.

The Event Possibilities Principle: Event possibilities refer to the likelihood of one noun being the agent of action as opposed to another. Since it is more likely in the real world that a dog would bite a man than the other way around, learners would likely misinterpret (3) as "The dog bit the farmer."

(3) The dog was bitten by the farmer.

In processing instruction, teachers provide students with structured input activities, taking into consideration the principles above. In a structured input activity, students are forced to attend to form in order to comprehend a sentence.

B

Teaching Procedure

1. Explicit Explanation

Explain how a past tense sentence is constructed in English. Then inform students of why they tend not to notice the past tense marker -*ed* and thus misinterpret past tense sentences.

2. Structured Input Activity

Have students read six sentences and decide whether they describe an activity that was done in the past or usually happens in the present. Then, check the answers together.

Sentences	Present	Past
(1) They watched television at night.	☐	☐
(2) They watch television at night.	☐	☐
(3) I walk to school on Mondays.	☐	☐
(4) I walked to school on Mondays.	☐	☐
(5) We played soccer on weekends.	☐	☐
(6) We play soccer on weekends.	☐	☐

Identify the principle in <A> that the teaching procedure in <B> focuses on. Then explain how the structured input activity in <B> helps students correctly process the target form for meaning.

| Your Answer | _____ |

_____

_____

_____

_____

_____

1. Topic : How to teach grammar

2. Focus

주어진 교실 수업에서 form-meaning relationship을 이끌어 내고자 하는 processing instruction을 통한 문법을 가르치는 과정을 이해할 수 있어야 한다.

3. Characteristics of the lesson procedure

(1) Explicit explanation

과거시제 구성 방법에 대한 설명을 명시적으로 진행하고, 반드시 '-ed'에 대한 form에 주목할 필요성에 대한 언급을 한다.

(2) Structured input activity

학생들은 structured input activity를 토대로 현재와 과거시제를 구분하기 위해 target form('-ed' marker)에 대한 연습에 참여하게 된다. 활동 안에서 학생들은 시제(form)만 달리 하고, 같은 의미를 가지고 있는 두 문장을 쌍으로 비교하도록 되어 있다. 따라서 동일한 의미의 sentence pair 안에서 형태 차이로 인해, 즉 각 문장이 past tense marker '-ed'를 가지고 있는지 아닌지에 따라서 (즉, 형태에 주목하여) 시제를 구분할 수 있도록 한다. 이와 같이 form-meaning relationship을 기반으로 하여 진행되는 학습 과정을 input processing (언어적 정보의 표면적인 형태, 문법 구조보다 정보의 내용과 그 의미를 먼저 인식하고 인지적으로 처리하는 것) activity의 한 유형이다.

4. Keyword list

input processing, processing instruction, form-meaning relationship, structured input activity

모범답안

The structured input activity in <B> is based on the Lexical Preference Principle. In this activity, students are exposed to the pairs of sentences in the activity, in which each pair has the same lexical meaning but different tenses. Thus, it requires them to focus on the lexical meaning first and the form (the past tense marker '-ed') second. In other words, through a form-meaning relationship in this activity, they distinguish the present from the past tense by noticing the past tense maker '-ed,' resulting in naturally processing it.

Plus⁺

Input Processing

Because it may be difficult for learners to attend to meaning and form in the input at the same time, a more explicit technique, input processing, was proposed by VanPatten (1996). It is important that the text used for input remain reasonably natural, and that the learners make the necessary connections between form and function in authentic contexts of L2 use. Consider the following exercise in Figure 1.

Figure 1

Instructions: Listen to the following sentences and decide whether they describe an action that was done before or is usually done.

1. The teacher corrected the essays.	Now ( )	Before ( )
2. The man cleaned the table.	Now ( )	Before ( )
3. I wake up at 5 in the morning.	Now ( )	Before ( )
4. The train leaves the station at 8 am.	Now ( )	Before ( )
5. The writer finished writing the book.	Now ( )	Before ( )
6. The trees go green in the spring.	Now ( )	Before ( )

---

26 Read the lesson procedure and write the TWO lesson objectives. Do NOT copy more than FIVE consecutive words from the passage. [5 points]

2015 전공A 서술형 1번

The following is a sample lesson plan of culture-integrated language learning for 2nd year middle school students.

Lesson Procedure

(1) Students watch a video clip that shows an experiment, which is summarized below.

The experiment shows that American mothers used twice as many object labels as Japanese mothers ("piggie," "doggie") and Japanese mothers engaged in twice as many social routines of teaching politeness norms (empathy and greetings). An American mother's pattern might go like this: "That's a car. See the car? You like it? It's got nice wheels." A Japanese mother might say: "Here! It's a vroom vroom. I give it to you. Now give this to me. Yes! Thank you." American children are learning that the world is mostly a place with objects, Japanese children that the world is mostly about relationships. Relationships usually involve a verb. Verbs are more important in Asian languages than in English. Asians tend to use an expression like "Drink more?" rather than "More tea?" when they perceive there is a need. Americans are noun-oriented, pointing objects out to their children, naming them, and telling them about their attributes. Nouns denote categories.

(2) Students share their own experiences about noun-oriented expressions as opposed to verb-oriented ones, and discuss different ways of thinking for those expressions.

(3) Students do Activity 1 in order to learn a variety of noun-oriented English expressions.

<Activity 1> Fill in the blanks with appropriate words.

Verb-Oriented Expressions	Noun-Oriented Expressions
He works hard.	He is a hard worker.
My head aches.	I _____.
He is very humorous.	He has a good _____.
…	…

(4) Students discuss why noun-oriented expressions are more frequently used in English than verb-oriented ones.

(5) Students engage in the following activity to reinforce their awareness of the cultural difference between the West and the East.

> Q: If you have a bad cold, which of the following wouldn't you say?
> A: ① I've got a stuffy nose.
>   ② I have a runny nose.
>   ③ My nose is sick.

Your Answer

_____

_____

_____

_____

_____

_____

문항분석

1. Topic : How to plan a lesson

2. Focus

주어진 수업의 주요 목표 두 가지를 파악하고, 명확한 action verbs를 사용하여 기술할 수 있어야 한다.

3. How to write today's aims/objectives

Objectives should be specific and measurable, which is why we use action verbs in writing educational objectives.

- Depending on what you want students to be able to DO at the end of a lesson, it will help us choose the right action verb for writing an instructional objective. Instructional objectives often will depend on the overall curriculum plan and the level of the learners, but it also involves the teacher's influence in designing a lesson.
- Verbs such as remember, learn, or know are not action verbs. These are more general verbs and are better for writing goals, not specific learning objectives. Because they are not action verbs they are difficult to measure. It's hard to describe how much you want a student to remember, learn, or know, so we use more specific action verbs instead.

4. Keyword list

action verbs

모범답안

The aim of the lesson is to enable students to explain the cultural and linguistic differences of the West and the East. Also it requires students to practice the variety of noun-oriented and verb-oriented expressions.

Plus⁺

Lesson Plan

1. Objectives

They are most clearly captured in terms of stating what students will do—that is, what they will perform. What does it mean? First, let's look at what not to do in designing objectives. Try to avoid vague, unverifiable statements like "Students will learn about the passive voice", or "Students will practice some listening exercises", or "Students will discuss the homework assignment". In stating objectives, you should be able to identify an overall purpose that you will attempt to accomplish by the end of the class period.

Terminal objective

Students will successfully request information about airplane arrivals and departures.

Enabling objective

- Students will demonstrate comprehension of the lesson's ten listed new vocabulary items through accomplishment of the main task.
- Students will show comprehension of an airplane schedule by responding to a preliminary list of ten questions.
- Students will produce questions with when, where, and what time in the main task.
- Students will produce appropriate polite forms of requesting in the main task.

In the lesson plan, terminal and enabling objectives are clearly specified with explicit identification of the elements of the lesson that will accomplish given objectives. This way the teacher can, before teaching, be certain about the purpose of the lesson, and after the lesson is completed, make at least an informal assessment of the students' success.

2. Variety, Sequencing, Pacing and Timing

- **Variety** : Is there sufficient variety in techniques to keep the lesson lively and interesting? Most successful lessons give students a number of different activities during the class hour, keeping minds alert and enthusiasm high.
- **Sequencing** : Are your techniques or activities sequenced logically? Ideally, elements of a lesson will build progressively toward accomplishing the ultimate goals.
- **Pacing** : Is the lesson as a whole paced adequately? Activities should neither too long nor too short.
- **Timing** : Is the lesson appropriately timed, considering the number of minutes in the class hour?

Chapter 05

Classroom Assessment

01 Read the passage and follow the directions. [2 points] 2023 전공A 4번

> A test taker is sitting in front of a computer, examining some sample items, and quickly learns how to take computer-based tests. Meanwhile, a computer program begins to 'guess' his ability level, and keeps trying to 'match' the test with his current language ability. This is how this technique works.
>
> The computer program usually begins by showing an item of moderate difficulty, for example, an item that the test taker has a fifty percent chance of getting right. If he gets this item right, the computer program reestimates his ability level in real time and shows either an item of equal difficulty or a slightly more challenging item. If the test taker gets his first item wrong, however, the computer program will show either an item of equal or slightly lesser difficulty. The test taker keeps taking the test until, for instance, he gets several items wrong in a row. To put it another way, the computer program repeats its matching work until it collects enough information to determine the test taker's current English ability level.

Fill in the blank with the THREE most appropriate words.

> The testing procedure described above enables us to make more individualized and educationally useful tests. It can also provide test takers with a better test-taking experience with fewer items, and with increased precision. This testing procedure is commonly referred to as _____.

Your Answer _____

1. Topic : Computer adaptive testing

2. Focus

현재 진행되는 교실 수업에서 교사들의 가장 어려운 문제는 학생들이 갖고 있는 언어 능력에 따른 수준 차이다. 따라서 대부분의 교실 수업에서 학생들 간의 학습 차를 줄이기 위한 방법으로 level-differentiated instruction을 진행하고 있다. 학습과정에서 학생들에게 적절한 과업을 제공하거나, 학생들을 유사한 능력의 동일한 소집단으로 구성하여 수업을 하도록 권고하고 있다. 반면 학습과정에 대한 연구와 시도는 다양하지만, 평가의 측면에서 현행 교사들은 어려움을 겪고 있는데, 그 어려움의 대안으로 제시되고 있는 CAT(computer adaptive testing)를 이해하고 있는가에 대한 문항이다.

3. Computer-adaptive testing(CAT)

Computer-adaptive testing(CAT) uses a database of questions to match the difficulty of each test item to the abilities of the learners being tested. Learners take a CAT test at the computer and because the computer can instantly mark each answer, the following question can be tailored or adapted. If a learner correctly answers a question, the computer will ensure that the next question will be more difficult. If a learner incorrectly answers a question, the next question will be easier.

One of the great advantages of CAT testing is that randomization of test items can ensure that learners of a large class taking a test in the same room may all take slightly different tests as their correct and incorrect answers prompt the computer to take them to different levels. However, the effort in setting up CAT testing is also difficult and learners may not like the fact that they cannot review or change the answers to any questions they have already answered.

4. Keyword list

computer adaptive testing, level-differentiated instruction, mixed level grouping, same ability grouping, level-appropriate task

---

Answer computer adaptive testing / computerized adaptive testing

02 Read the passages in <A> and<B>, and follow the directions. [2 points]

2023 전공B 11번

A

A high school English teacher, Mr. Choi, wanted to learn how to write selected-response items (e.g., multiple-choice items) more efficiently. He wrote several items before the workshop began, and found some of them were flawed according to the guidelines he learned during the workshop. The following are some of the guidelines along with examples of flawed items.

> **General Guidelines for Writing Selected-response Items**
>
> ① Make certain that there is only one, clearly correct answer.
> ② State both the stem and the options as simply and directly as possible.
> ③ Present a single clearly formulated problem to avoid mixed content.
> ④ Avoid negative wording whenever possible. If it is absolutely necessary to use a negative stem, highlight the negative word.

Item 1

My forehead itches every day during the summer. Using sunscreen hasn't helped much. I think I'd better go to the _____ to get my skin checked.

    a. dentist
    b. optometrist
    c. pediatrician
→   d. dermatologist

Item 2

Where did Henry go after the party last night?

    a. Yes, he did.
    b. Because he was tired.
→   c. To Kate's place for another party.
?   d. He went home around eleven o'clock.

Item 3

I never knew where _____.

       a. had the boys gone

→   b. the boys had gone

       c. the boys have gone

       d. have the boys gone

Item 4

According to the passage, which of the following is not true?

       a. My sister likes outdoor sports.

       b. My brother is busy with his plans.

→   c. My sister and I often do everything together.

       d. My brother is more energetic and outgoing than I.

'→' indicates the key; '?' indicates a possible answer.

B

After the workshop, to improve the quality of the items, the teacher revised some items according to the guidelines. The following are the revised items.

Item 1

I think I'd better go to the _____ to get my skin checked.
    a. dentist
    b. optometrist
    c. pediatrician
→   d. dermatologist

Item 2

Where did Henry go after the party last night?
    a. Yes, he did.
    b. Because he was tired.
    c. It was about eleven o'clock.
→   d. To Kate's place for another party.

Item 3

I never knew _____.
    a. where had the boys gone
→   b. where the boys had gone
    c. the boys where had gone
    d. the boys had gone where

Item 4

According to the passage, which of the following is NOT true?
    a. My sister likes outdoor sports.
    b. My brother is busy with his plans.
→   c. My sister and I often do everything together.
    d. My brother is more energetic and outgoing than I.

Based on <A>, identify the ONE most appropriately revised item in <B> according to guideline ②, and the ONE most appropriately revised item according to guideline ③. Then, explain each of the items with evidence from <A> and <B>.

Your Answer

_____

_____

_____

_____

_____

_____

1. Topic : Multiple choice item testing

2. Focus

Multiple choice item testing을 보다 효과적으로 작성하기 위해 Mr. Choi는 객관식 문항을 출제한 후 workshop에 참가하였다. 이때 workshop에서 제시한 guideline을 토대로 기존 출제 문항을 살펴보니 몇 문항에서 오류가 발견되어 수정·보완하고자 했다. 따라서, 본 문항에서는 Mr. Choi의 이전 문항 중 poor item을 파악하고 어떤 지침에 따라 오류로 판단되며, 문항이 어떻게 개선(good item)되었는지에 대한 평가 문항분석 문제이다.

3. Item analysis

Item 1 in \<A\>	My forehead itches every day during the summer. Using sunscreen hasn't helped much. I think I'd better go to the _____ to get my skin checked. 　　　　a. dentist 　　　　b. optometrist 　　　　c. pediatrician →　　d. dermatologist
Item 1 in \<B\>	I think I'd better go to the _____ to get my skin checked. 　　　　a. dentist 　　　　b. optometrist 　　　　c. pediatrician →　　d. dermatologist

➡ Item 1 in \<A\>는 'Guideline ② State both the stem and options as simply and directly as possible'에 대한 부분을 지키지 못하여 poor item이 된 것이므로, Mr. Choi는 기존의 stem이 직접적인 질문이 될 수 있도록 명확하고 단순하게 Item 1 in \<B\>로 수정·보완하였다.

Item 3 in <A>	→	I never knew where _____. a. had the boys gone b. the boys had gone c. the boys have gone d. have the boys gone
Item 3 in <B>	→	I never knew _____. a. where had the boys gone b. where the boys had gone c. the boys where had gone d. the boys had gone where

➡ Item 3 in <A>는 'Guideline ③ Present a single clearly formulated problem to avoid mixed content'에 대한 지침을 따르지 않고, 복합적인 요소와 간접의문문의 어순 및 시제에 대한 두 가지 요소를 평가하고 있어 poor item으로 평가된다. Mr. Choi는 주어진 stem과 options에 대한 재정비로, options의 동사들을 동일하게 제시하여 간접의문문의 어순에 대한 평가만 이루어질 수 있도록 Item 3 in <B>로 수정·보완하였다.

4. Keyword list

stem, options, selected-response items(multiple choice items), distractor

---

모범답안

Item 1 in <B> is appropriately revised based on guideline ② in that the original complicated stem is changed into a simple and direct one sentence. Also, following guideline ③, Item 3 in <B> presents a clear single problem about an 'indirect question' by changing tenses in the original options into the same past perfect 'had gone'.

03 Read a teacher's and a student's journal entries and follow the directions.
[2 points] 2022 전공A 1번

Ms. Ahn's Journal

I think I need to change my approach to teaching speaking skills. In my conversation class, I usually have my students listen to dialogues and then practice the main expressions using pattern drills, which I thought would help them speak with both accuracy and fluency. However, when I assessed their speaking performance last week, most students had difficulties speaking fluently. They frequently had long pauses in their speech, but were quite accurate. In order to address this issue, I'm going to add more fluency activities such as discussion, role-plays, and information-gap activities.

Nayun's Journal

Today, I got my final exam results. Compared to the mid-term exam, my score has improved a lot. I'm very proud of myself because I studied a lot for the test. My English teacher usually includes lots of reading comprehension questions on exams, so this time I read all the reading texts in the textbook multiple times and took many practice tests. However, I'm a bit disappointed with the test in a way. I really want to improve my English writing skills, but I just don't have time to practice them. Well... I don't know.... I want to change how I'm studying, but I can't give up on getting good English test scores.

Fill in the blank with the ONE most appropriate word.

> The above two journal entries demonstrate _____ effect in that the teacher and the student each write about what they do for their teaching and studying with regard to tests.

Your Answer _____

문항분석

1. Topic : Assessment principles (Washback effect)

2. Focus

현 교실 수업은 학생들의 실질적인 의사소통 능력을 고양하는 데 초점을 두고 있으므로, 각 학습에 따른 교실 평가도 학생들의 직접적인 언어 수행에 대한 평가를 강조하고 있다. 또한, 각 언어 학습의 연계성이 중시됨에 따라 각 학습 후의 평가와 차후 학습과의 긴밀한 관계가 형성되므로 평가를 구성할 경우, 해당 평가가 이후 학습에 미치는 영향을 반드시 고려해야 한다.

3. The importance of washback

Washback provides the information that washes back to students in the form of useful diagnoses of strengths and weaknesses.

Case 1

In my courses I never give a final examination as the last scheduled classroom session. I always administer a final exam during the penultimate session, then complete the evaluation of the exams in order to return them to students during the last class. At this time, the students receive scores, grades, and comments on their work, and I spend some of the class session addressing material on which the students were not completely clear. My summative assessment is thereby enhanced by some beneficial washback that is usually not expected of final examinations.

4. Keyword list

washback, validity, reliability, authenticity, construct validity, content validity, criterion-related validity, predictive validity

Answer washback

04 **Read the conversation and follow the directions.** [2 points] 2021 전공B 1번

> *(T1 is the head teacher, and T2 is teaching English writing this semester at the school.)*
>
> T1 : Good morning, Mr. Lee. How are your writing classes going?
>
> T2 : Good morning, Ms. Park. They're going well, but I find scoring students' writing quite challenging.
>
> T1 : What makes you say that?
>
> T2 : I rated my students' writing assignments last night. But when I look at them today, I feel I would give different scores.
>
> T1 : Why do you think that happened?
>
> T2 : Well, I'm pretty sure it was because I was doing it late at night. I think I was too tired.
>
> T1 : Mmm.... I don't grade my students' writing assignments when I'm tired. That way, I can avoid being inconsistent. I just put them away until the next day.
>
> T2 : I bet that would be very helpful with keeping scoring reliable.
>
> T1 : Yeah, it helps.
>
> T2 : Another issue is that over time, I tend to stray from the rating criteria. I need to find a way to stick to it for consistency in scoring.
>
> T1 : Well, why don't you go back every once in a while and check the last few essays you've marked to see that you're still following the rating criteria?
>
> T2 : That's a good idea. It'll help keep me on track.
>
> T1 : Exactly.
>
> T2 : Thanks for your advice.
>
> T=teacher

Fill in the blank with the ONE most appropriate word.

> Teacher 1, the head teacher, is giving advice on the issue of _____ reliability that Teacher 2 is facing when scoring students' writing.

Your Answer _____

문항분석

1. Topic : Assessment principles (Reliability)

2. Focus

의사소통 평가의 중요성에 따라 교실 수업과 평가 간 관계에서 내용타당도의 중요성이 대두되고 있지만, 각각 진행되는 평가의 신뢰성이 보장되지 않을 경우 평가로서의 역할을 충실히 이행하기가 어렵다. 따라서, 신뢰도가 보장되는 타당성 있는 평가가 현 교실 수업의 가장 중요한 화두가 된다. 현 교실 수업은 large class로 이루어져 있으므로 평가에 대한 교사의 신뢰도를 유지하기 위해 학생들의 학습 과정 및 결과에 대한 평가가 더욱더 객관적으로 진행될 수 있는 여러 장치들이 필요하다.

3. The type of scorer reliability

(1) The case of Inter-rater reliability

Ratings of Contestants' Compositions

Students	Criteria	Teacher A	Teacher B
Giho Lim	Content	2	5
	Organization	1	4
	Vocabulary	3	4
	Grammar	2	5
Bomi Cho	Content	3	1
	Organization	5	1
	Vocabulary	4	2

1=lowest ↔ 5=highes

(2) Intra-rater reliability

When I am faced with up to 40 tests to grade in only a week, I know that the standards I apply—however subliminally—to the first few tests will be different from those I apply to the last few. I may be 'easier' or 'harder' on those first few papers or I may get tired, and the result may be an inconsistent evaluation across all tests.

4. Keyword list

reliability, inter-rater reliability, intra-rater reliability, validity, internal consistency reliability

Answer   intra-rater

05 Read the passage in <A> and the tests in <B>, and follow the directions.
[4 points] 2022 전공B 10번

┌─────────────────── **A** ───────────────────┐

Mr. Lee and Ms. Min are both middle school English teachers for 1st graders, but their students' English writing proficiency is quite different from each other. The two teachers have developed tests to assess their students' abilities to write using comparatives and superlatives as the target forms.

┌──┐
Mr. Lee's Assessment Note

• I taught my students to write simple sentences using comparatives and superlatives and provided sentence drill activities to practice them in previous lessons. After that, I designed a writing test to assess my students' abilities to make a simple sentence using one of the target forms.
└──┘

┌──┐
Ms. Min's Assessment Note

• My students learned how to use comparatives and superlatives in sentences. After they were able to write sentences using the target forms accurately, I offered a story-writing activity in class. Then, I made a test to assess how well the students put sentences together to write a story using the target forms.
└──┘

└──┘

B

Test 1

Directions : Based on the pictures, fill in each blank with an appropriate comparative or superlative.

1. tall → _____

2. long → _____

3. big → _____

Test 2

Directions : Describe the two people circled in the picture by using one of the words listed below.

1. taller
2. younger
3. older

Test 3

Directions：Choose the correct answer.

> My friends and I loved watching soccer on television, but we couldn't play it. We didn't have a team. Eventually, we made a soccer team and we were happy. Last Wednesday, we had a game, but it rained a lot. Our shoes got wet and heavy. The other team's players ran faster than us. So we took off our shoes.

Q. How was the weather last Wednesday?
   a. sunny   b. rainy   c. cloudy   d. snowy

Test 4

Directions：Describe the sequenced pictures using comparatives and/or superlatives. You should write more than THREE sentences with appropriate connectors.

Based on <A>, identify ONE test in <B> that each teacher developed, respectively. Then, explain your answers with evidence from <B>.

Your Answer

1. Topic : Classroom testing

2. Focus

학생들의 정확한 목표언어 지식 및 사용을 측정하기 위해 교사는 측정 목적에 부합하는 평가 과제에 대한 선택 및 준비를 해야 한다. 평가의 목적과 평가 과제에 대한 차이가 있을 경우, 교사는 측정하고자 하는 언어 요소나 능력을 정확하게 평가할 수 없으므로 해당 교실 평가를 타당도 있는 평가로 보기 어렵다.

3. Choosing the best assessment task(s) for our unit

We can evaluate their suitability against the following criteria. These same criteria should be used to guide design or modification decisions.

1	The task is authentic and set in a realistic context.
2	They are worthwhile learning activities in their own right.
3	The assessments permit a holistic rather than a fragmented approach.
4	The tasks are not repetitive for either student or assessor - they should work as a productive use of time for all those involved.
5	The assessment prompts student self-assessment.
6	The tasks are sufficiently flexible for students to tailor them to their own needs and interests.
7	The assessment is not likely to be interpreted by students in a way fundamentally different to that of the designer.
8	The task does not make assumptions about the subject matter or the learner which are differentially perceived by different groups of students, and which are irrelevant to the task.

4. Keyword list

classroom testing, assessment purpose, assessment task type, authentic, self-assessment

모범답안

Ms. Lee develops Test 2 while Ms. Min Test 4. In Test 2, students should make a simple comparative sentence to describe the circled two people using one of given target words. In Test 4, students need to write more than three sentences with appropriate connectors to make a story using comparatives and/or superlatives.

06 **Read the passage and follow the directions.** [2 points] 2014 전공A 기입형 7번

> At a high school English writing contest, contestants were given the instructions in the box and completed their compositions.
>
> > Listen to a taped radio interview of Barbara Carrel, a famous writer, about her adventure to Africa. While listening, take notes. Then using the notes, write a story about her adventure. You will be given 30 minutes to complete the story.
>
> Each contestant's composition was evaluated by two English teachers using the same rating scale. Below is part of the two teachers' scoring results.
>
> ### Ratings of Contestants' Compositions
>
> | Students | Criteria | Teacher A | Teacher B |
> |---|---|---|---|
> | Giho Lim | Content | 2 | 5 |
> | | Organization | 1 | 4 |
> | | Vocabulary | 3 | 4 |
> | | Grammar | 2 | 5 |
> | Bomi Cho | Content | 3 | 1 |
> | | Organization | 5 | 1 |
> | | Vocabulary | 4 | 2 |
>
> 1=lowest ↔ 5=highest

Complete the comments on the situation above by filling in each blank with ONE word. Write your answers in the correct order.

The procedure used in the contest exemplifies (1) _____ testing in terms of the number of skills assessed. One potential problem with the scoring process is low (2) _____ reliability, which is most likely due to the subjectivity of the raters.

Your Answer (1) _____

(2) _____

1. Topic : Assessment

2. Focus

주어진 평가의 성질에 따른 유형(i.e., performance test, integrative test)을 분류하고, 채점 방법과 2인 이상의 채점 시 유의해야 할 평가 원리 등을 파악하고 있어야 한다.

3. The characteristics of the given test

주어진 test에서는 수험자가 한 사람에 대한 인터뷰를 듣고 나서, 그것을 바탕으로 이야기를 스스로 작성해보도록 요구된다. 두 가지 언어 스킬(i.e., listening, writing)을 사용하여 평가가 이루어진다는 점에서, 이 test는 integrative test로 분류된다. 이 test는 학생들의 performance를 관찰하고 채점을 진행하는 과정에서 채점자의 주관적인 판단이 개입될 우려가 있다. 또한, 2인이 채점에 참여함에 따라 각 항목에 대한 채점 기준이 일치되지 않았을 경우 inter-rater reliability가 낮아질 수 있는 위험이 있다. 한편, 학생들의 performance를 평가하기 위하여 분석적 채점 방법(analytic scoring rubric)을 사용하는데, 즉 언어 능력의 하위 범주(i.e., content, organization, vocabulary, grammar)에 대한 채점이 이루어지고 있다. 이러한 하위 능력에 대한 점수를 기반으로 하여 학생들의 언어 능력에 대한 장단점을 판단할 수 있다.

4. Keyword list

analytic scoring/holistic rubric, inter-rater reliability, integrative test, performance test

Answer (1) integrative (2) inter-rater

Plus +

Types of Scoring

Writing can be assessed in different modes, for example analytic scoring, holistic scoring, and primary trait scoring. If evaluating the same piece of writing, each mode of scoring should result in similar "scores," but each focuses on a different facet of L2 writing.

1. Analytic scoring

In this mode, students' writing is evaluated based on detailed grades for elements of writing such as vocabulary, grammar, composition, or mechanics. Results are based on multiple sub-grades (e.g., 4 out of 5 on vocabulary, plus 3 out of 5 on grammar plus 4 out of 5 on content, etc.)

2. Holistic scoring

Holistic scoring results in a more general description for categories, but includes the different elements of writing implicitly or explicitly. The result is usually a global grade, such as A, B, C, D, E.

3. Primary trait scoring

If the class or the assignment focuses on a particular aspect of writing, or a specific linguistic form, or the use of a certain semantic group, primary trait scoring allows the instructor and the students to focus their feedback, revisions and attention very specifically.

07 **Read the passage and follow the directions.** [4 points] 2020 전공B 6번

A high school teacher wanted to develop a test in order to assess his students' English reading ability. He developed the test based on the following procedures:

- Step 1: Construct Definition
  He started by clarifying what his test was intended to measure. He defined the construct of his English test as the ability to infer meanings from a given reading passage.

- Step 2: Designing Test Specifications
  According to the construct definition in Step 1, he specified the test as consisting of a total of 20 multiple-choice items: 1) 10 items asking test-takers to infer meanings and fill in the blank with the most appropriate words or phrases (i.e., Fill-in-the-Blank), and 2) 10 items for finding the best order of scrambled sentences (i.e., Unscrambling).

- Step 3: Developing Test Items & Piloting
  He finished item development. He piloted the test to examine whether the items had satisfactory test qualities.

- Step 4: Analyzing Item Facility & Item Discrimination
  He analyzed item difficulty. To increase internal consistency, he removed the items with a high value of item discrimination.

- Step 5: Analyzing Reliability & Validity
  Reliability was assessed by Cronbach's coefficient alpha. To investigate the concurrent validity of the test, he asked his colleagues to review the test items based on the test specifications.

- Step 6: Administering the Test
  After making the necessary revisions, he administered the test to his students.

Based on the passage above, identify TWO steps out of the six that have a problem in the process of test development. Then, support your answers with evidence from the passage. Do NOT copy more than FOUR consecutive words from the passage.

Your Answer

_____

_____

_____

_____

_____

1. Topic: Classroom testing

2. Focus

고등학교 학생들의 읽기 능력을 측정하기 위한 평가 도구 개발 과정을 보여주고 있다. 특히, 개발된 평가 도구의 각 항목들에 대한 난이도가 평가 원리(validity, reliability 등)에 근간을 두고 정확하고 적절하게 이루어졌는지에 대한 점검을 해야 한다.

3. Two steps that have a problem in the process of test development

(1) Step 4 : Analysing Item Facility & Item Discrimination

개발된 평가 도구의 각 항목에 대한 난이도와 변별력이 적절한지에 대한 평가 가 이루어져야 한다. 교사는 시행하고자 하는 평가가 적절한 난이도와 정확한 변별도를 갖추었을 때 internal consistency가 높아 평가의 신뢰도를 확보할 수 있다고 판단할 수 있다.

> ▶ **Reliability** : The consistency or stability of assessment results
> • It is considered to be a characteristic of score or results, not the test itself.
> • A test is reliable if it produces consistent scores.
> ▶ **Item Difficulty** : The ration of correct responses to total responses for a given test item. Hence, this index says something about how the items fared for this given group of students—whether the items were easy or difficult.
> ▶ **Item Discrimination** : How well an item performs in separating the better students from the weaker ones. To increase internal consistency the items with zero/negative item discrimination should be removed.

(2) Step 5 : Analyzing Reliability & Validity

시행할 평가에는 최종적으로 신뢰도와 타당도 검사가 주어져야 하며, 신뢰도 는 Cronbach's coefficient alpha에 의해 평가된다. Validity 중 공인타당도 (concurrent validity)를 검사하기 위하여, 교사는 현재의 평가 결과가 기존의 타당성을 입증받고 있는 평가 결과와 동일한지에 대한 검사를 해야 한다. 또한, 구성타당도를 입증받기 위해서 현재 진행되는 평가가 주어진 평가 구성 및 세 부표준과 일치하는지에 대한 검사를 해야 한다.

Concurrent validity measures how well a new test compares to an well-established test. It can also refer to the practice of concurrently testing two groups at the same time, or asking two different groups of people to take the same test.

① Advantages
- It is a fast way to validate your data.
- It is a highly appropriate way to validate personal attributes (i.e. depression, IQ, strengths and weaknesses).

② Disadvantages
- It is less effective than predictive validity to predict future performance or potential, like job performance or ability to succeed in college.
- If you are testing different groups, like people who want jobs and people who have jobs, responses may differ between groups. For example, people who already have jobs may be less inclined to put their best foot forward.

모범답안

Version 1

To increase internal consistency, in Step 4, the teacher should remove items not with high but with zero/negative item discrimination. In Step 5, as for the concurrent validity, he should ask his colleagues to check the correlation between the current test and previously validated test, not review the test referring to the test specifications.

Version 2

To increase internal consistency, in Step 4, the teacher should remove items not with high but with zero/negative item discrimination. In Step 5, as for the construct validity, he should ask his colleagues to review the given test referring to the test specifications.

08 **Read the passage and follow the directions.** [4 points] 2017 전공A 9번

Mr. Lee wants to determine how well the scores from the College Entrance Exam (CEE) predict academic success in college. The scatter plot below includes high school seniors' CEE scores from 2014 and their college Grade Point Averages (GPAs) in the fall of 2016. Their CEE scores are placed on the horizontal axis and their college GPAs on the vertical axis.

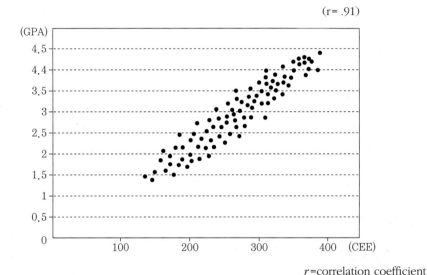

(r = .91)

r =correlation coefficient

Students	CEE (Fall 2014)	GPA (Fall 2016)
A	389	4.43
B	246	2.58
C	304	3.15
D	322	3.27
E	211	2.10
F	328	3.62
G	314	3.18
H	288	2.83
I	372	4.00
J	368	3.85
·	·	·
·	·	·
·	·	·

Based on the information in the passage, identify the type of validity within the context of criterion-related validation and explain it with evidence.

Your Answer

_____

_____

_____

_____

_____

문항분석

1. Topic : Testing principles

2. Focus

준거타당도의 일종인 예측타당도(predictive validity)에 대한 이해도를 측정하는 문제이다. 주어진 그래프와 표에 대한 적절한 해석을 통하여 개념을 구체적이고 명확하게 서술하여야 한다.

3. How to draft a testing

(1) Validity(타당도)

① Content validity(내용타당도) : 특정 평가가 측정하고자 하는 내용을 평가하였다면 그 평가는 내용타당도를 지닌다고 할 수 있다. 교실 평가에서 내용타당도가 높으려면 학습한 내용으로 평가를 구성해야 한다.

Content validity is determined by checking the adequacy with which the test samples the content or objectives of the course or area being assessed. For the language teacher, the degree of test validity is derived from a meticulous analysis of the content of each item and of the test as a whole.

② Construct validity(구성타당도) : 구성타당도는 평가가 평가 목표 또는 평가 기준의 이론적인 구성을 배경으로 하고 있는지를 말한다. 예를 들어 의사소통 능력을 측정하고자 할 때 의사소통 능력을 구성하는 이론적인 개념인 조직적 능력, 화용적 능력, 전략적 능력 등이 모두 포함된 평가를 실시한다면 구성타당도가 높다고 할 수 있다.

Construct validity refers to the degree to which scores on an assessment instrument permit inferences about underlying traits. In other words, it examines whether the instrument is a true reflection of the theory of the trait being measured.

③ **Face validity**(안면타당도): 안면타당도란 학습자의 관점에서 보았을 때 해당 평가가 측정하고자 하는 것을 제대로 측정하고 있는지를 느끼는 정도이다.

Face validity concerns about whether the test looks as if it is measuring what it is supposed to measure. That is the look of a test can influence the test taker.

④ **Criterion-related validity**(준거타당도): 시행된 평가 결과가 동일 능력을 측정하는 믿을 만한 다른 평가 결과와 비슷하다면 준거타당도가 있다고 할 수 있다.

ⓐ 공인타당도(concurrent validity): 현재의 평가 결과가 기존의 타당성을 입증받고 있는 검사와 동일한지의 여부를 의미한다.

ⓑ 예측타당도(predictive validity): 어떤 평가에서 좋은 결과를 얻은 피험자가 이와 관련된 미래의 실제 생활에서도 성공적으로 그 능력을 수행하고 있다면 예측타당도가 높다고 할 수 있다.

⑵ Authenticity(진정성)

목표언어의 과업과 제시된 언어 평가 과업이 일치할 경우 혹은 실제 상황이나 실제 생활에 관련된 과업을 그대로 모사하는 경우 진정성 있는 평가라 할 수 있다.

Authenticity is defined as the degree of correspondence of the characteristics of a given language test task to the features of a target language task. For authenticity in a test, a task is likely to be enacted in the "real world." Thus, the sequencing of items that bears no relationships to one another lacks authenticity.

⑶ Washback effect(역류효과)

역류효과란 평가가 다음 학습에 미치는 영향으로, 부정적인 역류효과보다 긍정적인 역류효과가 높아야 한다. 즉, 학생의 장단점에 대한 정보를 제공함으로써 내적 동기, 자신감, 언어적 자아, 언어 사용 전략 등을 높이도록 평가를 구성해야 한다. 마지막으로 역류효과를 높이기 위해서는 학생이 자신의 수행 결과를 언제든 교사와 토의할 수 있는 창구를 마련해 주어야 한다.

(4) Reliability(신뢰도)

① **Inter-rater reliability(채점자 간 신뢰도)**: 둘 이상의 채점자가 채점을 할 경우 불확실한 채점 기준, 선입견, 부주의 등에 의해서 평가 신뢰도가 낮아질 수 있다.

Two or more scorers yield inconsistent scores of the same test, possibly for lack of attending to scoring criteria, inexperience, inattention, or even preconceived biases.

② **Intra-rater reliability(채점자 개인 신뢰도)**: 한 명의 채점자가 채점을 하더라도 채점 기준이 불확실한 경우, 장시간의 채점, 선입견 등에 의해 신뢰도는 낮아질 수 있다.

A common occurrence of low intra-rater reliability results from unclear scoring criteria, fatigue, biases toward particular students, or simple carelessness.

(5) Practicality(실용성)

Practicality pertains primarily to the ways in which the test will be implemented, and, to a large degree, whether it will be developed and used at all. That is, for any given situation, if the resources required for implementing the test exceed the resources available, the test will be impractical, and will not be used unless resources can be allocated more efficiently.

4. Keyword list

content validity, face validity, construct validity, criterion-related validity, concurrent validity, predictive validity, authenticity, practicality

---

모범답안

The College Entrance Exam(CEE) has a strong predictive validity given that its scores from 2014 correlated highly with the examinees' college GPAs in 2016. For example, Student E who gets the lowest score from CEE gains the worst GPA while Student A of the highest score shows the best performance in their college.

09 Examine part of a test evaluation checklist by a head teacher and a student's reflective journal about the test, and follow the directions. [4 points] 2016 전공A 13번

Mr. Kim, a head teacher of high school English, wanted to evaluate the achievement test of English reading in order to find to what extent the five major principles of language assessment (practicality, reliability, validity, authenticity, and washback) were applied to the test.

TEST EVALUATION CHECKLIST

Test-takers: 2nd year high school students

Content	Scale		
	1	2	3
Subjectivity does not enter into the scoring process.	☐	☐	■
Classroom conditions for the test are equal for all students.	☐	☐	■
Test measures exactly what it is supposed to measure.	■	☐	☐
Items focus on previously practiced in-class reading skills.	■	☐	☐
Topics and situations are interesting.	☐	☐	■
Tasks replicate, or closely approximate, real-world tasks.	☐	☐	■

1=poor, 2=average, 3=good

Post-Exam Reflection

I studied really hard for the test because I wanted to move to a higher level class. But I got 76 and I was so disappointed. Since there were no errors in scoring, my score was dependable, I think. The topics were very relevant to my real life. But what was the problem? Did I use the wrong study skills? Actually I was very surprised when I first saw the test. Lots of tasks were very unfamiliar and I believe I've never done those kinds of tasks in class. Furthermore, after the test I actually expected the teacher to go over the test and give advice on what I should focus on in the future. It never happened. No feedback or comments from the teacher were given. I was not sure which items I got wrong. I will have the same type of test next semester and I'm not sure how I can improve my reading skills and get a better grade.

Identify TWO well-applied principles and TWO poorly-applied principles among the five principles of language assessment stated above based on all the data. Then support each of your choices with details from the post-exam reflection ONLY.

Your Answer

_____

_____

_____

_____

_____

_____

1. Topic : Principles of language assessment

2. Focus

교실에서 진행되는 평가 원리에 대한 세심한 고려를 통해 바람직한 교실 수업 방향을 이끌어낼 수 있다. 과거의 평가가 이전 수업의 정리이자 학습자 간의 성취평가로써 종합적으로 이루어졌다면, 현재 진행되는 classroom testing은 이전 수업의 정리이자 새로운 수업의 시작점이 되는 형성적인 평가로 이루어져 있다. 따라서 학생들은 평가를 통하여 이전 학습의 강점과 약점을 파악하여 새로운 학습 방향을 세워야 한다.

3. Five principles of language assessment

(1) Validity

측정하고자 하는 것을 측정하고 있는지에 대해 content/construct/face validity 등으로 이루어져 있다. 또한 학생들의 현재의 평가가 앞으로 학생들의 학습 수행 능력의 지도가 될 수 있도록 평가의 목적이 주어졌을 경우에는 predictive validity 등을 고려하여 평가를 구성할 수 있다.

(2) Authenticity

실제 언어 사용을 토대로 평가가 구성되어 있는지, real-world task로 평가 과제가 제시되어 있는지, 평가 항목 간의 맥락이 갖춰져 있는지 등을 반영하는 원리이다.

(3) Washback effect

평가가 그 다음 학습에 미치는 영향으로, 이전의 평가에 대한 강점과 단점에 대한 진단적 정보를 토대로 다음의 학습을 계획하고 준비하도록 현 평가의 구성을 이루도록 하는 원리이다.

(4) Reliability

두 명 이상의 채점자가 평가를 진행하여도 동일하거나 유사한 결과가 산출되어야 한다는 평가 원리이다. Scorer reliability로 inter-rater reliability와 intra-rater reliability로 구성되어 있다.

(5) Practicality

평가가 실용적이고 합리적으로 시행되고 있는지에 대한 원리이다.

4. Others

(1) Norm-referenced testing

상대평가형의 대집단 평가로 학생 간의 등급을 나누기 위한 평가

(2) Criterion-referenced testing

절대평가형의 교실 평가로 학생 개개인의 성취 기준에 토대를 두고 진행되는 평가

(3) Formative assessment

Evaluating students in the process of "forming" their competences and skills with the goal of helping them to continue that growth process

(4) Summative assessment

- Aiming to measure, or summarize what a student has grasped
- Occurring at the end of a course or unit of instruction

5. Keyword list

reliability (inter-rater/intra-rater reliability), validity (content/construct/face/predictive validity), washback, authenticity, norm-referenced/criterion-referenced testing

---

모범답안

According to this data, this test has high reliability and authenticity, which shows reliable and fair scoring and the use of topics relevant to students' real lives. However, it has low validity and no washback. To be specific, it deals with tasks the students have never done in class. Besides this, he or she receives no comments or feedback about the test results for further study.

10 **Read the passage and follow the directions.** [2 points] 2015 전공A 기입형 3번

Mr. Lee's English listening test consisted exclusively of four-option, multiple-choice items. After scoring the test, he calculated the response frequency for each item. Part of the results is presented below.

Option Item	Upper Group (N=100)				Lower Group (N=100)			
	A	B	C	D	A	B	C	D
1	50%*	27%	13%	10%	10%*	45%	25%	20%
2	13%	10%	70%*	7%	25%	27%	28%*	20%
3	20%	25%	18%	37%*	21%	26%	16%	37%*
...								
17	4%	0%	61%	35%*	66%	0%	29%	5%*
...								

* indicates the correct response.

Complete the comments on item analysis by filling in each blank with ONE word. Write your answers in the correct order.

Items 1 and 2 seem to be fulfilling their function. Item 3 has the problem of item (1) _____. Therefore, option D of item 3 needs to be revised or item 3 needs to be discarded. Item 17 has a problem with its (2) _____: No one from the upper group and lower group chose option B, and many upper group students incorrectly chose option C.

Your Answer (1) _____

(2) _____

文항분석

1. Topic : How to draft multiple choice item testing

2. Focus

Multiple-choice test의 quality를 평가할 때 고려해야 할 두 가지 대표적 개념 (i.e., item discrimination, item facility)에 대해서 이해하고 있고, 그것을 통해 주어진 데이터를 명확히 분석할 수 있어야 한다.

3. Principles

(1) **How to draft a good test**

Multiple-choice item test를 개발해야 할 점은 적절한 item facility (난이도)이다. 즉, 너무 쉬운 문제는 변별력이 떨어지고, 너무 어려운 문제는 아무도 맞추지 못하는 쓸모없는 문제가 될 수 있으므로 주의해야 한다. 또한, 문항 변별도를 고려하여 상위 그룹 학습자들과 하위 그룹 학습자들에 대한 변별이 명확히 이루어져야 한다. 상위 그룹 학습자들이 하위 그룹 학습자들에 비해 정답 수가 현저히 높을 경우 변별이 잘 되고 있다고 평가될 수 있다.

(2) **Item facility**

문항 난이도로서 문항이 얼마나 쉬웠는지, 즉 정답을 맞힐 확률이 어느 정도 인지를 나타낸다. 0과 1 사이에서 값이 나오며 1에 가까울수록 정답률이 높은, 즉 쉬운 문제이다.

(3) **Item discrimination**

문항 변별도로서 상위 그룹과 하위 그룹을 어느 정도 변별해 내는지의 정도를 말한다. 변별지수는 −1~+1의 값을 취한다. 최소한 0.25~0.35의 변별도를 지녔을 때 문항 변별도가 있다고 할 수 있다.

(4) **Distractor analysis**

오답은 정답을 아는 사람과 모르는 사람을 분류하는 기능을 한다. 선다식 테스트를 향상시키기 위해서는 각각의 개별적인 오답이 얼마나 제 기능을 하고 있는지를 아는 것이 중요하다. 너무 많은 학생이 오답을 선택했을 경우 그 오답지는 학생들의 수준에서 정답과 변별해 내기 어려운 선택지이며, 한 명도 선택하지 않은 오답지일 경우 오답으로서의 매력도가 없다고 볼 수 있다.

4. Keyword list

item discrimination, item facility, distractor analysis

Answer (1) discrimination (2) distractors

11 **Read the dialogue and follow the directions.** [2 points] 2017 전공A 1번

Student—teacher Meeting

T : Well, looking back over the last twelve weeks, I can see that you have written many drafts for the three essay writing assignments.

S : Yes, I have. I have a lot of things here.

T : Of all your essays, which one do you think is the best?

S : I think the persuasive essay I wrote is the best.

T : What makes you think so? Maybe you can tell me how you wrote it.

S : Well... I think the topic I chose was quite engaging. I enjoyed the writing process throughout. And it feels good being able to see the progress I've made.

T : Yes, that's the benefit of this kind of project. I can see some improvement in your use of transitions. Your ideas are nicely connected and organized now.

S : Thanks. What else should I include?

T : Well, did you work on the self-assessment form and the editing checklist?

S : Yes, I did. I completed them and included them with all of my drafts right here.

T : Perfect! I'll be able to finish grading all of your work by the end of next week.

T=teacher, S=student

Complete the following by filling in both blanks with ONE word. (Use the SAME word.)

_____ can include essays, reports, journals, video or audio-recorded learner language data, students' self-assessment, teachers' written feedback, homework, conference forms, etc. As collections of these items, _____ can be useful for assessing student performance in that they can lead students to have ownership over their process of learning and allow teachers to pay attention to students' progress as well as achievement.

Your Answer _____

1. Topic : All about assessment

2. Focus

주어진 대화에서 교사와 학생이 이야기하고 있는(학생이 그동안 작성해 왔던) writing assignments 모음집을 무엇인지 명확히 파악하고 대안 평가로서의 주요 장점을 이해하고 있어야 한다.

3. Traditional assessment vs. Alternative assessment

Traditional assessment	Alternative assessment
• One shot, standardized exams	• Continuous long-term assessment
• Timed, multiple-choice format	• Untimed, free-response format
• Decontextualized test items	• Contextualized communicative tasks
• Scores suffice for feedback	• Formative, interactive feedback
• Norm-referenced scores	• Criterion-referenced scores
• Focus on right answer	• Open-ended, creative answer
• Summative	• Formative
• Oriented to product	• Oriented to process
• Foster extrinsic motivation	• Foster intrinsic motivation
• Non-interactive performance	• Interactive performance

4. Advantages of portfolio

포트폴리오란 학생들의 언어 수행 성취도를 보여주는 결과물을 모아 놓은 작품 모음집이다. 포트폴리오의 가장 큰 장점은 학생들이 자신의 성장 정도를 파악할 수 있다는 것과 자신이 관심 있어 하는 주제를 선택함으로써 동기를 부여하고 자발적인 참여를 유도할 수 있다는 점이다. 학생과 교사 모두에게 학생들의 장점과 약점에 대한 교정적인 정보를 제공하기도 한다. 또한 학습자 개인마다 각각의 포트폴리오가 있기 때문에 수준별 학습, 개별화 수업에 적용하기 쉽다.

5. Keyword list

portfolio, alternative assessment

Answer Portfolios

Plus⁺

Discrete Points Testing and Integrative Testing

Should language be tested by discrete points or by integrative testing? Traditionally, language test have been constructed on the assumption that: language can be broken down into its component and those component parts are duly tested.

1. What is DISCRETE POINTS TESTING?

Language is segmented into many small linguistic points and the four language skills of listening, speaking, reading and writing. Test questions are designed to test these skills and linguistic points. A discrete point test consists of many questions on a large number of linguistic points, but each question tests only one linguistic point.

Examples of discrete points testing:

1. Phoneme recognition
2. Yes/No, True/False answers
3. Spelling
4. Word completion
5. Grammar items
6. Multiple choice tests

Such tests have a down side in that they take language out of context and usually bear no relationship to the concept or use of whole language. Discrete point test met with some criticism, particularly in the view of more recent trends toward viewing the units of language and its communicative nature and purpose, and viewing language as the arithmetic sum of all its parts.

2. What is INTEGRATIVE TESTING?

Language competence is a unified set of interacting abilities which cannot be separated apart and tested adequately.

Whereas discrete items attempt to test knowledge of language one bit at a time, integrative tests attempt to assess a learner's capacity to use many bits all at the same time, and possibly while exercising several presumed components of a grammatical system, and perhaps more than one of the traditional skills or aspects of skills. Therefore, communicative competence is so global and requires such integration for its pragmatic use in the real world that it cannot be captured in additive tests of grammar or reading or vocabulary and other discrete points of language. This emphasizes the simultaneous testing of the testee's multiple linguistic competence from various perspectives.

12 Read the dialogue and follow the directions. [4 points] 2018 전공A 13번

T: Come here, Sumin. How was your vacation?

S: Pretty good. Thank you, Ms. Kim. Actually, I'm so happy to be taking English classes from you this year.

T: Good! You're really welcome in my class. Okay, then, let's talk about the test you had.

S: You mean the reading test you gave us in the first class? Actually, I was wondering why you gave us a test instead of going directly into the textbook.

T: Right, your class hasn't had a lesson yet. It was mainly to see how much you are ready for this semester and give you individual attention for any strong and weak points you have.

S: I see. So, how were the results?

T: Hmm... Overall, you did quite well. Especially, you did well on the grammar questions. But it appears you had a bit of trouble with some words in the reading texts.

S: You're right. Some words are really hard to memorize although I keep trying.

T: I understand. Well, why don't you try to learn them through a context particularly relevant to you? That will be helpful, I believe.

S: Thank you for your advice, Ms. Kim.

T=teacher, S=student

Fill in the blank with the ONE most appropriate word. Then, support your answer with evidence from the dialogue.

Tests can be categorized according to the purposes for which they are carried out. In this respect, the test that Ms. Kim and Sumin are talking about is an example of a(n) _____ test.

Your Answer _____

_____

_____

_____

_____

_____

1. Topic : Diagnostic test

2. Focus

평가의 유형 중, 진단평가의 목적 및 특성 등을 이해할 필요가 있다.

3. Kinds of test(목적에 따른 평가의 분류)

(1) Proficiency tests

If your aim in a test is to tap global competence in a language, then you are testing proficiency. Proficiency tests have traditionally consisted of standardized multiple-choice items on grammar, vocabulary, reading comprehension, aural comprehension, and sometimes on a sample of writing. Such tests often have content validity weakness, but after several decades of construct validation research, some great strides have been made toward constructing communicative proficiency tests.

(2) Diagnostic tests

This test is designed to diagnose a particular aspect of a language. A diagnostic test has the purpose of determining which features of English are difficult for a learner and should therefore become a part of a curriculum. These tests offer a checklist of features for the administrator to use in pinpointing difficulties. It is not advisable to use a general achievement test as a diagnostic, since diagnostic tests need to be specifically tailored to offer information on student need that will be worked on imminently. Achievement tests are useful in analyzing the extent to which students have acquired language features that have already been taught.

(3) Placement tests

Certain proficiency tests and diagnostic tests can act in the role of placement tests, whose purpose is to place a student into an appropriate level or section of a language curriculum or school. A placement test typically includes a sampling of material to be covered in the curriculum (that is, it has content validity), and it thereby provides an indication of the point at which the student will find a level of class to be neither too easy nor too difficult, but appropriately challenging.

(4) Achievement tests

An achievement test is related directly to classroom lessons, units, or even a total curriculum. Achievement tests are limited to particular material covered in a curriculum within a particular time frame, and are offered after a course has covered the objectives in question. Achievement tests can serve as indicators of features that a student needs to work on in the future, but primary role of an achievement test is to determine acquisition of course objectives at the end of a period of instruction.

(5) Aptitude tests

This test predicts a person's future success prior to any exposure to the second language. This is designed to measure a person's capacity or general ability to learn a foreign language and to be successful in that undertaking. Aptitude tests are considered to be independent of a particular language. Today, the measurement of language aptitude has taken the direction of providing learners with information about their preferred styles and their potential strengths and weaknesses.

4. Keyword list

proficiency tests, diagnostic tests, placement tests, achievement tests, aptitude tests

---

모범답안

diagnostic. This test is designed to diagnose how ready the student is for the upcoming semester, and what strong and weak points she has. As a result, it reveals that she had acquired grammatical knowledge well but lacked some vocabulary knowledge.

13 Read the passage in <A> and the part of the individual conference in <B>, and follow the directions. [4 points] 2020 전공B 10번

A

The students in Mr. Lee's class did an oral presentation. Mr. Lee gave his students the following rubric in advance and let them know that their performance would be evaluated across four categories: (a) content & preparation, (b) organization, (c) language, and (d) delivery. After the students' presentations were over, Mr. Lee had a conference session with each student to discuss his or her strengths and weaknesses.

PRESENTATION ASSESSMENT FORM

Evaluation Categories	Scale 1 poor 2 3 4 5 excellent				
Ⅰ. Content & Preparation					
1. Interest & Value of topic	1	2	3	4	5
2. Informativeness of content	1	2	3	4	5
3. Preparedness	1	2	3	4	5
Ⅱ. Organization					
1. Introduction (giving an overview)	1	2	3	4	5
2. Main body (supporting details & examples)	1	2	3	4	5
3. Conclusion (summarizing the presentation)	1	2	3	4	5
Ⅲ. Language					
1. Accuracy (accurate use of grammar)	1	2	3	4	5
2. Appropriateness	1	2	3	4	5
3. Fluency	1	2	3	4	5
4. Pronunciation	1	2	3	4	5
Ⅳ. Delivery					
1. Confidence (not overly dependent on notes)	1	2	3	4	5
2. Gestures & Facial expressions	1	2	3	4	5

B

(The following is part of the individual conference that Mr. Lee had with one of his students, Yuna.)

Mr. Lee : Your presentation was pretty good.

Yuna : Thank you, Mr. Lee.

Mr. Lee : Yeah, you were really prepared. And so you got a perfect score on that area.

Yuna : I tried my best to make my PPT slides as informative as possible.

Mr. Lee : I know! They were really impressive. And your topic was really good.

Yuna : Thank you! How was my pronunciation?

Mr. Lee : Overall, I think your language was easy for the other students to follow. But you may want to try to use your language more appropriately. For example, some expressions you used like *you guys* and *you know*, may not be appropriate in this kind of presentation.

Yuna : I see. Thank you for your feedback.

Mr. Lee : I also noticed that you referred to your cue cards too frequently without looking at the audience.

Yuna : I did?

Mr. Lee : Yes, you did. Your presentation would have been much better if you had shown more confidence in your presentation task.

Yuna : I agree.

Mr. Lee : Other than that, everything looked fine.

Identify TWO of the four evaluation categories that Mr. Lee thinks reflect Yuna's weak points. Then, provide evidence for each identified category from <B>.

Your Answer _____

_____

_____

_____

_____

_____

문항분석

1. Topic : How to evaluate students' oral presentation

2. Focus

학생들의 말하기 능력을 측정하기 위한 rubric 및 말하기 과제로 oral presentation 을 제시하고, 어떻게 평가를 할 것인지 알려준 뒤, 해당 평가를 통해 학생들의 장/ 단점이 무엇인지 파악하도록 하는 conference를 진행하고 있다.

3. Scoring methods

(1) Holistic scoring

A holistic rubric describes in general terms the qualities of excellent, good, fair, and unsatisfactory assignments. These descriptions can be tied to grades or stand on their own.

Hyunsoo	Description
Grade B (writing)	The 'B' paper shows: • an ability to interpret and develop ideas in the writer's own words • a clear organizational pattern • vocabulary that is adequate in expressing ideas • generally correct use of punctuation or spelling, although with occasional errors • grammar that is usually accurate, and does not interfere with the reader's understanding

(2) Analytic scoring

Classroom evaluation of learning is best served through analytic scoring, in which many as six major elements of writing are scored, thus enabling learners to home in on weaknesses and capitalize on strengths.

Content	30
Organization	20
Vocabulary	20
Syntax	25
Mechanics	5
Total	100

4. Keyword list

holistic scoring, analytic scoring, conferencing

모범답안

Yuna reveals her weak points in terms of Language and Delivery. First, she uses inappropriate expressions such as 'you guys' and 'you know.' During the presentation, also, she refers to cue cards too frequently, which results in showing low confidence.

14 Read the English test task specifications in <A> and the teacher's reflective journal in <B>, and follow the directions. [4 points] 2019 전공A 12번

Test Task Specifications

Category	Description
Purpose	To determine students' current levels and place them into the most appropriate speaking courses
Time allocation	2 minutes (1 minute for preparation and 1 minute for speaking)
Task type	Picture-cued tasks
Scoring method	Analytic a. Criteria: Content, Fluency, Accuracy, Pronunciation b. Each criterion is worth 5 points and the score for this task is added up to 20.
Scoring procedure	a. Two examiners: a primary examiner who conducts the test and a secondary examiner who observes the test b. If there is a difference of more than 2 points in total, the examiners discuss rating disagreements based on the recorded test to arrive at a rating that they agree upon.

B

I understand that some students have potential strengths in learning languages, and in order to check my students' aptitude in English, I conducted a speaking test with picture-cued tasks. For each task, students looked at pictures and prepared for 1 minute and then described them for 1 minute. I found that 1 minute was not enough for my students to prepare their answers, so I felt that I needed to change the time allocation for the task. In addition, although my rating and the other examiner's rating seemed consistent, I realized that my approach, providing a global rating with overall impressions using a single general scale, was not very effective because the scores didn't give much helpful information to students. ... There was one student's test yielding very different scores, so we (primary and secondary examiners) had a discussion about the recorded test and found that I gave the wrong score by mistake. It was good that we recorded the test even though both of us were present during the test.

Identify TWO categories that the teacher did NOT follow in the test task specifications from <A>. Then, support your answers with evidence from <B>.

Your Answer

1. Topic: Test type and scoring method (Test task specifications)

2. Focus

목적에 맞는 평가 방법과 채점 방법을 적용하고 있는지를 확인하는 문제이다.

3. Placement test

A placement exam or placement test is a test designed to evaluate a person's preexisting knowledge of a subject and thus determine the level most suitable for the person to begin coursework on that subject.

Certain proficiency tests and diagnostic tests can act in the role of placement tests. A placement test typically includes a sampling of material to be covered in the curriculum (that is, it has content validity), and it thereby provides an indication of the point at which the student will find a level or class to be neither too easy nor too difficult, but appropriately challenging.

4. Holistic vs. Analytic scoring methods

(1) Holistic scoring method

Holistic scoring method provides a single score based on an overall impression of a student's performance on a task.

① **Advantages**: quick scoring, provides overview of student achievement.

② **Disadvantages**: does not provide detailed information, maybe difficult to provide one overall score.

③ **Use a holistic rubric when**: You want a quick snapshot of student performance level.

(2) Analytic scoring method

Analytic scoring method provides specific feedback along several dimensions.

① **Advantages**: more detailed feedback, scoring more consistent across students, provides more guidance for instructional planning.

② **Disadvantage** : time consuming to score

③ **Use an analytic rubric when** :
- You want to see relative strengths and weaknesses.
- You want detailed feedback.
- You want to assess complicated skills or performance.
- You want students to self-assess their understanding or performance.
- You want information for instructional planning.

5. Keyword list

test type, scoring method, placement test, aptitude test, holistic scoring, analytic scoring

---

모범답안

The teacher in <B> does not follow two test task specifications from <A>: Purpose and Scoring method. To be specific, she conducts a test to check students' potential strength (to see the students' aptitude) in English rather than place students into the level-appropriate speaking course. Also, instead of an analytic scoring method, the teacher utilizes a holistic scoring method using one general scale.

Build Up New
박현수 영어교육론 ⑪

Part

02

기출지문분석

Chapter

01 2019학년도 기출지문분석

Ⓛ Topic : How to promote student learning (Writing and speaking)

② Focus

쓰기 활동과 말하기 활동 중에 교사의 재량으로 학습을 더 증진시킬 수 있는 방법을 제시하고, 이 방법들 중 수업에 적절히 반영된 것과 반영되지 않은 것을 고른 뒤 주어진 자료에서 각각의 증거를 찾아본다.

③ Classroom Data 2019 전공B 8번

A

Mr. Kim and Ms. Jo, English teachers, attended a workshop for language teachers where they both gained a lot of useful information to promote student learning. Below is part of the information from the workshop.

Teachers need to...

(1) keep in mind that their course goals and/or procedures can be modified.
(2) offer students a variety of learning strategies to develop learner autonomy.
(3) involve students in self-/peer-evaluation instead of evaluating them alone.
(4) assess students frequently throughout the semester.

B

(Below are the two teachers' reflections after the workshop.)

Mr. Kim's reflection

To develop English writing abilities, my students engaged in writing activities. I simply assumed that paragraph writing would be enough for my students. However, I realized that I should change the initial course goal after assessing my students' first classroom writings. Their writing abilities were well above my expectations so I changed the goal set earlier and included essays. Since I believe that one-shot assessment at the end of the course is not effective for enhancing student learning, I carried out assessment periodically over the whole course period. I also believe assessment should be objective and that students' self-assessments are rather subjective in some ways. So, I did all the periodic assessments by myself, not asking students to evaluate their own work.

Ms. Jo's reflection

In my class, students were expected to develop debating skills in English. I organized my lesson in this way: brief mini-lectures, short video presentations to provide content for debating practice, followed by small group debating practice. I taught a range of learning strategies so that my students could become independent language learners utilizing those strategies whenever needed. For improving students' oral skills, I thought that arranging assessments multiple times, not just once, would be better. So I carried out assessments every two weeks during my instructional period. Based on the results of the assessments, I noticed that strictly following the lesson procedure was rather challenging to my students. However, I kept the same procedure over the course period since I believe maintaining consistency is crucial in order not to confuse students.

△ How to promote student's autonomy

(1) Begin new learning tasks with opportunities for students to ask questions and get help from their teacher or peers if they are having difficulty understanding the concepts.

(2) Provide students with meaningful choices consistent with learning objectives (e.g., what relevant topics they want to study) and exercises that encourage self-monitoring of their comprehension (e.g., becoming aware of their understanding of the materials) and tracking their learning progress (e.g., keeping track of their learning progress in a journal).

(3) Use specific praise that tells students what they did well and for which learning processes and skills they are being praised.

(4) Involve students in setting objectives and participating in decisions about how to individualize objectives in line with curriculum standards, plus individual and collective student interests and choices.

(5) In small group discussions, students can share their personal interests and then see how these fit with the teacher's list. By helping students define their personal learning goals and objectives, teachers can guide students to see whether these are consistent not only with their own interests but also how they can be aligned with curriculum standards and expectations.

(6) Appeal to student interest and curiosity by introducing the unfamiliar through the familiar.

(7) Reward success with praise and model how students can monitor their own progress and success with self-reward strategies.

5 Advantages of self-assessment

(1) Helps to develop important meta-cognitive skills.

(2) Increases self-awareness through reflective practice, making the criteria for self-evaluation explicit, and making performance improvement practices intrinsic to ongoing learning.

(3) Heightens their awareness of the goals and outcomes of the program and allows them to identify their strengths and needs in relation to those outcomes.

(4) Helps them identify how they learn best; reflect on what they can do as learners.

(5) Contributes to the development of critical reviewing skills, enabling the learner to more objectively evaluate their own performance—and others', when used in conjunction with peer assessment. With peer assessment they become more practised in giving constructive feedback, and receiving and acting on feedback received.

(6) Helps students to take control of their own learning and assessment, and giving them the chance to manage their own learning and development more independently.

(7) Gives students greater agency regarding assessment, thus enriching their learning.

(8) Possibly, in the long run, reduces the teacher's assessment workload— although on its own this benefit is not sufficient to introduce student self-assessment.

6 Keyword list

autonomy, agency, self-evaluation, peer-evaluation, formative test, summative test

Chapter

02 2018학년도 기출지문분석

1 Topic : How to make a communicative classroom

2 Focus

Experienced teacher의 조언이 실제 수업에서 실현된 점과 실현되지 않은 점을 고르고 증거를 제시해 보도록 한다.

3 Classroom Data 2018 전공B 8번

A

(Below are notes that Ms. Shin, a new teacher, took of her senior teacher's advice on how to make her class communicatively oriented.)

Senior teacher's suggestions

- Objective : Get class centered on language functions rather than grammatical structures.
- Error targeted : Focus only on global errors impeding communication of meaning.
- Strategy : Encourage the use of communication strategies.
- Feedback : Provide correction implicitly.

B

(Below is Ms. Shin's talk at the beginning and closure of her single-activity class.)

Today, you are going to practice how to make requests using the question forms you learned from the last class. To do this, you will be doing an activity in pairs where you need to fill in a book order form by asking your partner for the necessary information. While doing this, you will get a chance to use the question forms to make requests. If you can't come up with the exact words to express the meaning you intend during the activity, you can try using similar words you know or even gestures, instead. Now, I will hand out the copies of the order form. Then, you can begin the activity with the student next to you. You'll work in pairs.
OK, here are your copies.

⋮

All right, now it's time to wrap up. I think you all did a great job on the form-filling activity exactly as I told you when the class started. But there is one and only one language element I want to briefly point out today. I noticed some of you missed 's' in some verbs like "He come" while talking. It should be "comes" not "come" though meaning is still clear without 's.' Apart from this, you seem to be fairly familiar with making requests now. Next time, we will focus on how to ask for permission.

4 Functional syllabus

A notional-functional syllabus is a kind of communicative syllabus which organizes units with the foundation of some functions such as asking question, expressing opinions, expressing wishes, making suggestions, complaining, and apologizing rather than including units instructing noun gender or present tense ending (Wilkins, 1976).

5 Communication strategies

Communication strategies are ways that learners get round the fact that they may not know how to say something. Most communication strategies are directed at filling in the gaps in the learner's vocabulary knowledge. If they help the speakers achieve their intended message, they are labeled achievement strategies. But the speaker might decide that the message is simply not achievable. Then they might adopt what is called an avoidance strategy.

6 Error correction

교사의 오류 수정의 정도는 어떤 오류를, 어느 정도로 수정하느냐가 관건이다. 오류 수정의 정도는 수업 목표에 따라 달라진다. 만약 정확성(accuracy)에 초점을 둔 수업이라면 global error뿐 아니라 local error도 correction의 대상이 된다. 이때 교사의 correction은 학습자의 발화가 끝난 후 실시하는 것이 바람직하다. 반면 유창성(fluency)과 의사소통(communication)에 초점을 둔 수업이라면 전체적인 의미에 영향을 주는 global error만을 대상으로 하여 학습자의 활동이 끝난 후 follow-up treatment에서 전체 교실 활동으로 실시해야 한다.

7 Keyword list

language functions, grammatical structures, global errors, local errors, error correction

Plus⁺

Coherence & Cohesion

The teacher provides a model text and students read it by focusing on coherence and cohesion of a model text.

▶ **Coherence** refers to the <u>logical development of ideas</u> within a text and it is an important subskill for students to be aware of.

▶ **Cohesion** refers to the <u>grammatical and lexical connections</u> between individual clauses. The grammatical links can be classified such as <u>referents</u> (pronouns, the article "the", demonstrative), ellipsis (leaving out of words or phrases where they are unnecessary), and conjunction (a word joins phrases or clauses together).

교사는 text의 coherence와 cohesion을 키워주기 위하여 다음과 같은 다양한 활동을 진행할 수 있다.

1. Focusing on the topic and function of each paragraph
2. Examining how the writer has chosen to order his arguments
3. Showing how to make their text "reader friendly"
4. Asking students to circle all the pronouns and then to use arrows to connect them to their referents
5. Asking students to replace a sentence which is missing from each paragraph or to replace the first sentence of each paragraph
6. Matching clauses which have been separated
7. Gapping conjunctions which students must replace from a selection

Chapter

03

2017학년도 기출지문분석

1 Topic : How to manage a classroom

2 Focus

교사의 역할(teacher's roles)에 따른 수업 전개(classroom management)의 차이를 파악하도록 한다.

3 Classroom Data 2017 전공B 8번

━━━━ A ━━━━

Class A

Lesson objectives : Ss will be able to discuss and present their travel experiences using comparatives.

1. T tells a story about travel experiences.

> *Let me tell you about two trips I took, one to Singapore and the other to Bangkok. I really enjoyed my trip to Bangkok. It was more interesting than my trip to Singapore. Singapore was a little more boring than Bangkok. Although Singapore was cleaner and nicer; I thought Bangkok was a more fun city to travel in.*

2. T articulates the lesson objectives and asks Ss to form groups of six.

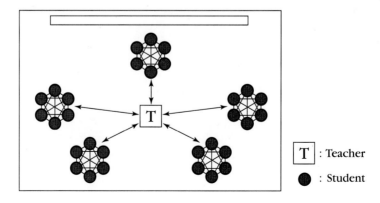

T : Teacher

● : Student

3. Ss begin a consensus building activity. During this activity, Ss compare locations according to a list of given adjectives (e.g., *safe, beautiful, historic*) on a worksheet.

(T helps Ss as needed.)

	Your chosen place	Your group's agreed-upon place
safe	*Busan*	*Daegu*
beautiful	*Jeju*	*Jeju*
historic		
...		
_____ (*your idea*)		

Ss compare and discuss their ideas using comparatives.

(T gives feedback. Ss correct ill-formed utterances.)

> S : Busan is beautifuler.
> T : Beautifuler?
> S : Beautiful, more beautiful.
> T : More beautiful?
> S : Busan is more beautiful.
> T : More beautiful. OK.

4. In groups, Ss discuss where the better and worse places to visit are.
(T walks around the classroom to see if all the Ss are participating in the discussion. If Ss are reluctant to join in group work, T encourages them to participate.)

5. Ss work on a summary together within their group. T allows Ss to choose a role within their group (e.g., leader, timekeeper, note-taker, reporter).
(T monitors their work and helps out as needed.)

6. Each group presents their summary to the class.
....

                                                    T=teacher, S=student

| | B | |

Class B

Lesson objectives :

(1) Ss will learn comparative forms;

(2) Ss will be able to make sentences using comparatives.

1. T explains the grammatical form of comparatives and writes the following chart on the board :

safe	safer
beautiful	more beautiful
cheap	cheaper
expensive	more expensive
...	...

(T stays at the front of the class the entire time, and Ss sit in orderly rows in silence.)

2. T instructs Ss to pay attention to the lesson.

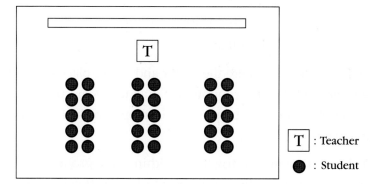

3. T plays a recording line-by-line, and Ss listen and repeat.

(T instructs them to repeat in unison.)

Recording	Students
A：What is cheaper, taking trains or taking buses? B：Taking buses is cheaper than taking trains.	What is cheaper, taking trains or taking buses? Taking buses is cheaper than taking trains.
A：Which one is safer? B：Taking trains is safer than taking buses.	Which one is safer? Taking trains is safer than taking buses.
....	....

4. T checks if Ss understand the comparative forms.

(T asks questions, Ss answer individually, and T gives feedback.)

> T：What is the comparative form of 'safe'?
> S：Safer.
> T：Good. What about 'beautiful'?
> S：More beautiful.
> T：Very good. Then what about 'cheap'?
> S：More cheaper.
> T：No, not 'more cheaper'. It's 'cheaper'.

5. Ss do more choral repetition.

(T plays the recording again, pausing it after key phrases, and Ss repeat them immediately.)

6. T asks Ss to repeat key phrases individually.

(T corrects Ss' errors explicitly.)

....

T=teacher, S=student

🔔 Teacher roles

(1) The controller

The teacher is in complete charge of the class, what students do, what they say and how they say it. The teacher assumes this role when a new language is being introduced and accurate reproduction and drilling techniques are needed.

In this classroom, the teacher is mostly the center of focus, the teacher may have the gift of instruction, and can inspire through their own knowledge and expertise, but, does this role really allow for enough student talk time? Is it really enjoyable for the learners? There is also a perception that this role could have a lack of variety in its activities.

(2) The prompter(facilitator)

The teacher encourages students to participate and makes suggestions about how students may proceed in an activity. The teacher should help students only when necessary.

When learners are literally 'lost for words', the prompter can encourage by discreetly nudging students. Students can sometimes lose the thread or become unsure how to proceed; the prompter in this regard can prompt but always in a supportive way.

(3) The resource person

The teacher is a kind of walking resource center ready to offer help if needed, or provide learners with whatever language they lack when performing communicative activities. The teacher must make her/himself available so that learners can consult her/him when (and only when) it is absolutely necessary.

As a resource the teacher can guide learners to use available resources such as the internet, for themselves, it certainly isn't necessary to spoon-feed learners, as this might have the downside of making learners reliant on the teacher.

(4) The assessor

The teacher assumes this role to see how well students are performing or how well they performed. Feedback and correction are organized and carried out.

There are a variety of ways we can grade learners, the role of an assessor gives teachers an opportunity to correct learners. However, if it is not communicated with sensitivity and support it could prove counter-productive to a student's self-esteem and confidence in learning the target language.

(5) The organizer

This is perhaps the most difficult and important role the teacher has to play. The success of many activities depends on good organization and on the students knowing exactly what they are to do next. Giving instructions is vital in this role as well as setting up activities.

The organizer can also serve as a demonstrator, this role also allows a teacher to get involved and engaged with learners. The teacher also serves to open and neatly close activities and also give content feedback.

(6) The participant

This role improves the atmosphere in the class when the teacher takes part in an activity. However, the teacher takes a risk of dominating the activity when performing it.

Here the teacher can enliven a class; if a teacher is able to stand back and not become the center of attention, it can be a great way to interact with learners without being too overpowering.

(7) The tutor

The teacher acts as a coach when students are involved in project work or self-study. The teacher provides advice and guidance and helps students clarify ideas and limit tasks.

This role can be a great way to pay individual attention to a student. It can also allow a teacher to tailor-make a course to fit specific student needs. However, it can also lead to a student becoming too dependent or even too comfortable with one teacher and one method or style of teaching.

Plus⁺

Plan and Flow

Too much free time can be a dangerous thing in a language classroom. An organized class that flows from one activity to another has a few benefits:
• Keeps students focused and in learning mode
• Maintains confidence in the teacher
• Prevents downtime, which leads to boredom and conversation

Don't stress about having a once-in-a-lifetime, cutting-edge curriculum planned for each class. What's more important is that students trust in your plan. They need to understand each activity, why they are doing it and what they will learn.

To help ensure a logical, efficient course plan that students trust, try scaffolding, backwards planning and balancing. To maintain class flow use scaffolding, in which you provide students with supplemental resources, instructions or activities that prepare or support them in order to make a given task more manageable. Here's a simplified summary of second language scaffolding for beginners.

For example, if you want students to read a news article and summarize it, you could :
• Have a class conversation on the topic beforehand to help familiarize them with it.
• Provide a vocabulary key with definitions and synonyms to refer to while reading.
• Have students work in pairs.

As students progress you will remove these "scaffolds" one by one. In a couple of weeks when students are more familiar with news articles, you could take away the vocabulary key and the pair work, keeping only the initial conversation. When you think they are ready, you will simply assign an article without any supplementary resources or activities.

Scaffolding helps you tailor activities so that they are neither too easy nor too difficult, keeping students from getting lost due to boredom or lack of motivation.

Chapter
04
2016학년도 기출지문분석

1 Topic : Action research – Peer observation

2 Focus

Teacher training의 일환으로 교사가 자신의 수업 개선을 위해 수업 내용을 녹화하여 자가 장학(self-observation)을 하거나 경험 많은 동료 교사에게 장학을 부탁할 수 있다. 본 문항에서는 기존 수업의 활동 및 교사 질문에 대한 개선과 학습자의 오류에 대해 보다 적절한 피드백 등을 제안받고 있다.

3 Classroom Data 2016 전공B 8번

Teacher: Ms. Song	Consultant: Mr. Cho	Date: Dec. 2nd
Before consultation	In my class, I taught grammatical structures as follows: . . . T : She will go swimming. (showing a picture of 'John riding a bike') "Ride a bike." S1 : John will ride a bike. T : Good. (showing a picture of 'Mary playing the piano') "Play the piano." S2 : Mary will play the piano. T : Very good. (showing a picture of 'Tom visiting a museum') "Visit a museum." S3 : Tom visit a museum. T : No, you should say, "Tom will visit a museum." . . . T : (showing a picture of 'people going to a movie') What will they do? S4 : They will go to a movie. T : Very good. (turning to S5, showing a picture of 'students singing a song') What will they do? . . . I expected my students to learn practiced structures, but they still had difficulty in using them in real context.	

Mr. Cho's advice	The following are pieces of Mr. Cho's advice: • Utilize an e-portfolio. • Use other types of questions. • Employ various authentic materials. • Provide other types of feedback. • Assign specific roles to students in group work.
After consultation	After the consultation, I made changes in teaching grammar as follows: T : Good morning, class. Winter vacation is coming soon. I will go to Jeju Island and travel around. Minji, what will you do this vacation? S1 : I go to Grandma's house in Busan. T : Minji, I go to Grandma's house? S1 : Oh... eh... I will go to Grandma's house. T : Perfect! What about Bora? Do you have any plans? S2 : Um... I... I take guitar lessons. T : I take guitar lessons? S2 : Uh... I will take guitar lessons. T : Good! What a great plan! Why do you want to do that? · · · ·

T=teacher, S=student

4 Question types

(1) Display questions

They seek answers in which the information is already known by the teacher. This type of elicitation has been criticised for its lack of authenticity since it is not commonly used in conversation outside the classroom. Extensive use of display questions could be a waste of time. However, it is said that display questions can potentially be central resources which language teachers and students use to organize language lessons and produce language pedagogy. Accordingly, they are an important tool in the classroom, not only for the teacher to be able to check and test their learners, but also as a source of listening practice. One of the first things a beginner learns in English is how to understand and answer display questions.

Ex   The teacher asks a learner 'What is the past simple form of leave?'

(2) Referential questions

They require answers which contain information unknown by the teacher, and they are frequently used to call for evaluation or judgement. They are commonly used in regular conversation outside the classroom, hence are believed to encourage students' higher-order thinking skills and authentic use of the second language in the classroom. Many teachers agree that teachers' use of referential questions could prompt students to provide significantly longer and syntactically more complex responses than the use of display questions.

Ex 1 What do you think about this topic?

What do you think about animal rights?

Ex 2 T: Last week we were reading "Kee Knock Stan" (title of a story). What is "Kee Knock Stan," (display Q) Hyunsoo?

S: I cannot understand.

T: Yes.

T: What do you think the postman at the post office would do? (referential Q)

S: I think I would divide it if the letters are to Hong Kong or other places.

T: Yes, I think that's a sensible way, right? Good.

Chapter 05

2015학년도 기출지문분석

1 Topic : Reflection on today's lesson

2 Focus

Sumi와 Inho의 learning log와 교사의 teaching log에 있는 수업에 대한 comments를 통하여 수업의 장단점을 파악하고, 단점에 대해서는 적절하고 구체적인 해결책을 제공할 수 있어야 한다.

3 Classroom Data 2015 전공B 논술형 2번

Bulletin Board

Sumi

I loved today's lesson! When the teacher asked questions about the words and expressions related to cooking using the recipe from a cooking magazine, I was able to clearly figure out the meaning of what we were supposed to learn. It was really motivating to use the recipe for learning about the words and expressions used practically for cooking. But I made a few errors, such as telling the difference between "slice" and "chop," that I think I will repeat again despite the teacher's correction. When I make errors, I want him to give me some time to think about why I make them and how I can correct them myself.

Inho

When the teacher asked us to bring a recipe from a cooking magazine yesterday for today's lesson, I wondered why. But when he asked questions about some words and expressions related to cooking using the recipes we brought, I realized why. When asking and answering about them using the cooking material with the teacher and then with my partner, I came to clearly understand the meaning of the words and expressions. Plus, it was very fun and exciting. But I didn't like that he corrected my errors when I misused the word "pan" in "boiling water in the pan"; I prefer getting correction from my friends because it makes me feel more comfortable.

My Teaching Log

What I put emphasis on in today's class

I always want my students to have a clear understanding of what I teach, so today I tried to teach the points using materials used in real life rather than the ones in the textbook. To my surprise, they really loved the way I taught today. They participated in the lesson with a lot of enthusiasm.

The things I have to improve in the next class

While leading the activity, for convenience' sake, I corrected the errors that students made. Considering their opinions, however, I have to use alternate ways to give them a chance to correct their errors individually or in pairs.

⚠ Error treatment

유창성을 넘어서 정확성에도 목적을 둔 교사는 학생이 생성한 오류를 수정할 것인지 아닌지에 대한 판단을 하고, 수정을 할 경우 언제, 어떤 방식으로 피드백을 제공할 것인지 결정하고 적절한 피드백을 선택하여 제공해야 한다.

• Should learners' errors be corrected?
• When should learners' errors be corrected?
• How should errors be corrected?
• Who should do the correcting?

교사는 학습자들의 참여를 유도하기 위해서 학생의 오류를 하나의 학습 과정으로 인식하고, 오류 수정은 학습 목표에 따라 진행해야 한다. 즉, 교실 수업의 목표가 정확성에 있는 경우 즉각적으로 피드백을 제공하지만, 의사소통에 초점을 둘 경우 의사소통 활동이 끝난 후에 피드백을 제공하는 것이 바람직하다.

When the focus is on meaning, it is inappropriate to interrupt the flow of interaction. In these situations, the teacher can make a note of errors for follow-up treatment later. When the focus is on form, the teacher might well interrupt before the students have finished their turn.

◈ Error Treatment Sequence (Lyster & Ranta, 1997)

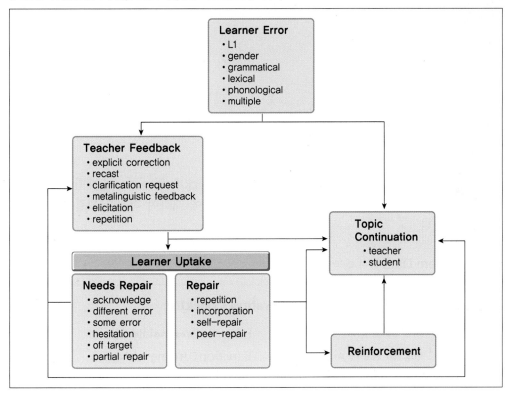

Build Up 영어교육론

2014학년도 기출지문분석

Chapter 06

1 Topic : Class observation

2 Focus

동료 교사의 수업 참관 후 작성된 observation checklist와 notes에 대한 분석을 기반으로 수업의 특징에 대해 이해하고, 예상되는 문제점에 대하여 적절한 해결책을 제시할 수 있어야 한다.

3 Classroom Data 2014 전공B 논술형 2번

Observation Checklist

Instructor : Sumi Kim Unit : 4. Personal Health
Topic : How to treat acne Function : Giving advice
Period : 2/8 Date : Nov. 11

Areas	Criteria	Scale*
Lesson Preparation	• have a clearly developed lesson plan	1 — ②— 3
	• prepare interesting multimedia materials	1 — 2 —③
Instructional Strategies	• give clear directions	1 —②— 3
	• use an appropriate grouping strategy for group activities	①— 2 — 3
	• provide level-appropriate activities	1 —②— 3
Affective Aspects	• create a warm and accepting atmosphere	1 — 2 —③

1=poor, 2=average, 3=good

336 Part 02 기출지문분석

> **Notes**
> • A fun video clip on acne. Ss loved it.
> • T was kind and patient.
> • Group activity (same-ability grouping)
>   — Higher-level students did well. Had no problems.
>   — Lower-level students had a hard time completing the task. Seemed like they needed some help.

⚃ Level-differentiated lesson

(1) Managing mixed level class

대집단 수업의 가장 큰 문제점 중의 하나는 학생들의 언어능력에 차이가 난다는 것이다. 따라서 혼합된 능력을 지닌 학생들(mixed ability students)을 지도한다는 것은 교사에게 수업에 대한 계획 및 수행상의 여러 가지 문제점을 일으킨다.

Many teachers see mixed level classes as especially problematic. Yet in a real sense all classes have students with a mixture of different abilities and language levels. Within the school environments, students are often streamed—that is re-grouped for language lessons according to their abilities. In other situations, however, such placement and streaming are not possible and so teachers are faced with individuals who have different language knowledge, different intelligences, different learning speeds, and different learning styles and preferences. There is particular concern for the needs not only for students who are having difficulty at the lower end of the scale, but also for "gifted" students.

(2) Different student actions

학생들에게 상이한 자료 및 내용을 제공하기가 어려울 경우, 동일한 자료에 대한 상이한 반응 및 답변을 유도하는 것도 하나의 방법이 될 것이다.

① **Give students different tasks**: 동일한 읽기 자료를 제공하고 학생들에게 저마다 다른 답변을 하도록 요구한다.

For example, group A might have to interpret the information in the text by reproducing it in graphic form (or in charts and tables). Group B, on the other hand, might answer a series of open-ended questions. Group C—the group we perceive as having the greatest need of support—might be offered a series of multiple-choice questions; their task is to pick the correct response from two or more alternatives because we think this will be easier for them than having to interpret all the information themselves.

② **Give students different roles** : 과제 진행 시 학생들에게 저마다 다른 역할을 제시한다.

If students are doing a role-play, for example, in which a police officer is questioning a witness, we might give the student playing the police officer the questions they should ask, whereas the student playing the witness has to come up with their own way of expressing what they want to say. We will have done this because the student or students playing the police officer clearly need more guidance than the others. If students are preparing for a debate, we might give Group A a list of suggested arguments to prepare from whereas Group B (whom we think need less support) are told to come up with their own arguments.

5 Tiered tasks

수준별 그룹으로 진행하되, 과업 수행 결과물은 유사하다.

Example 1

다음은 '*The spirit of London*'이라는 읽기 자료를 토대로 구성된 3개의 과업 자료이다.

Top Tier

Task A: for weaker students

1. How much of London's history does *The spirit of London* show?
2. How do you go around it?
3. What special effects does it have?
4. What can you see in the modern-day section?

Answers

ⓐ light, sound, music, and smells   ⓑ police, punks, and tourist

ⓒ more than 400 years   ⓓ in a taxi

Middle Tier

Task B: for midlevel students

1. How much of London's history does *The spirit of London* show?
  ⓐ 400 years   ⓑ more than 400 years   ⓒ 300 years

2. How do you go around it?
  ⓐ in a taxi   ⓑ in a train   ⓒ on foot

---

3. What special effects does it have?
   ⓐ lights   ⓑ sound and music   ⓒ smells

4. What can you see in the modern-day section?
   ⓐ police   ⓑ punks   ⓒ tourists

Bottom Tier

Task C : for stronger students

1. How much of London's history does *The spirit of London* show?
2. How do you go around it?
3. What special effects does it have?
4. What can you see in the modern-day section?

- Matching work : Task A gives all the answers on the page for support. They are jumbled for challenge. Weaker students manipulate the given material, and can use logic to help match the task items, together with the information in the reading text.
- Multiple choice questions : Task B gives multiple-choice answers to help the average students. This is slightly different from the conventional "one answer only is correct" multiple choice, since in questions 3 and 4 there are more than one correct answer.
- Open questions : Task C gives open questions—with no extra support—to challenge the stronger students in the group.

Example 2

Tiered task의 보다 간단한 형태로 학생들의 수준을 두 단계로 나누어 동일한 과업을 진행하되, 교사가 과업의 support를 다르게 제공한다. Dual-choice gapfill이 이에 속한다.

The Dead Sad Animal Rap	MISSING WORDS
Listen to the rap. What are the missing words? Humans... ⓐ ... the dear old dodo, It was... ⓑ ... It couldn' fly Humans... ⓒ ... all the passenger pigeons From the... ⓓ ... American sky.	killed / shot easy / simple hunted / shot south / north

As they listen, weaker students circle one of the words in the box to fill each gap. Stronger students get the same task sheet, but with the missing words box cut off. The task is therefore more challenging for them.

2013학년도 기출지문분석

Chapter 07

1 Topic : Dictogloss

2 Focus

Dictogloss 활동을 진행하는 각 단계 및 절차에 대한 이해를 토대로 각 단계 안에서의 문제점들을 파악하고, 학생들의 이해를 돕고 흥미를 이끌어내며 고른 참여를 이끌어낼 수 있는 실질적인 dictogloss 방법들을 제시할 수 있어야 한다.

3 Classroom Data 2013 논술형 1-2번

A novice high school teacher, Ms. Kim, uses dictogloss as a classroom task for the first time. She plans to use News Script to have students practice passive voice. The teacher's task description is below.

Task Description

- Inform students that the class will work on the dictogloss task with a specific focus on passive voice.
- Have students write down key words while they are watching the 7-minute-long news clip once.
- Ask students to work in groups of 8 for 20 minutes to reconstruct the story.
- Have students watch the clip one more time.
- Distribute the transcript and ask them to review it at home.

After the class, Ms. Kim wants to find out what students think about the dictogloss task. She asks the leader of each group to give comments. Their written comments are presented below.

1st group leader :

The story seemed interesting, but it went on and on. After watching it, we could barely remember anything we heard, except a few words like *boy, locked, shivering,* and *scared*. The teacher asked us to listen carefully for examples of passive voice, but we couldn't notice many. There were too many new and confusing expressions.

2nd group leader :

It was our first time to do this activity, so it was very, very difficult. Also, we didn't know anything about the story before watching the clip, so we were lost.

3rd group leader :

When we worked in groups, some students hardly had any chance to talk. So we could not share our ideas well.

Lesson procedure

Required steps for a Dictogloss activity

Step	Students	Teacher
1. Preparation	• Study vocabulary activities to prepare for the text. • Discuss the topic (predict vocabulary and content etc.). • Move into groups.	
2. Listening for meaning	Listen to the whole text.	Reads the text at normal speed.
3. Listening and note-taking	Take notes listing key words.	Reads again at normal speed.
4. Text reconstruction in group	Work in groups to reconstruct an approximation of the text from notes (one learner acts as the writer).	• Helps groups. • Offers guidelines.
5. Text comparison between groups	Compare group versions of the text. Pay attention to points of usage that emerge from the discussion.	• Facilitates class comparison of versions from different groups. • Facilitates discussion and correction of errors.

* Steps 4 and 5 encourage learners to pay close attention to language form (i.e. word forms, word order, spelling, grammar rules, etc.)

New Build Up 영어교육론 **Ⅲ**

Chapter 08 2012학년도 기출지문분석

1. Topic A : How to develop a scoring rubric and rating scales

2. Focus

Scoring rubric 구성 시 가장 중요한 항목 중 하나인 구성타당도(construct validity)의 정의를 잘 이해하고 있고, 그것이 실제 시험(혹은 rubric)에서 문제가 되었을 경우에 어떠한 결과를 야기할 수 있는지에 대하여 예측할 수 있어야 한다. 더불어, 학생들의 실질적인 output에 대한 평가를 객관적으로 진행하여 scoring을 제공할 수 있어야 한다.

3. Classroom Data 2012 논술형 3-1번

A third-grade high school English teacher, Ms. Park, wanted to diagnose students' speaking ability and decided to use picture description as a performance assessment in her class. Ms. Park developed a scoring rubric and rating scales to evaluate students' performances. Then students were given a series of pictures and asked to describe them for three minutes as fully as possible. However, her head teacher, Ms. Yoon, commented on the initial scoring rubric and Ms. Park revised it. The following are pictures, transcripts of two students' picture descriptions, and Ms. Park's initial and revised scoring rubrics in tables.

<Pictures>

<Speech Transcripts>

<Jitae>	<Mina>
A family of three, uh, playing badminton.. erm.. on beautiful sunny day. It also look like, uh, they have set up, set up a tent and picnic in mountains. Wh.. Whi.. While they are away playing badminton, a eːr theːː dog, maybe a st.. st.. strayːː dog find their picnic and steal some food. The dog, dog runs away with a (0.8) sandwich in mouth. As soon as they come back to the camp siteːː, the family shocked to see the picnic, well, you know, ruined. He isːː hmm.. they obviously had, hmm, no idea what is going on. Then, after (1.2) packing up, I think, they head home? or motel, I mean, a place to stay. You can see people have, like, depressingːː erm depressed faces. To make thingsːː worse, it is getting dark. Th.. The.. Their car is still in the mountains.	I, er, I see happy family. hmm.. Father? Son? Some peopleːː people are playing (3.1) outside, at ground. Two eːr childrenːː playing with something like b.. ball. Big guy look at a boy and girlːː He is sitting on the chair. Oh, there is animal, one animal (2.4) a (2.0) dog or? (3.8) A big tent is open. It come in the mountain, oh fromːː the mountain? and run to the home. And dog try, tries to get some food and eːr eating that later. They are very (3.2) su.. sur.. surprised. Girl is angry. They? are angry. They have nothing to eat (2.9) no sandwiches or kimbab for the camping? He want to go home soon. It is dark eːr outside. (0.5) They take the.. the.. their car and areːː going back.

* Transcription Convention
(0.8) - Interval between utterances (in seconds)
eːr, theːː - Lengthening of the preceding sound |

<Table 1> Ms. Park's <u>Initial</u> Scoring Rubric

	Jitae			Mina		
	Excellent	Good to Fair	Needs Work	Excellent	Good to Fair	Needs Work
Pronunciation	○			○		
Grammatical Accuracy		○			○	

<Table 2> Ms. Park's <u>Revised</u> Scoring Rubric

	Jitae			Mina		
	Excellent	Good to Fair	Needs Work	Excellent	Good to Fair	Needs Work
Pronunciation	○			○		
Grammatical Accuracy		○			○	
Fluency					○	
Cohesion	○					
Vocabulary	○				○	

Ms. Park's initial scoring rubric in <Table 1> has a big problem regarding the principle of validity. Also, if she used the test results from <Table 1> it would be problematic. In Ms. Park's revised scoring rubric two ratings are missing : ("Fluency" for Jitae and "Cohesion" for Mina).

⚃ Some examples of classroom testing

(1) Example 1

If you are trying to assess a person's ability to speak a second language in a conversational setting, asking the learner to answer paper-and-pencil multiple- choice questions requiring grammatical judgments does not achieve **content validity**.

(2) Example 2

I once administered a dictation test and a cloze test as a placement test for a group of learners of English as a second language. Some learners were upset because such tests, on the face of it, did not appear to them to test their true abilities in English. They felt that a multiple-choice grammar test would have been the appropriate format to use. A few claimed they didn't perform well on the cloze and dictation because they were not accustomed to these formats. As it turned out, the tests served as superior instruments for placement, but the students would not have thought so.

➡ 위와 같은 평가 상황은 안면타당도가 매우 낮으나(low face validity), 구성타당도가 매우 높다(high construct validity).

(3) Example 3 : Oral Interview

The scoring analysis for the interview includes several factors in the final score: pronunciation, fluency, grammatical accuracy, vocabulary use, and sociolinguistic appropriateness. The justification for these five factors lies in a theoretical construct that claims those factors to be major components of oral proficiency. So if you were asked to conduct an oral proficiency interview that evaluated only pronunciation and grammar, you could be justifiably suspicious about the construct validity of that test.

(4) **Example 4**： Written Vocabulary Quiz

Likewise, let's suppose you have created a simple written vocabulary quiz, covering the content of a recent unit, that asks students to correctly define a set of words. Your chosen items may be a perfectly adequate sample of what was covered in the unit, but if the lexical objective of the unit was the communicative use of vocabulary, then the writing of definitions certainly fails to match a construct of communicative language use (Brown, 2004).

1. Topic B : Teaching and learning methods

2. Focus

제2언어 습득과 관련하여, 인지주의 접근법과 사회문화적 접근법에서 강조점을 두는 학습 원리들을 이해할 수 있어야 한다. 더불어, 그 두 가지 접근법을 기반으로 하여 Jitae의 학습 방법의 문제점을 인지하고 그 문제점을 극복하기 위한 적절한 활동들을 제시할 수 있어야 한다.

3. Classroom Data 2012 논술형 3-2번

Context

Ms. Park recognized Jitae's problem regarding the third-person singular subject-verb agreement after reviewing his speech sample from the performance assessment. Then Ms. Park had a conference with Jitae. She found that, in the first grade of middle school, Jitae was explicitly taught how to put -*s* at the end of verb stems and then practiced the subject-verb agreement through transformation exercises (e.g., *run → runs*). Since then, Jitae has been exposed to the grammatical morpheme through reading materials but has not been given chances to use the form in conversation. After checking up on Jitae's knowledge, Ms. Park was convinced that he still retained the grammatical knowledge about the rule. In the classroom, however, Ms. Park has observed Jitae making the same errors frequently in conversation.

4. CR tasks

학습자들에게 해당 규칙이 적용된 일련의 예들을 제공한 뒤 규칙을 도출하도록 하고 그 규칙을 자신의 상황에 맞게 적용, 연습하는 단계로 이루어진다.

Deductive means of teaching grammar tend to emphasize from over meaning, and promote passive rather than active participation of the learners in the learning process. Such approaches are believed to intimidate learners. Instead, awareness-raising inductive approach helps to develop learners' own understanding of language, and to build confidence in themselves as learners. Further, allowing the learners to take responsibility for discovering target rules favorably affects retention. Consciousness-raising tasks, which can be either deductive or inductive, offer an effective means of teaching grammar.

A CR task can be defined as a grammar activity where students are provided with L2 data in some form and required to perform some operation on or with it, the purpose of which is to arrive at an explicit understanding of some linguistic property or properties of the target language.

Plus⁺

Traditional Approach & Input Processing Approach

1. Traditional approach

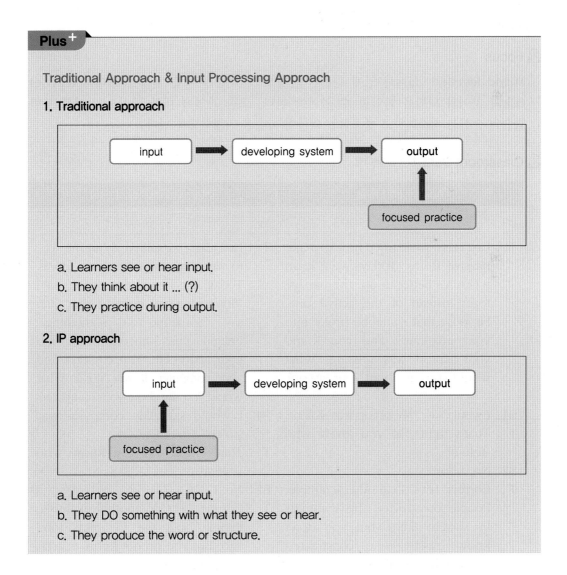

a. Learners see or hear input.
b. They think about it ... (?)
c. They practice during output.

2. IP approach

a. Learners see or hear input.
b. They DO something with what they see or hear.
c. They produce the word or structure.

Chapter 09 2011학년도 기출지문분석

1. Topic : Level-differentiated lesson

2. Focus

Mixed levelled class 운영에 관련된 문항으로, 수준별 학습 과정을 토대로 teacher talk의 차이와 역할을 파악할 수 있어야 한다. 또한 과업에 대한 난이도 차이를 통한 학습의 손실을 최소화하고 성공적인 외국어 학습을 지향하도록 한다.

3. Classroom Data 2011 논술형 1번

Advanced Level	Intermediate-low Level
T : Last class, we learned how to make passive forms. Today, we'll learn when it's better to use the passive form instead of the active one. Suppose that someone broke into your apartment and you found your laptop was missing. What would you say about your laptop?	T : Last class, we talked about the way to say that something was done. Today, we'll see why people say, "Something was done," rather than say, "Someone did something." Imagine this. Someone broke into your apartment. You couldn't find your computer. It was gone! What would you say about your computer?
S1 : I would say, "My laptop was stolen."	S1 : I would say, "My computer was stolen."
T : That's right. Do you know who stole it?	
S2 : No, I don't.	T : That's right. Do you know who stole it?
T : Correct. Let's do another example. People constructed the Pyramids in ancient times, but you don't know exactly who constructed them. What would you say about the Pyramids?	S2 : No, I don't.
	T : Correct. Let's do another example. People built the Pyramids long ago. But you do not know exactly who built them. What would you say about the Pyramids?
S3 : The Pyramids were constructed in ancient times.	S3 : The Pyramids were built long ago.

T : Great. Can anyone tell us when passive sentences are preferred to their corresponding active sentences?

Ss: When we don't know who did something.

T : Good. Let's go through a passage together. Try to understand the passage, while also paying attention to the passive forms used in the passage.

TASK

Step 1

T : I'm going to read you the passage twice. First, I'll read it at normal speed and then I'll read it again as slowly as possible. As you listen, write down as many words and phrases as possible.

> Have you ever seen the Pyramids of Egypt? Have you ever wondered why they were built and how they were built? The Pyramids were built because the kings wanted to live after they died. They thought why they would live after they died. The Pyramids were constructed on the west side of Nile River. They were built there because the sun rises in the east and sets in the west. They believed why the king and the sun god would be born and born again, just like the sun. The Pyramids were very difficult to build, but the whole world can enjoy them.

T : Great. So we can say the same idea two ways. We can say, "People built the Pyramids long ago." Or, "The Pyramids were built long ago." Now, when is it better to say, "The Pyramids were built long ago"?

Ss: When we don't know who built them.

T : Good. Let's go through a passage together. Try to understand the passage. Let's see if you can find any sentences like "The Pyramids were built long ago."

TASK

Step 1

T : I am going to read you the passage twice. Both times, I will read it very slowly and clearly. As you listen, write down any words you hear.

> Have you ever seen the Pyramids of Egypt? Have you ever wondered why they were built and how they were built? The Pyramids were built because the kings wanted to live after they died. They thought why they would live after they died. The Pyramids were constructed on the west side of Nile River. They were built there because the sun rises in the east and sets in the west. They believed why the king and the sun god would be born and born again, just like the sun. The Pyramids were very difficult to build, but the whole world can enjoy them.

Step 2

T : Now, in groups of three, share your notes and see whether your group can come up with its own version of the text. Once your group has reconstructed the text, check it to make sure the meaning is similar to the text you heard. Also check it carefully for grammatical mistakes.

Step 2

T : Now, let's rewrite the text. First, in groups of three, put together all the words that each member heard. Then, working in your group, try to make sentences with those words. And then compare your group's sentences with other groups' sentences. Using all the sentences available, rewrite the text. And check it to make sure the meaning is similar to the text I read.

Step 3

T : Now, I'll pass out the original text that I read to you. Compare your group's text with the original one. How is the original different from yours? Look at both content and passive forms. And then make a presentation about the differences you've found between the two texts.

Step 3

T : Now, I will give you the original text. On the text, I've already underlined some parts. [Only the passive forms in the text are underlined.] Mark the parts in your group's text that you think match those underlined parts. Make your group's text as similar as possible to the original text.

The lesson plans are for the second class period. In the first class period, students learned how passive sentences are formed. One of the aims of today's class is to help the students learn when passives are preferred to their corresponding active sentences.

🔔 Task difficulty

말하기 활동의 난이도와 관련하여 교사가 고려해야 하는 세 가지 요소는 자료, 과업 그리고 학습자 요인이다.

Text	• How dense/complex are the texts that learners are required to process? • How abstract/concrete is the content in relation to the learners experience? How much contextual support is provided?
Task	• How many steps are involved in the task? • How relevant and meaningful is the task? • How much time is available? • What degree of grammatical accuracy is provided? • How much practice or rehearsal time is available?
Learner	• The level of confidence • Motivation of learners • Prior knowledge of content • Degree of linguistic knowledge • Skill, extent of cultural knowledge • Degree of familiarity with task type itself

Build Up ⁿᵉʷ

박현수 영어교육론 Ⅲ 기출문제

Guideline for Pre-service Teachers

초판인쇄 | 2023. 5. 25.　**초판발행** | 2023. 5. 30.　**편저자** | 박현수

발행인 | 박 용　**발행처** | (주)박문각출판　**표지디자인** | 박문각 디자인팀

등록 | 2015년 4월 29일 제2015-000104호

주소 | 06654 서울시 서초구 효령로 283 서경빌딩　**팩스** | (02)584-2927

전화 | 교재주문·학습문의 (02)6466-7202

저자와의
협의하에
인지생략

정가 25,000원
ISBN 979-11-6987-301-7